# RIGHT PLACE, RIGHT TIME

To WALTER

Jim Bowen

# RIGHT PLACE,
# RIGHT TIME
## ...now with added extras!

'We've been together now for forty[ish] years,
an' it don't seem a day too long.'
(I think it might to Phyllis!)

JIM BOWEN

Palatine Books

First published in 2002 by Carnegie Publishing Ltd

This revised and extended edition published in 2005 by Palatine Books,
Carnegie House,
Chatsworth Road
Lancaster LA1 4SL
www.carnegiepublishing.com

*British Library Cataloguing-in-Publication data*
A CIP record for this book is available from the British Library

ISBN 10: 1-874181-35-7
ISBN 13: 978-1-874181-35-4

Typeset in Adobe Garamond by Carnegie Publishing
Printed and bound in the UK by CPI, Bath

# *Contents*

# *Acknowledgements*

To Phyllis, who struggled with me throughout this marathon. To Lynne who ghosted by proxy. To Bernard, Steven and Christine, whose work you will enjoy if you stick with it, and to all those people I have mentioned herewith for not going to their solicitor. Finally may I thank you dear reader for buying the book. If by chance you've borrowed it ... well, that's all right!

# The Second Best Comedian in Britain

I'VE MADE some wicked jokes on TV about my pal Jim over the past few years, such cruel remarks as, 'The acoustics at the London Palladium are terrible, I could hear every word he said.' 'If you flattened out his wrinkles he'd be eight feet tall.' 'Julius Caesar said funnier things while they were stabbing him.' And 'is there no beginning to his talents?'

When a newspaper article appeared claiming that comedians were more important to society than doctors or priests, I disagreed. 'No one on his deathbed is going to say, "I think the end is near, fetch me a comedian". If you were on a plane and the pilot announced, "Both engines have failed and we're about to crash into the ocean, but, thank heavens, we have a comedian on board," how would that cheer you up? Unless it was Jim Bowen.'

Don't imagine that Jim wasn't a co-conspirator in this sustained detriment. The theft of my gag lines was widely publicised at the same time that I was presenting The National Lottery Live on BBC1. In the midst of transmission he walked on, thrust a large battered volume into my hands and said, 'Here's your lousy joke book back. It wasn't worth pinching the damn thing.'

And during my seventieth birthday special on BBC1, described by me as a god of comedy, Jim entered seated on a palanquin carried by slaves, his mind apparently ruined from hosting countless game shows and muttering, 'Super, smashing, lovely, now that's safe, let's look at what you could have won,' over and over again.

You might be wondering why would anyone pick on such a kind and lovable man, especially a fellow jester who professes to be a good friend?

The answer lies in the title of an old song recorded half a century ago by the Ink Spots: 'You Always Hurt the One You Love'.

From Jim's earliest TV appearance on such shows as Up for the Cup and The Wheeltappers' and Shunters' Social Club, I was a fanatical admirer.

I repeated his surreal catchphrases at every opportunity until my wife feared we would both go mad: 'Dip your bread in, tell 'em nothing, make 'em buy a programme.'

When I met the man in person at ATV's Borehamwood studios I knew we were friends for life in ten seconds flat.

So when I next needed a famous human target for an insult, Jim became the obvious focus of my tough love. 'Jim's just like the great Charlie Chaplin. Chaplin never said anything funny either.'

No one laughed louder than Jim.

And that's a big clue to his permanent popularity – he's a deeply modest, unassuming and vulnerable human being and it's these qualities that shine through his comedy and win the hearts of the audiences.

Just a few comedians are loved, truly loved, by the public and their fellow performers. Eric Morecambe was one of the few. George Formby and Jimmy James were even more loved than they were laughed at. No one in our business ever encountered Tommy Cooper without feeling an immediate fondness for that endearing awkward clown. And when Jim took his first steps into the limelight as one of Granada's new-found funnymen in The Comedians, he did more than any of that dazzling company of fools could equal. He was the one you cared about.

Oh, you laughed at them all, at their jokes and perfect timing and varied comic strengths, but when they left the screen there was only one member of the team who was engendered genuine public affection. People don't just like Jim; they love the man.

That's what made Bullseye such a comfortable family favourite for so many years and that's why Jim's wry comedy will always earn more laughter than the same patter delivered by anyone else. He doesn't hide behind a manufactured persona. There's no assumption of false sophistication, no vanity, no dissembling; what you see onstage or on screen is the real guy.

It's the same deal on the pages of this book. What you get is plain Jim, entertainingly funny and serious by turns but always unvarnished and honest.

### [*I say, how terribly obsequious!*]

Oh, and as for the heading of this piece, 'The Second Best Comedian in Britain', go ahead. Ask Jim who the number one comedian is. He'll say, 'I don't actually know. I let all the others argue over that.'

# CHAPTER ONE

## The Early Years

I FIND MYSELF writing the introduction to a book which already exists, if you know what I mean ... well ... what I'm really saying is that this version of *Right Place, Right Time* is the *de luxe* version, the GT model if you're a car person. In this publication is an assembly of tales 'out of school', as it were, stories that perhaps you shouldn't know about, secrets even. Nothing in her to threaten the nation's security, but enough I hope to justify this extended piece of writing.

It's still the story of my life, with the added benefits of new extra treats, further recollections and perhaps a few more chuckles.

The even better news for those of you of an accountancy nature is that the price remains the same! How's that for currying favour and tempting a purchase rather than encouraging the acquisition of a library ticket?

*I say, how very devious!*

The underlying thought which prompted the creation of this book, apart from the fact that I felt confident enough to assume it made interesting reading was that I really do believe that if ever anyone was in the right place at the right time it was me. From the children's home in Liverpool to the heady geriatric days enjoying a very comfortable life, Lady Luck has been my constant ally. A wonderfully happy marriage alongside a successful career in the riskiest of all professions had been monitored by good fortune in abundance. From this grateful writer ... enjoy the next couple of hundred pages.

∼

1937 was a good year for me, but not too good for my mum, an unmarried lady from somewhere on the Wirral. Being unmarried and a mother in 1937 was not a good thing to be and as a consequence my popping out was an embarrassment to her. I had to go, and go I went – to a children's home in Liverpool, where I was scrubbed up awaiting collection by some unsuspecting couple who chose to have a second-hand product (of whatever quality!). Adoption in the thirties was a complicated affair and Joe and Annie Whittaker were to become very familiar with the conditions and requirements demanded of an aspiring mum and dad. My real name was Peter Williams, but that was to be a temporary title as I was on the short list for being posted to a new home where both my Christian name and surname were to change. I've thought long and hard about this adoption business over the years and it's never ever given me a problem. I do have a problem with the ill-informed do-gooder, however, who encourages the adopted child to search out his real parents; in many cases the search takes the lid off a can of worms causing distress and pain for all parties involved. Just be grateful that you came out of the hat!

These simple lines completely capture the emotions of adoptive parents:

*Not flesh of my flesh,*
*Nor bone of my bone,*
*But still miraculously my own,*
*Never forget for a single minute,*
*You didn't grow under my heart, but in it.*

How could any adopted child think of hurting parents who thought like that?

I've always felt a bit special, being chosen as it were. Chosen that is, not necessarily by the parents to be; they didn't have a say in the final choice. The authorities tried to match the baby with the parents but it was very much a lottery. The nearest comparison I can think of to the adoption procedure is going to Battersea dogs' home for a friend. The only flaw in that comparison is that when you go to Battersea dogs' home you can choose the one you want, probably the one with the prettiest face, whereas in the adoption game you had to have the one you were given. I bet my parents to be thought they'd lost the raffle when they looked at me!

I was collected by the Whittakers one spring morning in 1938 and taken home to 303, Dill Hall Lane, Clayton-le-Moors near

**I say, isn't he just like his dad!**

Accrington, Lancs. The locals knew that Joe and Annie had no children, and that Annie had shown no signs of pregnancy by way of swelling, or by having cravings for aniseed balls and Marmite on toast; in fact she had shown no signs at all of anything untoward happening within the parochial confines of Clayton-le-Moors.

It came as a surprise to the locals, therefore, when Annie was seen walking down Whalley Road, wheeling a pram containing a nine-month-old baby. Inquisitive eyes peered through the lace curtains that provided camouflage for the inhabitants of the surrounding streets; word spread throughout the parish that, despite the non-appearance of three wise men, or a bright shining star in the East, a baby had appeared in Clayton-le-Moors in a pram wheeled by Annie Whittaker. Now Annie was a good church-going lass but it defied even the most devout believer that she would have robbed a manger of its contents, and as far as they knew there was room in most of the neighbouring inns, Joe would have researched all that; besides, Bethlehem was the other side of Preston so that idea was definitely out. It had to be something in the air, or perhaps she'd just borrowed the pram for effect.

The contents of the pram had to be looked into, so one of the local residents would have to solve the mystery. As Annie walked down the main thoroughfare, carefully steering the childbearing pram (remember this was a new experience for her), she was accosted by one of the news gatherers of the village who stopped her in her tracks and peered into the pram. 'Whose is the baby, Annie?' enquired the newshound. 'Oh, he's mine and Joe's,' replied Annie proudly. Confusion reigned in the mind of the enquirer because all she could think of to say was: 'I say, isn't he like his dad!'

My new mum (and from that moment on, my only mum), must have chuckled inwardly at this naïve but well-intentioned remark. Comments like this were to follow her round for many a year as she caringly offered me the chance to enjoy a normal family life, which could so easily have passed me by. Of the many children in that home in Liverpool, I was the one drawn out of the hat to go and share Joe and Annie's life. How lucky can you get? Talk about being in the right place at the right time!

Life in the early forties was not too easy for us, though we in the north west of England escaped the brunt of the hostilities affecting Europe. We still couldn't get bananas though!

**Mum and me.**

**A holiday snap by the author – Mum and Dad promenading in Blackpool.**

We did, however, take the traditional week's holiday in Blackpool every year until I reached double figures. Oh, how I looked forward to that week! We stayed at the North Bank private hotel (actually it was a boarding house), but it was on the north promenade next to the legendary Imperial Hotel where people stayed for a fortnight sometimes. They wore straw hats and had walking canes and I'm fairly sure that some of them lived in semi-, or even completely, detached houses. Apparently in some of these residences you could find grapes on the sideboard and no one in the family was poorly!

*I say, how very posh!*

I distinctly remember the first sighting of the sea, as we alighted from the steam train that brought us to North station Blackpool, direct from Accrington. The smell of the ozone mingling with fish and chips still remains embedded in my olfactory bank. The Saturday we arrived was always spent booking the shows we wanted to see during the week. We always went to first house because after the shows we sometimes went to Beth's café at Gynn Square for a fish supper that tasted magnificent.

The pleasure beach was always on the list of places to visit, though I remember I wasn't allowed on too many rides (I often wonder if it was too expensive). I remember the famous stars that appeared in Blackpool during the forties; how I idolised them. George Formby, Frank Randle, Dave Morris, Jimmy James, Winifred Atwell, and Albert Modley, the list was endless. Sandy Powell, the funniest ventriloquist I ever saw, whose dummy's lips moved less than his. Jewel and Warris were the top double act in the country at the time and I remember their act involving a large water tank in which Jimmy Jewel had to test this pen that allegedly could write under water! The theatres of Blackpool were my Disneyworld. I would stand outside them just reading the posters. I fantasised about their lifestyles. What was it like to own a Rolls Royce? Where did they get their suits? They wouldn't be staying at North Bank private hotel at £7 a week full board (use of cruet 6d. extra). They wouldn't have to put down a shilling deposit on the bath plug. They would have afternoon tea in the sun lounge at the Imperial hotel, with cream cakes and those thin see-through china cups with fancy handles and cucumber sandwiches with the crusts cut off. They wouldn't take a 'Jug of tea for the sands' (2s. 6d. plus 5 shillings deposit). They wouldn't have Sunday lunch in a café that had an advert in the window saying you could get 'Mash for Baby' for 6d. No, they would probably saunter into lunch at their leisure, take up their reserved table and choose from a much more varied menu than ours. I wasn't at all envious really!

You'll hear more of my theatrical dreams later on; all I'm doing here is planting the seeds of anticipation as the career swings from one side of the social and intellectual pendulum to the other ... and back!

Let's stay on the lighter side for a few lines; these stories are all about Blackpool and they're jokes, just in case you're not sure.

I remember the landlady at the hotel explaining why she sat the fat boy in the bay window at mealtimes. 'People passing will think that the food must be good here if he looks like that!' Remember this was just after the war and there weren't as many fat folk about, because there wasn't just as much spare food going around and chocolate was still on ration!

Then there was the story of the lady who was trying to get across the tram track, which as you know traversed the pavement on the promenade on some stretches. She stood hesitantly waiting to cross when a kindly tram driver took pity on her and stopped. 'Will I get electrocuted if I step on the rail?' she asked. 'Only if you put your other leg on the wire over the tram!' the driver replied. I think the lady crossed over safely.

Of course I must tell you about the act staying in digs in Blackpool for the summer season. The food left a little to be desired. In fact it left an awful lot to be desired, especially in the meat department. Every meal the landlady served was salad. Breakfast, lunch, dinner: every meal contained greens of one sort or another. This went on for several weeks; in fact the act had begun to grow larger front teeth! One particular lunchtime, as she was bringing in the predictable fare she dropped a fork on the carpet. 'Oh!' she exclaimed, 'that's a sign of a stranger coming to visit.' 'I hope it's the bloody butcher!' said the act. He didn't stay there for much longer.

I grew up enjoying primary school life at All Saints C of E Primary School in Clayton-le-Moors, where I did well, and when Mum and Dad moved to Nelson to open a greengrocer's shop, I continued the trend, passing my eleven plus exam when I was nine. This achievement was of particular significance as it was to have a profound effect on my relationship with my dad. In later years it influenced my behaviour towards our son Pete.

Dad had always said to me, 'Jim, whatever you do get a good dressed up job like teaching or banking; security and respectability is what you should aim for. Don't be like me without any qualifications and having to take whatever job comes up. Make something of yourself'. He constantly talked about his station in life and how he wanted me to do better, though why I could never understand. Dad was always a success in my eyes.

It was therefore with much excitement that I ran to meet Dad as he came home from his job in a local dyers and finishers factory in Nelson, to tell him that I had passed my eleven plus almost two years ahead of time. I expected at least a cry of delight and a slap on the back from him. His reaction was a very subdued 'Oh good'. That was it. No arms round the shoulder, no celebratory hug, no

**Dad, ready to serve his country.**

cheers, no ... no anything. I was absolutely mortified; I mean to say, all that effort to please him and then ... nothing! The whole experience scarred me for life. What I failed to realise was that Dad was a member of the 'show no emotion' brigade. In my selfish innocence I had forgotten that he had spent four of his teenage years watching his pals disappear in the woods of Ypres as he served his country in the R.A.M.C. throughout The Great War. Being subjected to such dreadful traumas before you reach twenty is bound to influence your emotional behaviour in later life. The stiff upper lip really did mean something then. Crying wasn't part of the equation. If it had been, then nothing would have got done. Too many soldiers were being killed far too quickly to have time for grief. There wasn't time to spare for Dad and his pals to cry, they were too busy laying their comrades to rest.

Don't ever forget Remembrance Sunday will you? Look around at this fine country of ours, and even with all its shortcomings, I'm sure you'll think it's worth two minutes a year just to remember the folks who paid the bill.

I can understand Dad's reaction to traumatic situations now. However, there can be no excuse for any shortcomings in the emotion department on my part. I had everything to be grateful for. I had no first hand experience of tragedy, Joe and Annie saw to that and yet I was still to fall short, despite everything. Dad's stiff upper lip had rubbed off and it shouldn't have done. Luckily the people who were to come into my life were compensators, thank God! Otherwise I could have led a very lonely life. I met the right people at the right time (there it is again!).

I started at Nelson Grammar School in September 1949 and I began to fail. I lost sight of the big picture and during the next three years I was to discover that I wasn't all that good at anything, except perhaps running. I actually made the school cross-country team during my third year at Nelson G.S., after which I was transferred for geographical reasons, we moved house! My end of term results became ever more disappointing to Mum and Dad and I found myself losing direction. Dad's advice on reaching ever upward wasn't in the frame and I was unknowingly becoming a burden emotionally to my special parents. Remember, they chose me. How's that for ingratitude?

Padiham, near Burnley, was to be our next home in the form of a newsagent's shop. It was also an off-licence, so that enabled Mum and Dad to work seventeen hours a day, from delivering the morning papers at 6 a.m. to closing the shop at 10.30 p.m. when the pubs closed. I'll bet they loved that! The new address meant that I could attend Accrington Grammar School, where I would take my GCE examinations. I didn't actually sit the examinations; I was just present in the room where they took place. I sat in the room for the duration of eight subjects and managed to fail nine. Now that's bloody good isn't it? My only valid contribution to school life at Accrington was my selection for the school cross-country team. Dad didn't conceal his sadness at my performance too well; he just went very quiet as I tried to salvage some credibility for myself in the household. I got a job emptying dustbins first. You can imagine what went through Dad's mind can't you. 'Get a job with prospects, you know, teacher, banker, make something of yourself'. I really filled the bill didn't I: a dustbin man. Well done, Jim! I don't think so.

Actually fortune smiled at me when I took up the appointment of 'waste disposal executive'. It was during those few months of treading down ashes, broken marmalade jars, empty Scott's porridge oats boxes (they were really strong, they were!), and other such delights, that the realisation of what could lie ahead dawned on me. The foreman of our mobile team was a knowledgeable man whose academic achievements made mine look glorious, and whose advice I listened to avidly. We were six-handed as a team and were in command of the latest model of dust collection cart (it had slidey up doors, two on each side, and big canvas bags hooked on the back. You remember the ones don't you?).

We began work at 5 a.m. every morning and completed our allotted round, after which we went to the waste tip to discharge our load. It wasn't the cleanest of occupations but I sort of felt I was paying the price for getting it wrong. It was one frosty morning in November as we all sat on a wall eating our ash-laden jam butties when I was regaled by the ramblings of my team leader. He spoke sagely to me in cultured tones: 'Tha knows, Jim. I've bin thinkin' ... When tha considers how long this world's bin' goin' round, an' then tha thinks how long it's likely to go round; we're only 'ere for a bloody weekend!' What an outrageously simple outlook on life, and how accurate it was. I took on board his words and promptly spoke to Dad about the imminence of everything, and asked if I could be given a second chance to fulfil his ambitions for me. I wanted to go back to school to take those infernal examinations again, this time to actually pass them. I was allowed to speak with my former headmaster, Ben Johnson, tyrant of this parish, who very kindly allowed me back through the portals of this fine building. Accrington Grammar School has nothing but happy memories for me now. The year of '55 was a great one. I took nine subjects at GCE 'O' level and passed ten. Now that IS bloody good! My dustman experience led me back on to the road of achievement. Thank you for offering me a learning process that fortunately I chose to grasp. I also learned to appreciate the true value of gainful employment in whatever field. My pals at the council yard in Padiham taught me more about life in the few months I worked with them than I had amassed in my sixteen years to date. I think also that working in that far from comfortable environment gave me an awareness of life in the less affluent lane; it made me remember that everyone on this earth has a part to play, if we are to get through it all. It made me reject shirkers, and it made me very conscious of the value of being a team player. Thank you very much boys.

# CHAPTER TWO

# Cold Comfort, Camaraderie and Confusion

Now I had to join the army.
*I say, how very patriotic!*

I had little choice in the matter. It was called National Service. Every young able-bodied male living in the United Kingdom of Great Britain was expected to do his duty to Queen and country when he reached the age of eighteen. The tour of duty was a compulsory two years, after which he was released, or demobilised as it was called. I was summoned to Hilsea Barracks in Portsmouth, a naval town, as you will recall. I shall only remember it with military connotation, however. The brown envelope arrived at the newsagent-cum-off-licence in Green Lane, Padiham, one morning in July 1955. It suggested that I appear at Hilsea Barracks in order that I might train to defend our homeland against attack. I was to become a member of the Royal Army Ordnance Corps, or more briefly the RAOC; the chaps in this branch of the army look after ammunition and sundry supplies like potatoes, boots, uniforms and all the other stuff that equips the army to function effectively.

The train journey from Padiham to Portsmouth was financed by Her Majesty in the form of a travel warrant, so I left Lancashire feeling particularly important and quite prepared to at least give the whole idea a fair chance. Leaving home wasn't as traumatic for me as it was for Mum and Dad. Mum could remember the last time uniform was part of her life, and Dad knew what was in store for me at Portsmouth. Fortunately he didn't tell me!

Hilsea Barracks was a huge training camp, so large in fact that it had its own railway station. It was here that I first came into

**Sergeant Shelton's heroes. Hilsea barracks.
I'm second from right, in the middle row, hidden by rifle.**

contact with a gentleman whose parents weren't married. His name was Shelton (we never got on first-name terms); he was a Sergeant. He was no more than five feet three inches tall (in metric that's very short), but he had the presence of a giant. This was because the army had given him three stripes. Basically what we're talking about here is God. We are looking at ultimate power in uniform. We're talking about a being that thrives on generating fear for fun. He swept into my life with such force that even now over fifty years on, I shudder.

Ninety lost souls alighted from the train at Hilsea barracks, gauche youthful and helpless, searching for that mother figure we had left earlier in the day. I can tell you now we searched in vain. The last thing we would find at Hilsea Barracks was a figure of comfort. We were greeted by a corporal (two stripes only) who herded us into three groups of thirty, each group lined up in three rows of ten. These were called platoons and three of those formed a company. We became 'C' company. It became apparent quite early on that corporals had the same bestiality licence as sergeants, so from the off, so to speak, we were put in fear for our lives. The noise emitting from the mouths of these corporals was deafening, not to say terrifying. Needless to say, therefore, we immediately came to terms with 'blind obedience'. The first few days at Hilsea were absolutely horrendous. We were chased from pillar to post for no apparent reason. We painted coal white, we polished the studs on the soles of our boots immediately before wearing them on a route march, in fact we did exactly as we were instructed at all times without so much as a raised eyebrow. The whole training programme lasted six weeks and as the weeks progressed the platoon corporals became less and less human and Sergeant Shelton's parents became less and less married. Room inspections became a nightmare as we stood to attention by our beds, rigid with fear in case the inspecting officer found a speck of dust ... anywhere. We had dozens of pieces of kit, all of which had to be immaculate and laid out on the bed in precise geometric pattern. Woe betide any recruit whose knife and fork were not gleaming and in exactly the right position on the bedcover, i.e. 2 inches either side of the mess tin, parallel to the seam of the bedcover. By the end of the training we could polish for Europe, march for England, and fight for survival (probably for self, not necessarily for country!).

After basic training we were posted to serve in a trade for the remainder of our National Service. The departure lounge at Hilsea Barracks that September morning had a strange feel about it (it wasn't a departure lounge, actually, it was a shed). All of us had come through the whole experience alive and well. Now there's a surprise. Not only had we survived the ordeal but also we felt better people for it. In modern parlance the six-week struggle we had faced together had bonded us. The rigours that we had been subjected to gave us a sense of achievement, a sense of pride, not only in ourselves but in our fellow soldier. It started to make incredible sense to us all. Sergeant Shelton became a hero to us. We began to realise why the training had to be as it was. I suppose looking back at the whole period you could say we had been chronologically microwaved. We had grown ten years older in six weeks!

*I say, how terribly clever!*

We all boarded our respective coaches to travel to wherever we had been posted. I was scheduled to attend The School of Ammunition at Bramley in Berkshire where I was to study for nine months to become an ammunition examiner. This job carried with it an

**School of Ammunition, Bramley. We got our stripes and a gun (note the fire bucket, just in case!).**

automatic promotion to corporal at the end of the course so I began preparing to become bestial. In fact the stripes were a technical step up the ladder rather than a marching up and down one. Nine months at Bramley equipped me to defuse a 40mm Bofors shell and to despatch ammunition of any shape, size or calibre to wherever the Queen deemed necessary (I think she had help from someone in this respect). On completion of the course I was posted to Nesscliffe Central Ammunition Depot near Shrewsbury where I was expected to defend my country.

With about thirteen months left of my contract with Her Majesty, I was now serving as a non-commissioned officer, with approximately one week's experience as an ammunition examiner. I looked forward to an interesting period in my life as I was given the task of supervising a workshop in which ammunition of a certain age was being refurbished. It was a fairly mundane routine as I watched the experienced workers scrape and repaint shells of all denominations from 8 a.m. to 4.30 p.m. every day. I never quite understood the rationale of re-painting shells to a high gloss finish when at the end of the day their function was to explode. I mean, paint an un-exploding door to a high gloss, yes; but a bomb? I then realised why Sergeant Shelton made us paint coal white at Hilsea barracks. Of course, it all made sense to me now. It was the blind obedience syndrome. My time at Nesscliffe did have its dramatic moments, however.

August 1956 was an interesting time to be serving your country, as about that time a bit of bother started bubbling in the Suez Canal area. Sir Anthony Eden was Prime Minister at the time and it appeared that there could be a chance that the canal might close down on a rather permanent basis. Geographically and strategically this route was of considerable importance to our trade and ultimately our economic well-being, so Anthony thought that it might be nice if we had some sort of influence on its survival. He decided to fly the British flag, and promptly sent some of our chaps out there to ensure fair play. This involved despatching out ammunition so that we could make our presence felt in a tangible way. It became the role of the RAOC to send ammunition by rail to merchant ships in place at Barry docks in South Wales. There it would then be loaded, under our expert supervision as ammunition examiners. The fully loaded ships would then sail east with their cargoes to find their place in Anthony's arsenal at Suez, where ultimately the idea was to fire this stuff at the people being difficult about the tenancy agreement on the Suez Canal.

Please note that at this stage in our military careers we had spent at least six weeks honing our pyrotechnic skills by repainting knac-kered ammunition in Shrewsbury. This vast experience we had gained obviously equipped us more than adequately to oversee the loading of hundreds of tons of various highly dangerous explosives on to Her Majesty's naval vessels. Very rational delegating we thought, as we fumbled through paperwork, casting a very inexperienced eye over the cargo as it was loaded on to the vessels.

It was with regard to the transportation of this ammunition to Suez that my career in the army stumbled somewhat. As senior tradesmen supervising the loading of this sensitive cargo, we were expected to know exactly what went on board and to know the details of the ages and strengths of the different categories of projectile. Imagine a very critical interpretation of the term 'sell by date'. As the stock of shells aged their potency lessened. For example, shells dating back ten years would travel further than shells which were twenty years old because the propellant would not have degenerated as much. There was a way of calculating the range of these shells, given their accurate age. Shells were loaded in large batches all supposed to contain ammunition of the same age. I wrongly assumed that all shells in each complete batch were the same age, without actually checking the sell by date. Accurate range calculations were made on the assumption that the whole batch was the same so checking was vital.

It transpired that during one loading operation someone noticed that the age of the shells in one particularly large consignment varied by as much as fifteen years! Fortunately the whole batch was off loaded before the ship sailed. Had this not been the case, the shells being used at Suez would not have performed as calculated by the gunners in the Royal Artillery, who relied totally on our figures when calculating the range of the projectiles. Basically, what would have happened had the rogue batch got through would have been that our shells would have landed on our troops. Even worse was the fact that none of us knew the detailed content of what we were handling; it could have proved disastrous on the dockside. This would not have been the best of military scenarios. Everything was done that was legally (or illegally) possible to keep the news of this awful blunder from our commanding officer, but sadly I was found out. I reported to my ultimate superior back at the Central Ammunition Depot at Shrewsbury, where I was dutifully reprimanded and immediately posted to Aldershot where I was to serve on a six-week course at the end of which I would be a Physical Training Instructor. The idea was that I would be as far away from explosives as possible in a gymnasium in Aldershot! This penance turned out to be a blessing in disguise some three years later, however, as you will find out. The only consolation was that all this confusion was taking place in the south-west corner of Wales; for God's sake it might have been happening in Blackpool. I ask you, how would that have affected the summer season? I'm only joking Wales. I married a Welsh girl, you know, but that's a couple of years on from here.

Suez died down soon and life in the RAOC afforded me the chance to form a dance band at Nesscliffe. This stood me in good stead with the Regimental Sergeant Major who gave us time off from ammunition and physical training to rehearse for dances in the sergeant's mess. For this we were rewarded with sandwiches, a beer or two, and a promise that guard duty would not feature too prominently in our lives. This was a two-edged sword for me because Bobby Charlton (now Sir Bobby) could have had the privilege of having me as his guard commander had I not been ordered to play for dances in the sergeant's mess. Actually Bobby never did guard duty; I think Sir Matt Busby had friends in high places because Bobby seemed to go home every weekend. I heard he had a little commitment at Old Trafford and I'm sure I never saw him play cricket. Perhaps he had a paper round. Another chap who missed out on being under my command in the guardroom was a certain Duncan Edwards. He seemed to have a similar arrangement with Sir Matt and the army. Anyway, whatever it was he must have been important to the nation's security because nobody asked any questions.

We were in fact very proud to have both Bobby and Duncan play for our battalion, and needless to say we never lost a game! We did, however, lose great talent all too prematurely at Munich in 1957. At least we were able to watch Bobby entertain us for many years after that fateful night. I met him many times after we left the army and I'm sure you'll know that he is the perfect ambassador not only for soccer but also for sport in general.

My time in the army was to influence me quite dramatically in the imminent years as a schoolteacher. Rightly or wrongly I look back and believe that the discipline of the army was on the whole a good thing. I watched the growth of self-esteem, pride in appearance, acceptance of decisions without dissent or question. I really didn't see too much erosion of imagination; in fact within this disciplined structure I could see a security that bred innovation and an awareness of life around one. I saw the real meaning of the term 'team player', a modern buzz phrase which describes well the way we all worked together within a highly disciplined environment. I can't help thinking that it might just be nice to try a bit of it again today. Surely discipline and order are prerequisites in a civilised world, where man should be able to speak reasonably freely, and walk with confidence in his own garden. I suppose the good news is that you can think what the hell you like! Still, I'm a senior citizen now so please allow me that little rant.

*I say, how old fashioned!*

CHAPTER THREE

# *My Blind Date*

AUGUST 1957 saw the termination of my contract with Her Majesty. I had been granted an early release from the RAOC to allow me to begin training as a teacher at Chester College. I had managed to gain a place at this most prestigious teacher-training establishment before I was called up for National Service. September saw me enter the halls of residence at the college, where I was to spend two happy years fulfilling the ambitions of both Dad and myself. I found the course work difficult at Chester, partly I suppose because I was out of the habit of thinking, and partly because I just wasn't clever enough. Suffice it to say that after two years before the academic mast I managed not to be found out, and I subsequently qualified as a human being fit to stand in front of children and hopefully educate and improve them. While at Chester I became Chairman of the Rag Committee, a position of dubious respectability in terms of intellectual recognition at the college, but one that I thoroughly enjoyed. The position enabled me to recruit a band from the student body at the college to play in the procession that rit- ualistically marched round the city raising money for local charities. The band remained in existence throughout my time at Chester and we played for many functions, none of which paid us any money. It must be said, however, that we weren't outstanding; in fact, with hindsight we were bloody awful! The end of my first term at Chester was punctuated by a group of us being invited to a formal dance at Chester's sister college in Liverpool, St Katharine's College (Taggart Avenue, Liverpool 17).

You may well wonder how I remember the address in such detail. It happened like this: a small group of us decided that it would be churlish of us to deny the ladies of St Katharine's College (Taggart Avenue, Liverpool 17), the pleasure of our most entertaining

**Outside Chester Town Hall, playing Ragtime in Rag Week.**

company. We therefore effected an invitation to ourselves from ourselves through the good offices of some socialite who had friends in high places at St Katharine's College (Taggart Avenue, Liverpool 17). The night of the dance came round and the group of us approached the college gates confidently, invitations in hand, and we entered this haven full of lovely young student teachers of the female persuasion. I do mean the real thing of course! We had each been allocated partners for the evening so we dutifully met in the common room and conducted pleasantries for a while with our respective hostesses. It was a bit like multiple arranged marriages without the vicar being there! It was a very posh affair with boiled ham sandwiches (brown bread if you please), and orange cordial by the glass. Alcohol was not allowed on the college campus (I don't think it was allowed in Childwall, actually; I mean, that's Liverpool 17). Bear in mind that both Chester College and St Katharine's College were C of E so we would have needed at least a curate for anything morally threatening to occur. My allotted friend for the evening was a very quiet lady from Burnley. I don't think she'd been out a lot as the whole affair was too much for her to cope with. She sat in a corner and kind of opted out of the scenario.

This kind of thing must not have gone on in Burnley, you know, sandwiches and neat orange juice. Come to think of it I hadn't experienced anything like this in all my army service, which as you know was spent in war-torn Shrewsbury, a well-known, up-market society town. Anyway the upshot of it all meant that she took her ball home, and that enabled me to attach myself to this lovely girl with the blue eyes. We chatted for a while, and would you believe it, she came from Shrewsbury! What a coincidence, Shrewsbury, the town where I fought for my country! (She came from Oswestry, actually, which is the next town to Shrewsbury, but it sounds more romantically coincidental if I say Shrewsbury.) She told me her name was Phyllis and her dad owned a butcher's shop in Oswestry. She was studying Physical Education and would qualify as a teacher at the end of the current academic year. She had a great sense of fun and we really hit it off together, so much so that we ended up as partners for the rest of the evening. We had a riotous time together, dancing to long playing records, eating portions of sherry-free trifle, and at the end of the evening we were all allowed into Phyllis's room for half an hour to drink coffee. We stayed very late into the night, so late in fact that we almost missed the 10.30 p.m. bus back to Chester. Oh yes! We were absolutely wild in those days.

The months went by and Phyllis and I became really good pals, visiting each other every weekend at either St Kath's or Chester College.

Towards the end of my first term I was to learn that Mum was not well and the chances of her seeing me qualify as a teacher were slim. In fact she left us alarmingly quickly as her illness became untreatable. Dad was incredibly brave about it all and carried on with his life, alone and very independent. He was not a religious man but always gave Mum chance to breathe in that department. Mum used to go to church regularly; I don't think she really understood religion but she believed it to be the right thing to do. Her belief was based on what she was taught as a child. In the early part of the century most children believed what they were taught by their parents. The mind of the child then was not as questioning as the mind of the computer-trained technocrat wizard of today. I'm sure Mum didn't really understand the *Te Deum* or the *Magnificat*, but she felt a lot better when she'd sung them. I just hope that when the chips were down for her, the time she spent in church was of some comfort to her. Having seen her most weekends towards the end of her time on earth I'm not sure that any amount of hymn singing or praying would have done any good. It taught me not to like God very much. I certainly didn't like the vicar who came to visit Dad when Mum eventually did die. 'God moves in a mysterious way' were his words of comfort as he entered the front room where Mum lay.

I'll tell you what I think shall I? 'It's a bloody funny way to move for a chap who's supposed to care for his flock. I wouldn't like him as my bloody shepherd if I were a little lamb'.

This was one of the more troubled periods of my early twenties, and even at this early stage of my relationship with Phyllis she was proving to be a tower of strength. She was there throughout Mum's illness and ultimate departure and as we approached the end of the academic year we became very close. The summer holidays were upon us, which meant we would be apart for several weeks. Before the holidays began I grasped the opportunity and asked her to marry me. Luckily she agreed, but it didn't turn out quite as simple as that. Phyllis's parents had not been too keen on my association with their eldest daughter, and did little to encourage the alliance. Looking back now I can fully understand their position. Here was this northern chap coolly sweeping into their daughter's life before she has had a chance to 'live a little'. They knew that there was a big world out there and knew that Phyllis's social parameters had been somewhat restricted. She spent most weekends helping her dad in the butcher's shop and many evenings delivering meat on her bike with the basket on the front (remember them?). They had worked to get their daughter into a respected profession and before she'd had a chance to see the world, or at least London, this chap swans in and wants to take her away from them, along with their plans for her. Who did this chap think he was?

As the weeks rolled by they began to soften towards me and eventually when we broached the subject of marriage they gracefully acquiesced. There was a price for me to pay, however. Phyllis's dad was one of the old school who had a very wry sense of humour and he insisted that I propose to his daughter in the living room of their home in the traditional way. I had to go down on one knee and ask for Phyllis's hand in marriage. Then I had to wait for his permission for the ceremony to take place. He made me wait

**The start of a wonderful marriage, though Phyllis thought she was marrying Buddy Holly.**

a while before he agreed. I suppose he had every right, he was paying for it!

At the start of my second year at Chester Phyllis took up an appointment at Wem Secondary School, where she taught Physical Education to the girls. I continued to work my way through my final year at Chester. The final term approached and the task of applying for jobs became a major feature in both our lives. The dilemma we faced was one that must have threatened many relationships in those early days. Should we live with my dad in Clayton-le-Moors, should we live in Shropshire near to Phyllis's roots, or should we just sod off and make a brand new start? The last of these three options was immediately thrown out as being far too adventurous for a couple who had spent their formative years in a fairly protected environment. Phyllis had experienced little more than a meat delivery round in terms of world travel, though she did spend some time in Childwall (Liverpool 17), and my CV as far as travel was concerned was restricted to military activities in Portsmouth, Bramley and Shrewsbury. (We won't talk about the Welsh episode.) These combined experiences hardly equipped a young couple to set up home in foreign parts. Take into account also that at the time this decision had to be made, we had no job prospects and even less money. That left us two options; was it to be Shropshire or Lancashire? You know damn well the option we chose don't you!

The end of my final term at Chester also meant that we both had to focus on the wedding. It was to take place at St Mary's Parish Church in Oswestry and the date was to be 3rd August 1959, Bank Holiday Monday. The arrangements had been made for the reception to take place at the Sun Hotel, immediately opposite the church; this meant that our taxi had to drive three times round Oswestry after the ceremony to allow the guests to get in to the hotel before we did! At this point I must tell you why the wedding ceremony was on a Monday: butchers' shops are closed on Mondays and Mr Jack Owen, father of the bride, didn't like to lose business. The day went well with the sun shining on all of us. Phyllis looked stunning and I just turned up. That was the way it was to be for the next forty-three years!

The reception came to a close and everyone went back to 'Owen Towers', 29 Victoria Road, a mere 400 yards from the hotel. The guests walked there, we got back in the taxi to do another three laps round the town, to ensure we got there after the guests. The whole wedding celebration, from start to finish, took place within a radius of 500 yards. The bill for the taxi was horrific! Early evening saw us depart for Blackpool in our 1955 Ford Prefect 100E model,

**Off on honeymoon to the West Coast – in a 1955 Ford Prefect with £14 in our pockets.**

registration number PLW 714. We had booked in to a boarding house in Bispham, a satellite of the entertainment capitol of the world that was Blackpool. I cannot remember to this day where the money came from for the honeymoon. I do know that we had to be very careful how we spent our meagre wedge. The end of the honeymoon drew to a close and, yes you guessed it, we travelled in our Ford Prefect the thirty-five miles to Clayton-le-Moors in Lancashire. Shropshire came third after we discussed the possibility of travelling the world.

I suppose conscience got the better of me and we both ended up teaching in Accrington, living with my dad. Economically it was the only option open to us, bearing in mind that when we returned from our honeymoon on the west coast of England (sounds better than Bispham), we had £14 in Phyllis's Post Office Savings Bank.

How we came to terms with the reality of our immediate circumstances as we began our married life defies logic. Here we were about to share a small house with my father, having literally a few shillings in the bank and no prospect of earning any salary for three months. The arrogant assumption of the whole scenario completely baffles me to this day. All we had was each other and what must have been an inordinately large, blinding ambition.

*I say, how terribly selfish!*

# CHAPTER FOUR

# Teaching: The Aspiring Years

Dad lived in a small terraced house in the up-market end of Clayton-le-Moors on his own and was coping quite well with his relatively recent loss. I think he was looking forward to us joining him but I'm sure he realised that it would be tight fit with three of us in 31 Harrington Street. The property comprised two bedrooms, a dining room, a front room or parlour (lounge to posh people), a small kitchen and a back yard. It was from this house that we both began our teaching careers, trying to educate the children of Accrington, and in the process educating ourselves in the art of cohabitation. Phyllis had been appointed P.E. teacher at Woodnook County Secondary School and I had been allocated a first year class at Hyndburn Park County Secondary School. We were on our way at last. The first month at our respective schools was not easy financially as we didn't get our salaries until the end of the first complete month. For four weeks we were visiting friends every evening, partly to eat their biscuits and partly to keep warm. Life at home with Dad was squashed up to put it mildly. It wasn't anybody's fault really. You see we had a front room or parlour (lounge if you're posh, I've told you once) but that was never used. Nobody in East Lancashire actually used their front room, unless the vicar came or it was a Sunday when relations came. Dad didn't have any relations so the front room was a no go area. This gave all three of us a combined living area less than that allotted to a gerbil sharing a cage with a tarantula. It was a nightmare for both Dad and Phyllis; I just turned up. During October we started to look for a house within our price range, but found little available with walls and a roof, so the prospect of getting a mortgage on dubious derelict buildings prompted us to look at newly built properties. Leonard Frankland was building some rather basic houses on

Sandy Lane in Accrington so we gave the site a visit. We found the site foreman who showed us round an almost completed house. The price was £1,690 (Baxi fire £7 extra). We were earning a combined salary of £74 per month. I'll write that again: combined salary £74 per month. The annoying part about that was that Phyllis was earning £41 of that £74.

*I say, how humiliating (well, it was in 1959!)*

We agreed to buy number fifty-three, Queen Elizabeth Crescent, and pushed the boat out and ordered a Baxi fire. Then we had the agonising wait for the house to be built. Every night after school we went up to the site to watch its progress. You know the saying 'A watched kettle never boils'; well the same applies to watched houses. It took ages for Leonard Frankland (builder-cum-snail of this parish), to finish the damn thing! I've never quite forgiven him, though the Baxi fire gave us much pleasure. It was a relief for us both to get into the new house and to give Dad his space back. Even after we moved, relations between Dad and me weren't great. We used to visit him every week and sit in complete silence in the living room. He seemed to take no interest in our careers at all; in fact we almost gave up trying to establish a rapport with him. We were both young and I was extremely ambitious, so that, along with the trying times we had had together in the shared accommodation in Clayton-le-Moors, did little to enhance relations. Phyllis throughout this period was absolutely impartial. Lesser women would have walked away. Thank God she didn't, though why I'm thanking God I don't know, because as you know, I'm not too keen on him.

The move into the new house was simple. We had little furniture and how we managed is a blur to me now, though we both had respectable jobs and were earning; perhaps we were given breathing space by the people we dealt with. I know the bank manager thought we were OK 'cos he helped us owe him money.

My job at Hyndburn Park School was teaching children who weren't exactly going to join MENSA, but they afforded me a most rewarding initiation in the art of communication. There were forty one boys and girls in class 1D at the St James's annexe to the main buildings of Hyndburn Park Secondary School. Conditions were appalling as the education system had to cope with 'The Bulge' syndrome. The year was 1959, just fourteen years after the end of the war. Soldiers by the thousand were coming home from war service to resume family life. Schools, infant, primary and secondary, all over Great Britain would have to accommodate the results of masses of activity in bedrooms (and kitchens) throughout the land for several years. My arrival at St James's annexe was to coincide with this influx of post war children into our schools. 1D was my special gang. Of the intake of over one hundred and sixty children that year the children of 1D were graded where the printer's name could be found on a poster. They were the children that time, parents and the overworked system forgot. They were to be my class. I was fresh out of college and determined to make my mark. In 1959 the policy of streaming children into groups of similar ability was in fashion. 1A therefore was the brightest group, so alphabetically 1D was the bottom of the pile in terms of academic achievement. The rosy faces that greeted me on my first day at the annexe were to become my best pals during the year to follow. The fact that they were in 1D became a source of pride to them as they worked enthusiastically to improve their standard of performance. No sense of inferiority pervaded 1D's classroom; nothing but the sweet smell of success was in the air in that satanic gloomy Victorian classroom, with its sliding partitions separating the wheat from the chaff. I made sure that they enjoyed being the chaff. The class as a whole helped me to perform well, not only as their teacher but as their confidante, their reassuring sounding board, their protection against failure; I was learning how to motivate and encourage children who hadn't known what it was like to be praised. I was enjoying the emergence of these hitherto ignored youngsters into the light of achievement; I showed off 1D as a positive force to be recognised within the walls of the school. No longer were they the also-rans, the hangers-on, as they began to establish themselves as winners. When the school had open days 1D were there, showing off their wares, gaining in confidence by the day; they were beginning to enjoy the respect their peers were showing them, they revelled in the encouraging sounds they were hearing, and they knew they were getting better at everything. Success breeds success they say, but also as a by-product comes that immeasurable commodity, self-belief. By the end of the Christmas term my mates in the class of 1D were extremely glad to be there, and they were looking at class 1A with a rather confident air. When we had completed the academic year the children were well prepared to face the main building at Hyndburn Park ... and so was I.

Educational philosophies go in cycles. They are, sadly, victims of fashion. Fashion is not a feature of our society which should be influencing such a vital element of our daily lives. Education is not to be tampered with; let common sense prevail. The experts said some years ago that streaming or selection of any kind is unhealthy in that it gives some children a sense of failure or inadequacy. Absolute rubbish. In the real world selection is an every day occurrence. Who gets promotion, who gets the last loaf of bread, who gets the best seat in the cinema? All these are selection processes. In order that our children can be better equipped to face the reality of challenge in the real world, we should subject them to challenge in the classroom. Challenge need not be daunting or discouraging. It should be made exciting and invigorating. Comprehensive education meant blurring of boundaries; losing streaming meant the same thing. The child in the classroom knows exactly where he is in the pecking order; he knows that some are better than others at all kinds of things. Don't patronise the child by trying to conceal the fact. He or she knows that if they aren't good enough then they won't be picked. The way forward is to face the differences in our charges, and with skilful management the differences can be made bearable. Elitism is a naughty word in the land of the mediocre. So challenge the mediocre and move on. Don't be frightened of excellence. It's there for everyone to enjoy at one level or another. Don't be put off by feasibility, it will compromise you soon enough. Look at optimums and be inspired by what you see. Let P.B. be your two favourite letters of the alphabet. Let them stand for Personal Best. You know you can do it!

*I say, how terribly inspirational!*

Discipline in the classroom occupied by 1D was severe. How dare I put that in print? The fact is, I can now because I am far distant from the current 'pupil rules OK' syndrome that permeates the environs of education today. Teachers now dare not even point a finger at a pupil for fear of reprisal. The ultimate sanctions have been taken from them. How can they be expected to perform their work if the principal tools of their trade have been removed? A prerequisite to any educative process is discipline. If the teacher is not in total control of the classroom he may as well go home; and many do. We're not talking machine guns here; we're talking about who is the boss. The sooner we credit the vast majority of our teachers with the integrity and dedication we know they have, the better. Teachers are not there to destroy or hurt their pupils, but there are times when they need to call upon resources that aren't always there for them. Parental support for a start would be nice. Perhaps the system itself could grasp the nettle and let the teacher win now and again. I'm heartily sick of reading about teachers being asked to jump through hoops on account of some little waster running home to a large dad, asking for protection from a newly qualified, enthusiastic teacher, allegedly nailing him to the wall and flogging him to within an inch of his life. I don't think so. Discipline has to be present and, as in most cases, if linked to a genuine desire to inform and educate it's possible to win. Come on, I did with 1D!

Even in my first year as a qualified teacher I was having aspirations as an actor, if only on the amateur stage. I had to join the teachers union (then the National Union of Teachers) where I quickly formed the Accrington Young Teachers Dramatic Society. My argument was that if we were to attract teachers into the Union, what better

**Accrington Young Teachers. My stage/acting debut. (I'm the vicar in the middle – typecasting?)**

way than by offering social opportunities for making new friends within the profession in the form of a dramatic society. The idea worked as we soon got over a dozen members, which enabled us to put on amateur productions in Accrington. These were usually comedies, either Lancashire based or of the Alistair Sim/Margaret Rutherford style. This enabled me to be in the plays and or produce them. The society remained alive for three or four years, during which time we put on several productions. I was the driving force behind the society and I was quite happy to undertake all the jobs entailed in getting the show on the road. I sold tickets, advertised the play, painted the scenery, in fact did everything needed to stage the show. I suppose even in those early days there was an innate desire to perform in an arena away from the classroom, and it's also interesting to note that they were all comedies. At that stage in my career, however, nothing was further from my mind than making a living on the professional stage in any shape or form. I spent as much time preparing for stage productions as I did preparing my schoolwork. I put that down to a level of energy that an ambitious 22 year old is gifted with, or that I was so frightened of not being noticed as I scrambled the ladder of recognition in those early days. Whatever the reason for my extremely energetic attitude to life in those heady days, it was to stand me in good stead in later years as I trudged my way round the highways and byways of club land in an attempt at carving out a living from the professional stage.

My second year at Hyndburn Park was spent in the main building, where I was asked to teach Physical Education, as the current P.E. teacher was leaving to take up an improved appointment in Preston. This was a great opportunity for me to progress because it meant I had a department of my own. I was quite comfortable with the challenge, as I'd done the PTI course in the army when my commanding officer removed me from the world of ammunition for a time (remember Wales and all that? Talk about good fortune!).

Physical Education was enjoying a high profile in the prioritised world of education during the early sixties. It was an element of the schools' curriculum which was deemed to be of increasing significance as leisure time was becoming more and more a feature of our lives. The experts thought that our children should be taught how to handle the increased spare time they were to have when they left school. So here was I in the vanguard of a movement that was to prove very advantageous as my career moved on. Educational gymnastics was a main element of the P.E. programme at this time and it occurred to me that if I was able to get the boys of Hyndburn Park up to a good standard within this field I could perhaps make a mark for the boys, the school and myself, and as a result I would become Minister for Education more quickly. This didn't quite happen but the boys didn't let me down and pretty soon we were gaining a reputation as a breeding ground for good gymnasts. P.E. organisers were coming to see the work being done in this rather unfashionable school with its central assembly hall doubling up as the gym. Eyebrows were being raised in high places and it was beginning to look like my career was moving in the right direction. I was extremely keen in those very early days and I joined in the extra-curricular activities with vigour. The school had a brass band, which practised twice a week after school and during lunch hour every day. I found time to work with the band, having played trumpet at Chester. Fortunately I managed to stay ahead of them technically by just a few days, but they never actually found me out! (I can tell you that many teachers are sometimes only just ahead of their pupils on many occasions during term time. The secret is to stay ahead!) I managed to do just that, teaching these keen musicians for the rest of my time at Hyndburn Park, and was able to enlarge the band considerably, encouraging the new second year pupils to take up a brass instrument. I even persuaded parents to invest in second-hand trumpets for their children. At the end of the second term of my new appointment I was giving P.E. dem-onstrations and conducting a large, if basic, group of brass players at parents' evenings. These extra-curricular activities were to stand me in good stead during the next couple of years. One of the most rewarding features of working with the band was the knowledge that several of the pupils carried on their interest in music after they left school; two at least joined regimental bands in HM Royal Marines. There the teachers were much farther ahead of them than I was!

It was during my second year at Hyndburn Park that I began to look around for greater opportunity to show off my teaching skills. I was, of course, a very experienced teacher now with at least, well, a year and a half under my belt! P.E. was well to the fore in modern educational policy and I was in the frame for a post of special

**Hyndburn Park enlarged Brass Band. Happy memories.**

responsibility at St Ambrose R.C. School, Rawtenstall, where a
vacancy had arisen. The appointment carried a salary increase of
£100 per year and the school had a fully equipped gymnasium!
What a luxury after the assembly hall surrounded by classrooms at
Hyndburn Park. The favourite for the job was an excellent P.E.
teacher who had demonstrated his boys' work to P.E. students from
Carnegie and Loughborough Colleges of Physical Education, both
highly prestigious establishments.

   The interview took place one Tuesday evening in May and the
job was to start in September. There were three candidates up for
the post. I looked round at my competition and really thought that
I was too inexperienced to make it. This was the first interview I
had been to where I actually faced my fellow applicants. The
procedure was that we would all be interviewed in turn and the
person who was to be offered the job would be called back in to
the governors to accept or reject. I was last to be called in to face
a panel of five people, none of whom I knew; I was feeling quite
nervous. As it all turned out, the favourite was offered the job but
then declined; this sent out a signal to my remaining competitor
that the job wasn't all it was cracked up to be, so he declined. Well,

would you believe it, I was called in, and guess what? I was offered the job. Obviously I would have to think long and hard about taking a job that was being offered to me as the last option. I mean, it's a question of pride. Who wants to be third choice out of three? If this board of governors think they can appoint me as an after-thought to take up a post of special responsibility, carrying an extra £100 per year then they can think again. I started work at St Ambrose R.C. Secondary School on 3rd September 1962!

I stayed at St Ambrose School for two years, during which time I met Percy Jones, a P.E. organiser who was to enhance my career in no small way. Percy was an innovator; he developed Educational Gymnastics to such an extent that he became a national authority on this highly specialist area of Physical Education. He was also my area organiser, which meant that I was close to the founder of this ground-breaking approach to what was called 'the indoor P.E. lesson'. I became his exhibition king, giving demonstration lessons to P.E. students from all over the country. I suppose my slightly extrovert teaching methods were good for selling the new approach to the subject. By late 1964 I was becoming quite famous within the relatively small world of the P.E. teacher. There came news of a brand new school being completed some ten miles away in the Ribble valley. Once again alarm bells began to ring in the career-oriented area of my persona. I enquired further into this new project to find it was a school with phenomenal facilities for every subject taught at secondary school. The P.E. facilities were amazing. One particularly inviting feature was that it contained two large gymnasia; and to complement that unique asset, there were playing fields accommodating soccer, hockey and athletics. There were tennis courts, netball pitches, in fact the facilities were the best that Lancashire Education Authority had to offer. It just so happened that the P.E. organiser for the area containing this new school was a certain Percy Jones, who was my organiser at St Ambrose R.C. School, Rawtenstall. I gently broached the subject of this new educational Disneyworld and suggested that I might apply for the soon-to-be advertised post as Head of the P.E. Department. The opportunity to demonstrate Percy's techniques and innovative teaching practices in the brand new environs of Billington St Augustine's R.C. Secondary School excited me to such an extent that I must have awakened Percy's imagination. He supported my application for the post and by some coincidence I was appointed. The icing on the cake for me was that Phyllis was appointed Head of the girls' P.E. Department. As we started our new jobs at Billington we felt able to move up in the property world as well. Langho is a highly fashionable area on the outskirts of Blackburn and a new development was being built, so there we were again, visiting building sites. We were in a slightly stronger purchasing position this time as we had established a respectable credit rating with the Midland Bank; as a result we purchased a property in this area of Blackburn, which not only moved us up the property ladder, but also moved us closer to our new jobs at St Augustine's. Things were looking really good for us; in fact we were quite enjoying our climb up the ladders of social respectability and professional achievement.

The job at Billington carried with it the opportunity to demonstrate our work in gymnastics to students around the country, as well as the chance for me to make a film of the boys of St Augustine's performing their skills in this relatively new method of teaching. It became known as 'The Billington Film' and was shown in P.E. colleges and teacher-training establishments throughout the country. Percy Jones was enjoying the limelight afforded him by having a

**Billington School, large gymnasium. A demonstration lesson for Carnegie students.**

brand new venue as a showcase for his innovative teaching practices, and as he was a greatly respected figure in the world of Physical Education, I was getting a good reputation for my work; the spin off for me was that I could look to move onward and upward with confidence. The world of P.E., however, was just as influenced by fashion as the rest of the education curriculum and the way forward was to be acutely aware of change. I suppose it's called career management in modern terms. The sad fact was that I was ambitious, and I was prepared to sell my soul. Even I didn't totally agree with the new alternatives the devil had on offer. This was the case at Billington. The latest craze (and that's what it was) to be presented to boys' P.E. teachers was ... wait for it ... Modern Educational Dance. This was to be the way to go if you were to progress significantly in the profession. I wanted to progress significantly. So, I sold my soul to Modern Educational Dance. Percy Jones was absolutely devastated. He was about to lose his premier disciple. I had been demonstrating his teachings for almost five years and here was I, changing my religion. I saw it as an opportunity to get on the fast track to becoming a lecturer in a training college, so I felt justified in changing horses in midstream.

In the midst of all this I still maintained my interest in variety. We talked earlier about how the theatre had always fascinated me, from being very small when Mum and Dad took me to Blackpool for our annual holiday. We used to arrive on the Saturday morning and after we had left our cases at the boarding house (North Bank Private Hotel, £7 per person per week, use of cruet sixpence extra), we went straight into the town to book our seats for the shows Mum and Dad wanted to see. I was happy just to tag along as long as we were going to the theatre. Over the seven nights we were away our budget allowed us to go to three shows. The stars we saw there completely mesmerised me. You remember, they included George Formby, Frank Randle, Jewel and Warris, Dave Morris, Jimmy James and many others. Now you see that's interesting; the first few names I listed there were comedians. Was that telling me something? I used to love watching them work; I revelled in the laughter they created. I suppose even at that early age I was hooked! The surprising thing was that I didn't realise that I was ... Not for me the Shirley Temple syndrome where I could sing, dance, juggle and play a musical instrument at five years of age. I was nine going on ten and could do nothing. I had no idea that one day I would play the London Palladium. It's called subliminal show business fetish!

The excitement of the pit orchestra striking up the overture, the house lights going down, the anticipation of seeing the artistes on stage, all this was the most exciting part of the holiday. The curtain going up for me was quite indescribable, the spotlights (I used to turn round to watch them), I used to try to imagine the sensation of being hit by one of those beams of light; people on the stage weren't real, they were gods, they were from space, I was a ham. I was one of those customers with sequins in their eyes. How could I see through them? I was a victim of Barnum. I was one of the suckers that were born every minute. I was the comedian's dream. I would laugh just to be part of the show. I was being severely stuffed by the showbiz bug and I was feeling no pain; it was a case of, 'Never mind the screaming, make me have it!'

*I say, how revealing!*

Mum and Dad never encouraged me to perform as such; in fact they almost repressed me, as it seemed to them that a nine year old was being precocious if he were 'showing off'. Television in my youth didn't feature too prominently in my life, so images of variety were restricted to the imagination, apart from my holidays in Blackpool where I could experience it first hand. The wireless was my only other link with show business, my only other tenuous connection, that which enabled me to enjoy the 'razzle dazzle' that was later to become my livelihood. Radio shows like Variety Band box, Workers Playtime, Saturday Night Out, and many more became a vital part of my life. Cyril Fletcher with his 'Odd Odes' was music to my ears, Frankie Howerd asking us to 'Titter ye not' and suggesting that his 'flabber had never been so gasted!', completely bemused me, and the razor sharp wit of Ted Ray told me that this was not the world of fools, but a world that appeared to be very fulfilling and exciting. I enjoyed comedians I suppose because I enjoyed laughter, and who doesn't, but I wasn't really thinking about actually being one myself. I wasn't behaving in a mature enough manner to convince anyone that there was any ambition in any direction at all. My life was sort of bumbling along and I didn't seem to be doing too much about it. I was only 16 and we've all been 16.

As I grew older I became even more interested in comedy. Perhaps it was because the premature end to my schooldays wasn't all that funny. Not a lot to laugh at when you're emptying dustbins for a career. My academic achievements warranted a comedic glance, though I'm not sure my dad would have seen it that way. National Service encouraged me to smile at life, and maybe it also encouraged me to start to cash in on what I thought was an element of talent in the laughter department. Early days, but I fancy there was a glimmer of aspiration in that direction. Chester College and Dad's ambitions for me were to stifle such thoughts for some time to come. As I entered the world of teaching, comedy was well down the list of priorities. I was newly married with no money; my mind focussed on progression through the ranks and ultimately my goal was to become a headmaster. A career as a comedian was not on the cards and any thoughts along those lines were immediately banished by a fervent desire to make a respectable man of myself, if only to please my dad. The first few years in the profession took all my energies as I struggled up the ladder to limited prosperity and a kind of acceptance by the establishment, such as it was in Accrington, *circa* 1960.

CHAPTER FIVE

# *The Future in Flux*

THE CAREER moved forward and as the promotions came along
my interest wavered a little as I sought fulfilment in the wider
aspects of the world around me. Teaching was fine, and the prospect
of a headship or even a lectureship was still interesting but not
exciting. I suppose as I got on top of each challenge along the road
my imagination was wandering back to the theatres of my childhood.
I was comparing my lifestyle with George Formby's or Frank Randle's
or even more significantly, Ken Dodd's. I tried to liken the start of
my day to the start of theirs. I couldn't see George Formby getting
up at seven thirty and walking to work. I couldn't see Ken Dodd
getting out of bed until after I had done dinner duty, though he
could well have been doing his books! In fact the whole comparison
exercise served to do nothing to enamour me of the routine I found
myself fettered to.

Something had to give. I had to make a concerted effort to get
into show business at whatever level I could. The answer lay in the
workingmen's clubs. I know it's a long way from the Opera House,
Blackpool, but at least I'm on the ladder; well perhaps not on the
ladder, but I knew which window cleaner would let me get on the
first rung. I was going to have to pursue this parallel career with
discretion. Working men's clubs don't mix too well with schools,
and if this scheme were to work the two worlds must literally be
kept worlds apart. Having spent three years dedicating myself totally
to teaching I felt I could venture into the twilight world of entertainment discreetly without invalidating my presence in the
classroom. It all started at the Regent pub in Blackburn where I
went for a lunchtime drink. There was a comedian advertised so I
waited to see the sort of thing he did in order to assess my position
more accurately. At around one o' clock the comedian went on and

to be truthful didn't do very well. I rather clumsily commented that I could do better; what I didn't realise was that the landlord of the pub was standing next to me. 'Oh really!' he snapped, and promptly went on to the stage and told the assembled crowd that there was some smartarse in the pub who thought he was a comic and would he come up here and prove it. The ball was firmly in my court. I went up on to the stage to minimal applause and found myself for the first time facing an audience who expected me to be funny to order, not when I felt funny but when they expected me to be. I stuttered through my very limited repertoire and somehow managed to survive the ordeal with an element of dignity intact. The landlord was agreeably pleased and invited me back for more that evening. I rushed home to tell Phyllis of my stage debut, and staggered her by further announcing that I had been booked back there that night. The fee mentioned was £3 for two spots of twenty minutes each.

It was then that the realisation of what I had agreed dawned on me. I didn't have enough material for two spots of twenty minutes each. I didn't have enough material for one twenty-minute spot. The thrill of being offered a chance to star at the Regent pub on a Sunday had clouded my judgement. I had been temporarily seduced by the offer of fame. The Regent pub was right in the centre of Blackburn, which as everybody knew was the Mecca of show business. To be spotted at the Regent pub meant instant stardom. It was well documented that anyone who appeared there on a Sunday night was guaranteed fame and fortune. It was Blackburn's equivalent of Opportunity Knocks. The fact still remained, however, that I didn't have an act to perform that night. I spent the next three hours writing down gags I had heard from every source, from fellow teacher, former pupil, current pupil, in fact any person who had been remotely funny within my recent memory span. I filled three postcards with gags; total running time eleven minutes. With space for laughter that could spread to fifteen minutes, still some nineteen minutes short of my obligation to the landlord of the Regent. The rest of the day was a blur. I remember going to the pub that night and doing my two spots. I don't remember how well I did; I do remember, however, that the whole episode taught me never again to say out loud anything about an act trying to earn his or her living by standing on a stage alone.

Despite the daunting Regent experience I started trying to get bookings around the area. I spent many evenings going to working men's clubs whenever there was an act on, just to watch, and maybe get a chance to do a few minutes. I was sure that the only way forward was to get on the stage wherever possible to try out new material and just get some stage hours in.

Quite early on in my show business career I decided that Whittaker wasn't really a suitable name for a potential star; and besides some cheeky sod called Roger would have made it difficult for me to stamp my own identity upon agents who would be clambering over each other to book me. We decided that a shorter name would be best. I modestly commented that I would be able to sign autographs more quickly for my adoring fans; and the concert secretaries in the clubs I was to headline in would stand a better chance of spelling a shorter name correctly. After a highly charged summit meeting Phyllis told me that Bowen was the answer. This choice was arrived at after we remembered that Phyllis's maiden name was Owen, and my middle name was Brown (that was my Mum's maiden name). B out of Brown plus Owen out of Owen gave us Bowen. It meant that Phyllis had the larger share of the named act, so she was happy. I was just delighted to come out of the argument alive with a new stage name. Jim Bowen it was to be.

Fortunately there were many opportunities to experiment with the act as the club scene was really vibrant, and the audiences were still up for being entertained. This was not to be the case for very long, however. As the sixties came to an end clubs were open seven nights a week, offering acts of all kinds, from speciality acts to guitar/vocalists (guit/voc in club terms), to comedians and others. It was a fact that comedians were always paid a little more than singers; the reason I know this is because, very early on in my club career, I learned that everyone in the club you were working at knew exactly how much each act was being paid, so there were no secrets at all!

From the workingmen's club circuit the next step was the variety club (Batley was the definitive version). What had happened was that the entrepreneurs had entered the entertainment arena and seen a golden opportunity to grab variety by the neck and give it a coat of luxury. They built huge cabaret venues, some seating up to a thousand people, and fitted them out like palaces. Breweries were keen to get in on the action so were offering bargain prices for their

**Jim Bowen it was to be – in 1966 in Blackburn. Are you sure?**

products, and also advancing loans by the handful at ridiculous interest rates. All this enabled the club owners to offer the customer top-flight entertainments in luxurious surroundings at knock down prices. Clubs like Batley Variety Club, Wakefield Theatre club, Caesars Palace, Luton, Golden Garter, Manchester, Blighty's,

Farnworth, Blazers, Windsor, the list was endless. Audiences flocked in their hundreds to be entertained in these venues by big stars, while at the same time eating and drinking at pub prices. It was a champagne lifestyle at beer and skittles prices. The era of the cabaret club was to last over a decade, during which time acts were given the chance to cash in on their current popularity. Television was directly responsible for artistes fees going through the roof, consequently any offer of work in television was manna from heaven to the cabaret act. Obviously the bubble was going to burst, but fortunately I had my little slice of the action during those heady days. By the end of the decade television was a very powerful force in the entertainment business, as its popularity grew. Its viewing figures grew quickly, which showed every one in the business that television and success were inextricably linked.

One night during a week's engagement at the Dolphin Bar at Cleveleys, Frank (it's the way I tell 'em) Carson called in for a drink prior to his appearance in a Blackpool nightspot. He was a big star then in 1970 so I was delighted when he came up to me after my first spot for a chat. 'How would you like to be on television?' he asked. What a question! 'Is the Pope a Catholic?' I felt like replying, but I resisted. 'Granada Television is making a new series about comedians and I know the producer', continued Frank, 'I'll mention your name if you like'. I was absolutely dumbstruck. Here was I, only four years working on the club circuit, and now being offered television work. Fantastic! I rushed home to Phyllis after the show and discussed with her how I would handle stardom. How would I come to terms with the adulation, the wealth, the lifestyle of a comedy superstar? Phyllis then pointed out that I was perhaps being a bit presumptuous. Had I actually been offered a television spot? Had I actually got a contract? What was the title of this new show that Frank had talked about? How well did I know Frank Carson? Had I better perhaps wait for the phone to ring? Basically Phyllis was just being difficult. In fact as usual she was being sensible so I restrained my anticipation and got on with my two careers; on the one hand climbing the chalk face of education, and on the other waiting for the phone to ring from Granada Studios. Work in the clubs was plentiful; fortunately there was enough work locally, so my teaching career remained more than a viable option should I cease to be funny, or should someone find me out! I was still obsessed with the world of comedy and did all I could to develop a style of my own (incidentally, so did every other 'stand-up' comic on the circuit). Around 1970 one comedian who really did have his own style was leading the pack.

I was in awe of this man who broke all the rules, and battered his audience into submission with his zany, unbridled, madcap brand of comedy that simply exhausted his audience. Ken Dodd broke the mould as far as comedians of that era were concerned. He added a lunatic dimension to life that blew all comedic analyses away. If anyone was responsible for me accessing show business it was Ken Dodd. He was the final straw that made me realise that what I wanted to do was what Ken Dodd did. I watched Doddy countless times and never tired of his performances. I never tired because I was watching a man generate so much pleasure and laughter, so much so that I just had to try to do the same. I never did, of course, but I gave it a bloody good try, even as an amateur.

My teaching career had reached a crossroads. I was going to have to make a decision to take the alternative, risky route to the upper echelons of my profession or just 'go with the flow' of the main-stream, and take my chances there. I decided that to 'go with the flow' wasn't me. Dance drama was to be the way forward, instead of the more acceptable, traditional teaching methods.

To do justice to this new approach to the subject it was advisable to spend a year at a dance/drama studio, after which I would be one of a handful of male P.E. teachers with a tangible qualification in this innovative approach to the subject. I applied to join the Laban Institute of Dance and Drama in Addlestone, Surrey, though I had little knowledge of this approach to the indoor P.E. lesson, so my application form was rather lacking in substance. Ironically my demonstration work in the field of Educational Gymnastics had been noticed by one of the staff at Laban, who fortunately for me recommended that I be called for interview. I duly went down to the studio at Addlestone where I spent a day convincing my inter-viewers that I wanted to do the course out of a genuine desire to spread the word about Laban. I am ashamed to tell you I convinced the panel that all my motives were honourable, and that my wish to study there had nothing to do with my wanting a job in a teacher training college. I know you'll believe that.

*I say, how terribly deceitful!*

So it was then that I began studying dance and drama at the Laban studio with twenty-eight ladies and five men, two of whom I wasn't too sure about. The course lasted a year (though it seemed like three), and towards the end of the year we all started applying for jobs. I had resigned from Billington School, leaving Phyllis as Head of Department, thinking that when I left Laban we could both move to wherever I was appointed in my new post as a lecturer in a training college. Oh to be wise after the event!

I didn't really enjoy my year at Addlestone, probably because I was there for the wrong reasons. I had always been honest with myself about my motives in life and perhaps in the Laban episode I wasn't being as honest as I might have been. There were other students at Laban, however, who were to show their true colours as the course progressed, and one such person did just that with a vengeance. Read on!

The *Times Educational Supplement* is a weekly publication which advertises every teaching and lecturing post in the country. Needless to say, as we entered the spring term at Laban we all began looking for vacancies in training colleges for P.E. lecturers. Many came up, and one by one my fellow students were appointed as P.E. lecturers at colleges around the country. That was to be expected as I had only done the two-year teacher's course at Chester, whereas most of my colleagues at Laban had completed three years at specialist P.E. colleges like Carnegie or Loughborough. I plodded on with my applications but was beginning to get a little dejected, as no one seemed interested in what I had to offer. I wasn't even getting invited for interview. It was beginning to look like I had sold my soul, but the price I was about to receive was minimal in terms of career enhancement. I was doomed to return to the classroom after all my efforts in the ethereal world of dance and drama. My newly acquired liberal, avant-garde, highly fashionable approach to the educating of P.E. teachers was not to be given a chance to even take root in any of the colleges that were advertising vacancies. One college, however, was wise enough to offer me an interview. Clacton teacher training college invited me down for interview during May of the final term at Laban. By now most of the appointments for the following year had been taken up so I was clutching at straws a little. Desperate is probably the word I'm looking for.

I found myself in the reception area at Clacton-on-Sea College with five other applicants. I knew four of them as a result of my work with Percy Jones demonstrating what the 'in thing' in P.E. was just a few years previous. What did surprise me, however, was that the other remaining candidate was on the Laban course with me at Addlestone. I found this strange because he hadn't mentioned it at the studio where we had been studying together just the day before. He knew that I was up for interview at Clacton but never said a word. What a strange way to behave I thought. Anyway we discussed together the probable requisites for the post, and I suggested that the job could involve coaching in canoeing, sailing and other water sports as it was situated by the sea. I was fairly thin on the ground in terms of experience with water sports and I knew he was. We both agreed that if the subject was broached, we would both admit to minimal experience, but would be prepared to attend the Easter P.E. School at Blackpool, where we would 'brush up' on the skills and techniques involved when coaching water sports. We were both confident enough to think that our Laban training would eliminate the other three applicants, as one of the criteria needed for the post was dance/drama. The usual interview routine took place; we all went in to the Principal's office where we all answered everything to the best of our ability. After about two hours we had all been interviewed so now the time came for us all to wait to see who was called back to be offered the job. I sat there smugly knowing I had made it. I knew because one of the interviewers was head of the P.E. department and had seen my demonstration work at a conference of senior P.E. organisers the previous Easter. He had also been at King Alfred's College, Winchester, where Percy Jones and I lectured to teachers attending the Summer School there. Basically I was home and dry. I mean, there was this senior lecturer who knew of my work, interviewing me for a job at his college; he did ask me about water sports and as agreed I explained that I would need to do the Easter course at Blackpool to do justice to the job's requirements. Honesty is the best policy I thought, so no problem there then. I sat confidently awaiting my recall to be offered the job. As the principal came out of the study I managed to resist the urge to stand up in anticipation of the panel's final decision. It was as well I did. 'Would you come in please Mr Cheatyballs?' asked the Principal. I was stunned beyond belief. They had offered the job to my counterpart from Laban. I was absolutely wrecked.

I left the college to walk down the promenade at Clacton, still in total disbelief. Phyllis had travelled to meet me after the interview, as it was half term at Billington and there she was, on the seafront as arranged. She knew straight away that our world had gone pear-shaped. 'What happened?' she asked. I then went on to describe how cheatyballs had surprisingly appeared on the scene and how he and I had agreed to be upfront about our limited seafaring experiences. I explained that one of the panel had been on one of my courses, and how he was obviously batting for me, during the interview, and finally how I nearly totally embarrassed myself by anticipating the outcome of the interview by prematurely standing up to return to the Principal's office to accept the job. We walked despairingly along the seafront in silence. The pace was slow, the mood sombre and the world was a very lonely place. We were in Clacton-on-Sea facing a future that looked particularly bleak with no job, no prospects and a self-esteem that had just bottomed out.

As we both ambled down the prom we heard footsteps behind us. Who should pull alongside but the friend I thought I had in the interview room some two hours earlier. The man who had given me hope and encouragement in my quest for elevation to the status of lecturer in physical education looked at me quizzically and suggested that my lack of experience in water sports had cost me the job. I then asked why cheatyballs was appointed. 'Oh, he had done water sports on courses at Blackpool and Loughborough and was quite confident in that area of the job, he was quite emphatic about that'.

I was stunned. The man hadn't stuck to his bargain with me, and he'd been totally dishonest with the selection panel. What made matters worse was the revelation that, had I been able to coach water sports, the job would have been mine by a mile. So much for integrity I thought. The aforementioned fellow student entered the ranks of the 'obliterati' who came into my life. I was to meet him years later in Clacton and my naïve belief in the philosophy that 'everything comes to those who wait' was to be well founded.

I had to learn to live with the disappointment of losing to a waster so I carried on with my studies at Laban watching the *Times Educational Supplement* for any suitable vacancies. Aspirations to become a lecturer were fading fast as the start of the final term was approaching, and it seemed that all the lectureships had been filled.

The more immediate problem was looming fast, and that was to get a job of any kind for the start of the new academic year in September. The creative elements of the school curriculum were well examined as part of the course, so a job in a primary school would be available somewhere as the fashionable 'integrated day' could be well enhanced by the experience acquired at Laban. The integrated day meant that subjects like English could be linked to Drama and in turn to Art, then on to Creative Writing and so on. Laban students were very much in vogue with Her Majesty's Inspectorate around the late sixties so the chances of getting a job in a school somewhere were more than good. I began looking for deputy head-ships in primary schools where I thought I could perhaps make my mark, even though I hadn't taught for any great length of time in one. Phyllis and I talked about where to apply and we eventually thought that the Lake District or north Lancashire would be worth a try. Several jobs were on offer in that area so once again I began posting my CVs off wherever there was a suitable vacancy. Several pre-interview visits to schools helped me feel the temperature of the water so to speak and ultimately the invitations for interviews came up. I attended several interviews around the North West but for one reason or another nothing came of them. Either the headmaster of the school didn't like me or I didn't feel I was the man for that particular position. Time was getting on and the prospects were looking grim on the employment front. Not only was I not making progress in the lecturing appointments, but also basic school teaching jobs seemed to be avoiding me. At this particular time in my life I was certainly not finding myself in the right place at the right time. Surely things must change.

CHAPTER SIX

# Decision Time:
# Laughs or Learning

B Y NOW we had sold the house in Langho in Blackburn, so we
had nowhere to live at the end of the Laban experience and
Phyllis had given up her job as Head of Department at Billington
School. Talk about burning your boats; we'd just made a bonfire
of our home and two careers. I had a real premonition that our
next address would be Pudding Lane, and our place of employment
would be Dotheboys Hall where I would probably rise to assistant
beadle and Phyllis could take up the appointment of housekeeper.
That's if everyone who applied for the position told the truth. I
mean, the luck we were having we could come up against another
cheatyballs!

Things were to change though. When I was on one of my sorties
into North Lancashire, looking at schools which were advertising
for teachers, I found myself in Brookhouse, a small village near
Lancaster where I met Cecil Wilkes, a fine gentleman who was
Headmaster of St Paul's Primary School. It was almost a social call,
as I really didn't think my future lay in a country school after the
hurly burly of life in Surrey (that's near London, you know). It
transpired that Cecil's very energetic deputy headmaster was due to
leave in the summer and he was looking for a replacement. The
job was just about to be advertised, and interviews were to take
place two weeks from then. I stayed quite a while with Cecil, who
seemed to be encouraging me to apply for the job. The more I
looked round the school, and the longer I talked to him, the more
I felt it appropriate to apply for the post. I said my farewells and
drove back to Addlestone to continue what remained of the course.

I watched the *Times Ed.* for the vacancy at St Paul's to appear, whereupon I sent off my CV and awaited a reply. It seemed weeks passed by before I got the call to attend for interview; it was a Friday morning in June and the sands of time were running out for this unemployed dance/drama expert. I really was leaving it till the last minute; missing out on this post would sound alarm bells in every corner of the workplace. Nothing would be sacred out there. Phyllis and I would be both unemployed and homeless, so this job was becoming increasingly vital to both of us.

The governors of St Paul's saw fit to interview three candidates and there we all sat, in the school hall, looking at one another, working out the odds, trying to decide who wanted the job most. I decided it was all of us. I was last to be called in to the headteacher's office where the vicar, two school governors and of course my friend Cecil were in attendance. It then dawned on me that I had a friend on the panel at Clacton. 'What good did that do?' I asked myself. Then I remembered there was no cheatyballs at this interview. After the panel had done with me I returned to my seat in the school hall and looked at the other two applicants and we discussed the pros and cons of the job. About twenty minutes elapsed before there was any sign of movement. Then Cecil came out of the room. 'Would you come in please Mr Whittaker?' he asked. The relief that washed over me on hearing those words will never ever fade away. Even now I recall vividly the excitement I felt as I walked back into that room. I'm ashamed to say I never even looked back at my competitors to wish them well. The vicar, John Mullineaux, turned out to be a most supportive element in the St Paul's experience over the next couple of years. During my time there we did exciting things in the drama department and I think my time spent at the Laban Studio proved to be good for the children at the school. I was now approaching thirty-two years of age and prospects were looking good for a headship very soon. Cecil was turning out to be the kind of boss an ambitious deputy dreamed of. I was given the freedom to do really innovative work with the pupils, and once again in my career, people in high places were taking notice. To make headmaster at thirty-three, which was now looking likely, would put me well on track to achieve my ambition to become a lecturer; so all was dropping into position on the education front.

*I say, how convenient!*

The show business side of things was still featuring prominently, and the tenuous offer of an appearance on television from a certain Frank Carson had not been entirely forgotten. But, as they say, a bird in the hand is worth twenty television contracts in the bush (or the post), so my eyes in 1970 were fixed firmly on the education ball.

During my first term at St Paul's we were granted an addition to the family, a daughter; we called her Sue. She was to be the best Christmas present Phyllis and I ever got. The parcel weighed 7 pounds 5 ounces and was delivered first class to Royal Lancaster Infirmary on 1st December 1969 at 3.30 a.m. She was to be a source of pride and joy to us for life. Everything seemed to be dropping into place for us. We became a planned threesome; I was on course at St Paul's to take the world of education by storm, and my adventures on the fringes of big-time show business were augmenting the family income, though a TV offer would have been the icing on the cake. I was having a marvellous time at St Paul's and we were doing exciting work with the children. Cecil, my boss, was very supportive as we experimented with creative ideas in dance and drama, producing some really interesting stage work, which not only thrilled the children but entertained the parents as well. It was looking like I was to have more contact with the stage, working with children, than I was in my own right as a comedian. I suppose I never lost sight of the possibility of making it as a comic, but as I became more and more involved at school, the notion of stardom became less and less significant. But things were not to remain like that for much longer. Mid-way through my second year at St Paul's School, plans for my future in education were to be seriously derailed by a phone call.

Frank (it's the way I tell 'em) Carson had remembered his visit to me at the Dolphin Bar in Cleveleys. He must have done because the phone call came from Johnnie Hamp who was Head of Light Entertainment at Granada Television. 'Is that Jim Bowen?' he enquired. I obviously owned up instantly as I realised that Carson had been as good as his word. 'I'm making a second series of The Comedians and I'd like you to come down to Granada Studios in Manchester to record some material for me.' I'd watched the first series and wondered if that was the television opportunity that Frank Carson had talked about; I was fairly certain it was, so you can imagine my reaction to this phone call. I'm not actually sure whether

I got to the studios before he'd finished the sentence or after he'd started it! The series had run for a year and had become a massive success. With its simple formula of one comedian telling a joke followed by another, and another, it caught the imagination of the viewing public and went to the top of the ratings. Here was I, getting a phone call from Johnnie Hamp, a television executive. I was to be on television so early in my part-time show business career!

*I say, how exciting!*

However, it wasn't as straightforward as I'd imagined. On my arrival at Granada television studios there were at least twelve other comedians, all thinking, like me, that all their Christmases had come at once. We were to try for the second series, and this meant that we were to become additions to an already established group of very experienced performers. Faces like Bernard Manning, Charlie Williams, Colin Crompton and Ken Goodwin all stared at us, nay glared at us, or so it seemed. We knew them all as they were in the vanguard of the first series and had become big stars as a result of appearing on the show. We were there, within touching distance of fame; all we had to do was perform well in front of an invited audience, for ten minutes. Simple I thought, but when the reality of what it could all mean dawned on us, the job became much more than just another gig (booking).

I remember I went on about halfway through the evening, which was good for two reasons. 1. The audience were still fairly fresh, and had laughter left in them. 2. Only half of the other comedians had had a chance to steal your gags! I did quite well in my efforts to impress Mr Hamp, so much so that I was included in the second series of The Comedians. It became decision time again. Only weeks after declaring my future career lay in the arms of education, I was being challenged by the chance to make a real impact in the world of entertainment. All the efforts made to take the fast track in the respectable confines of teaching, and the chance to become a head-master, were to be sidelined by the temptations of the instant gratification that goes with performing on a stage to an audience who want to laugh. The choice was simple. Was it to be laughs or learning? You know the answer.

I confronted Cecil Wilkes, my boss of two years and explained my predicament. I needn't have bothered. Cecil was a wise old bird who had seen the way my life and ambitions were leaning. He knew the question I was going to ask him and graciously gave me the answer I wanted to hear. I resigned my post at St Paul's C. of E. County Primary School and set out on the road to ... well we would have to wait and see. The best part of all in this time of indecision was that firstly, I left St Paul's with the blessing of everyone, and secondly, Phyllis was extremely comfortable with everything. It was finally to be, 'Goodbye education, hello show business'.

The early seventies were exciting for me because I was lucky enough to be earning my living doing exactly what I enjoyed most. I was able to do it with the support of appearances on national television, which made my job easier because people recognised me and therefore gave me a little more time to prove myself on stage, and a little more money for being there.

One year after deciding to make a career out of comedy Johnnie Hamp offered me a summer season at Clacton-on-Sea on the pier. This was an ideal start for me as it gave me twelve weeks' guaranteed work and valuable experience working in a theatre. Sundays were days off so I was able to do concerts in resorts far away from Clacton. The fees for Sunday concerts were about the same as the week's salary at Clacton, so the bills were being paid. Business on the pier at Clacton was not good. In fact after a few weeks the whole experience was becoming a cure for agoraphobia! The cast list included Jimmy Marshall, Pat Mooney, Sammy Thomas and Russ Abbot who was embarking on his solo career, though the Black Abbots were in the show in their own right. The whole season was a financial disaster for the promoters but we weren't too disturbed as we thought the Grade family could sustain the losses. The season for me, however, did have one particular highlight. I found myself walking along the prom one evening when, from behind, I heard the sound of approaching footsteps. 'How are you, Jim?' came the sound of a vaguely familiar voice. I turned round and who do you think I saw? There he was, Mr Cheatyballs, resplendent in shiny jogging suit and white trainers (he always was a poser). 'Well, what a pleasant surprise, bumping into you!' I exclaimed (I was in show business now so I knew how to fake it!). 'I'm so pleased to see you again, how is the world of the college lecturer?' His expression

**Me, Pat Mooney, Sammy Thomas (in grass skirt!), Jim Marshall and Russ Abbot. Clacton Pier, 1973. There are more of us on stage than in the audience!**

became slightly troubled as he explained to me that the Clacton College of Education was being closed down and his job was being phased out within the next few weeks. I commiserated with him for a couple of seconds, and then I explained I had to get on, as I was busy buying handkerchiefs. I did wonder whether or not to offer him a job as my driver, but I was never too keen on shiny jogging suits; besides he might tell me he had an advanced driver's licence when all he could drive was a lawnmower. 'Sod him!' I thought, and strictly between you and me I wasn't intending to buy any hankies at all! The summer season came to an end and it was back to the club circuit.

Many comedians, who weren't fortunate enough to appear with The Comedians on television, found it very hard work in the clubs because we were doing gags by the hundred on the box, invalidating them for use in the real world of club land. The audience believed that whoever did the gag on television had created it, so when another comic did it in their club, he was accused of pinching it! For a time in the mid seventies the life of a non-telly comic was very hard. Life on the clubs was becoming routine and demanding; travel was the order of the day and to give you some idea of our schedule it was not uncommon to drive over 120,000 miles each year. In these relatively early stages of my show business life little time was given to the future. The phone rang regularly and the work was plentiful, so thoughts of pensions and old age didn't come to mind. I was in my mid thirties, with a lovely wife and daughter and the future seemed quite secure. To further enhance my future Johnnie Hamp had offered me some guest appearances on a new series he was making called The Wheeltappers and Shunters Social Club. This meant more network television exposure and an even greater chance of surviving long term in my relatively new career.

Another element came into the family equation when on 4th March 1974, we were blessed with our best ever present, a son, Peter, 7 pounds 7 ounces. I knew he was called Pete because Phyllis had decided that in 1959!

I know I said that Sue was our best Christmas present ever; well Pete was as well. It's my book after all, so I'm allowed two best ever presents!

Pete was delivered first class just like Sue to the same address as Sue, even the same ward, at Royal Lancaster Infirmary. Although he was delivered first class, there was slight damage to the contents in transit. Pete was born with a cleft lip. There was a history of this condition in Phyllis's family, in fact Phyllis had lost a brother with the same problem many years earlier, but all the experts say the trait is not hereditary. We were living in Brookhouse at the time, and Phyllis's mum was in residence to oversee my wellbeing while Phyllis was in hospital sorting out the proposed increase in personnel. We got a phone call from the hospital around 10 a.m. from the sister in the maternity ward. 'Can you come down Jim?' she asked. I was standing in the hall and Phyllis's mum was at the doorway. She knew something was wrong. I'll never forget her face as she looked anxiously at me. 'Of course I can', I replied, 'Is everything alright?' The pause seemed forever as the sister replied, 'Pete's got a cleft lip, but otherwise he's in great shape and so is Phyllis.'

Phyllis's mum knew exactly what the sister had told me, and I knew exactly what was going through her mind. Remember, some thirty years before she had lost a son with the same condition. I reassured her that all was well and shot off to see Phyllis and our new son. On my arrival at the hospital I was greeted by the sister who remarked in a very matter of fact way that all could be easily sorted out, and would I like a cup of tea. Phyllis was in excellent shape and Pete was certainly making his presence felt! Within an hour Mr Maurice was on the scene. Now here was some special kind of guy. He was a plastic surgeon who specialised in cleft lips and palates. What a man! 'I'll sort him out in three months when he gets a bit bigger', he said. The presence of the man was enough to dispel any worries we had about the little package, damaged or not. We got home and explained to Sue that Pete was going to have to be mended, so that sorted her out. Phyllis's mum was a slightly different kettle of fish. She needed a little more reassurance that all would be well, and we could understand that. It was interesting and endearing that she asked if we would get Pete christened before he went to be mended. Of course we would, and we did. Pete reached the three-month marker and sure enough a letter came from the lip repairman inviting Pete to come in and take advantage of the offer made to him at birth. We accepted on his behalf. We took him to Sharoe Green Hospital in Preston where Mr Maurice, true to his word, mended Pete. Neither Phyllis nor I could comprehend the level of skill required to perform such minute surgery. We were just so pleased that such skills were available to us. Pete had to stay there for a week or so after which he was allowed home.

We were obviously very relieved it was all over, and we knew that the sleepless nights Phyllis's mum had endured were over, but we wanted to do something for Sharoe Green. The ward sister said that an aquarium would be wonderful for the children to look at as they lay in bed but Matron had refused because it would need maintaining and she didn't have the resources to cope. The vibes we got from the ward sister were that perhaps there might be a way of getting an aquarium into the ward without consulting matron. This involved a little deception but we decided that, in the circum-stances, a little deceit could go a long, long way. After all, once in place, it would be awfully difficult to remove it without causing a lot of ill feeling amongst the troops. We got the message. About three weeks after Pete had been discharged from the menders, two white-coated staff entered Sharoe Green reception area carrying a large fish tank and accessories. When asked for their credentials they confidently stated that they were from Manchester Regional Hospital Board with equipment for Ward 3. No further questions were asked, and the men dutifully installed the tank with its contents in the agreed position on the ward. The duty ward sister had no idea why this equipment had arrived but was delighted to sign on the dotted line accepting the delivery. Today, some twenty-seven years on, the tank is still there, fully operational with its self-cleaning system to minimise maintenance time helping to pass the time for children getting mended in Sharoe Green. What the nurses don't know is that on the base of the tank is a little brass plate. Do you know what's engraved on that brass plate? It says simply, 'Thanks from Pete'. I wonder who those two white-coated deliverymen were.

*I say, how very mysterious!*

Back at Lancaster Infirmary the staff were interested in how Pete's operation had gone, as babies with cleft lips were not uncommon. They explained that some new mums, when faced with the surprise, sometimes had a little difficulty coming to terms with their slightly different newborn. Phyllis made contact with the maternity ward at Lancaster and offered to bring Pete to the hospital whenever the staff on the ward thought that showing Pete to the troubled mum might reassure her about her baby's prospects. She was called upon several times and was always delighted to go. The relief she brought to the new mum by showing her a repaired Pete more than justified her visit. The wonders of modern surgery still amaze me and 'it's getting better every day!' (Mamas and Papas *circa* 1967!).

Almost the whole of the seventies was taken up travelling the country doing the act in venues of all shapes and sizes, and at all times of the day and night. One particular Sunday lunchtime I was booked to appear at South Shields British Legion up there in Tyneside. Now there's a venue that conjures up memories. I was the support act to the stripper who was a regular feature at these society meetings, which were well attended by the local residents, mainly male it must be stressed. On my arrival at the club I was informed that the young lady would entertain the chaps first at around 12.30 p.m., and then I would follow with a 40-minute contribution to the lunchtime proceedings. The lady, as agreed, went onstage and did or rather undid her bit and came off to what

I thought was limited appreciation on the part of the audience. The concert secretary then introduced me from his pulpit situated halfway down the smoke-ridden club. The prospect of doing well seemed remote so I resigned myself to surviving the allotted time doing minimal damage to the occasion. Things were not to turn out quite as I had expected. After about ten minutes I realised that I was doing fairly well, so the chances of my getting paid were beginning to look quite good (getting paid off was a common occurrence in these clubs). As I sailed through the act everybody in the room was responding well to my efforts, except for a table of eight men sitting jury-like right across the front of the room immediately in front of the stage. They all just stared, poker-faced, throughout the whole act. What was even more annoying was that every two or three minutes, one of the jurors would get up from his seat, go to the bar and get a pint of bitter for himself and then return to his seat. This went on continuously through the whole act. It was most distracting and had this happened to me earlier on in my club life it could have proved disastrous. I completed the act and left the stage still holding on to my dignity, and as a bonus, I enjoyed a warm reception from the lunchtime audience. I went to the bar for a drink, only to be accosted by one of the unsmiling fellows from the front table, who had been defying me to make them laugh. 'Why man you were bloody good up there today!' he remarked. I resisted the urge to end his life, and just casually remarked that it would have been nice to see some evidence of his enjoyment. 'Why no man, we couldna' laugh at yer, 'cos the first one of us to laugh has to buy the other seven a drink!' What a wonderful frame of mind to be in when you're going out to enjoy yourself. The good news was that they laughed at the stripper, so their Sunday lunch outing was not totally in vain.

Life in the clubs was getting harder as the audiences became more difficult to please. Club life, though, was still a large element of the working man's routine, and Johnnie Hamp hadn't missed that. On the back of his successful television creation The Comedians, he saw an opportunity to develop the working man's club into a variety package that would appeal to everyone who enjoyed a down to earth night out with no frills attached. The Wheeltappers and Shunters Social Club was born. Colin Crompton was to be the entertainments secretary (remember the fire bell, 'Best of order please!'), and Bernard Manning was the compère. It was a marvellous vehicle for all club acts, and competition to appear on the show was fierce, as the clubs were becoming even more selective about the acts they booked; faces that they had seen on television took preference. The series ran for four years and it helped many acts to prolong their shelf life, mine included. There are a lot of people out there who owe a lot to Johnnie Hamp, with his creative approach to television in the seventies. The end of the decade saw the end of an era in television entertainment.

# CHAPTER SEVEN

# 'I'll go and make a coffee,' said Phyllis

C OMEDY had been king for almost ten years, and we had been part of its reign. The style we had developed, that of the stand-up comedian, just telling jokes we had picked up or stolen, had run its course. Forty years earlier, before television, Max Miller carried on for years with the same act, and a good one it was too. But even the great Max would have had trouble sustaining interest if 12 million viewers had seen him every week. Television had been good to us but it made us work at our craft. We had to develop and change if we were to stick around in show business. Either that or we would have to think the way of Micawber and believe that 'something would turn up'. We all know that Micawber was an eternal optimist and I believe that there is a lot of Micawber in most people in show business; there has to be because it's an absolute certainty that, for 95 per cent of us, nothing turns up. In show business the phone ringing is usually the thing that makes up for little or nothing 'turning up'. That's almost always as good as it gets. But still we carry on in hope; it's called trying to pay the bills and feeding the dependants, but more importantly it's feeding the ego.

One of the venues where I used to work was Charlton Athletic Social Club, which was managed by a good friend, Ray Donn. Apart from having the best wig in show business, Ray was a thoroughbred showbiz nut. He worked for all the showbiz charities, not the least of which was the Variety Club of Great Britain, and he had great connections, if you know what I mean. One of Ray's dear friends was a man called Albert Stevenson, a producer at ATV.

Albert served in the Second World War, was taken prisoner by the Japanese very early on during hostilities, and spent six years enjoying their hospitality. I'm sure you don't need me to tell you that the Japanese were known for their kind and gentle treatment of our troops while they had them in their custody. The story goes that Albert was invited to speak at a Rotary Charter Dinner where he was duly introduced as the creator of New Faces, the hit television programme, and as a man who was captured by the Japanese and imprisoned for six years during the Second World War. Albert gave his speech describing in detail his work in television and his life as an influential producer, with all its vagaries and pitfalls. Everyone thoroughly enjoyed the speech and afterwards the Rotary Chairman asked if anyone had any questions. There was a pause before one of the gathered intelligentsia asked, 'What was it like in a Japanese prisoner of war camp?' The crassness of the question would probably have floored most speakers but not Albert. 'The first six days it bloody pissed down!' he replied. I wonder why I never joined Rotary. But I digress.

Albert had devised a new series for ATV called Up for the Cup. The idea was that football clubs should offer an entertainment team up for selection to perform in competition with one another on television. Each team should contain a male singer, a female singer, a speciality act (e.g. impressionist, juggler or ventriloquist), and a comedian. The programme was scheduled to go out at 6.30 p.m. on Saturday night. Each week the winning team would go forward into the next round, and ultimately, if successful, would appear in the final. It meant the team that won every round would appear on television on five Saturdays throughout the winter schedule. Ray Donn asked me to be part of the Charlton Athletic squad as the team's comedian. I hesitated at first as I thought I was too old and experienced to be taking part in what appeared to be a talent competition. (I ask you, too old at 43, such arrogance!) Ray explained the mechanics of the idea, and the possibilities that the show could offer in terms of television exposure, so after a brief moment's consideration I agreed. At the time I didn't know how well connected Ray Donn was to the wheels in the business. Suffice it to say that we won every round and came a close second in the final! How's that for knowing who your friends are? After that adventure Ray looked after me for a while and we were to have some exciting times together. I was becoming part of the furniture at ATV's studios in Birmingham, having spent several weekends recording Up for the Cup there. We had a wonderful time meeting the other acts, and of course we enjoyed the success that our team's performance produced. Bobby Davro was our speciality act as an impressionist. Even then in those early days in his career he shone like a beacon. It's funny you know, but sometimes the tingle down the back of the neck tells you that you're watching something special. That was the case with Bobby. I'm pleased to see that his talents have not gone unnoticed.

As we approached the final round in this significant series I was to come across Jon Scoffield. It happened this way.

I was in my dressing room after we had recorded the final of Up for the Cup when the door opened and in walked this tall imposing figure of a man. 'Do you know who I am?' he demanded. I did of course, as I had seen him striding round the edge of the studio as we were recording the final. I assured him that I knew exactly who he was and thanked him for the chance to appear in his studio, which on reflection was a fairly weak reply to his query. 'You're a very funny man; I'm going to make you a star', he snapped. He then just walked out of the room without even looking back. I was flattered by his comment, however brashly it had been delivered and duly went home to Phyllis where I related to her the whole episode. She was, as usual, extremely excited by the news, and to celebrate we dismissed the whole thing as show business behaviour and had a coffee each. Some weeks later, however, we were to be proved wrong. The Frank Carson syndrome had reared its head again.

Having established myself at ATV as a reasonable act, I was offered a spot on a high profile, prime-time, and network variety show to be transmitted on Thursday nights at 8 o'clock. It was to be called Starburst and was to be directed by, guess who, Jon Scoffield. The conversation Jon had with me in my dressing room those weeks before began to register. While I was having lunch at Elstree studios, where the series was being made, I noticed Jon walking through the restaurant. He said nothing but just gave me one of those knowing nods that told me he hadn't forgotten the dressing room chat all those weeks ago at Birmingham. I suppose that's why he was Head of Light Entertainment at ATV; he never forgot.

I appeared on Starburst several times and all seemed to be going well, in fact very well. Television was featuring large in my career and the phone rang quite frequently, so the future was looking assured, at least as assured it could do in this business of ours. 1980 had been extremely good for me in terms of profile adjustment and I was happy just to ride the route I was allocated by circumstance and opportunity.

I now take you back, dear reader, to a certain children's home in Liverpool in 1938, where a young unwanted waif was waiting for 'something to turn up'. In this case he was waiting for a spare pair of parents to help him through life, and 'something turned up' in the shape of Joe and Annie Whittaker. Here we have this same unwanted baby, albeit 42 years on, waiting for 'something to turn up'. All I ask you to do before you read on is turn to chapter one and just scan the script and you'll read the phrase, 'How lucky can you get?'. You're not going to believe this but that phrase applied in 1980 to the same waif again. How lucky did I get? I think you'll enjoy the next little segment of the book, 'cos I feel I know you now!

The comedy style we were still trying to sell in 1980 was becoming 'old hat'. The after-dinner scene was where it was all going, and we were all trying to adjust to the new demands made of us by this new type of function. The future was looking all right but the distant future was becoming a bit of a worry. I had two young children who would need feeding and educating for some years to come, I was 43 years old and just beginning to realise that pensions and security in old age were rather more imminent than I realised; but the Micawber element in my make-up was slightly fudging these issues.

A light at the end of the tunnel appeared when I was asked to take part in a drama series called Muck and Brass, starring Mel Smith, who at the time was a rising star (Alas Smith and Jones, remember?). It was a series about council corruption and deceit, concerning property and land sales. Mel played the lead role as the crooked entrepreneur who was involved in fraudulent dealings, which entangled me as a weak-willed building society manager who was ultimately ruined by his schemes. The series, which was made by ATV in Birmingham, ran for seven weeks on the network. I appeared in three episodes and was paid £1,000 for the entire shoot.

I was filming this series between travelling to cabaret and after-dinner bookings around the country, so the diary was encouragingly full. This busy and lucrative scenario only further removed the responsibilities of parenthood and considerations about old age from my mind. This misguided philosophy was that as long as the diary was full, there was little need to worry about the future. I never contemplated the possibility of long- or short-term illness, or the possibility of an accident precluding me from earning. Looking back this was an incredibly irresponsible attitude, which I now feel quite ashamed of. I suppose to my credit I did work hard to provide, and fortunately I got 'the rub of the green' to allow me to do so.

I was booked to speak at a dinner in Wrexham, during the filming of Muck and Brass, and was in my hotel room awaiting a message from the toastmaster calling me to the function room to do my little bit. It was a sportsman's dinner and I was to speak alongside Mike England, the former captain of Blackburn Rovers and Wales. The telephone in my room rang and I answered it. Instead of the voice of the toastmaster I heard someone who was to become one of the most influential people in my life. 'Peter Harris here', said the voice. 'You don't know me but I've been asked to ring you by Jon Scoffield who, as you know is Head of Light Entertainment at ATV. This is rather embarrassing for me, but could you tell me what you do.' I was a little taken aback by this question, but with damaged (but concealed) ego I managed to describe to Peter what I did to make a living. I did, however, question the validity of the call. 'Well,' continued Peter, 'I'm a staff producer at ATV, and we are proposing to make a pilot game show involving darts and general knowledge, and Jon Scoffield thinks you could be the man for the job. When can we get together to discuss the project?'

The prospect of hosting a game show at this stage of my career was timed to perfection. Micawber was rearing his most welcome head and he was looking in my direction. Something was about to turn up.

*I say, how very fortunate!*

'I can be wherever you like, whenever you like', I replied, trying not to sound too keen; I mean, this chap had to ask what I did for a living so why should I try to accommodate him? I'll tell you why, because this man on the other end of the phone could be offering me a lottery win, and the lottery wasn't operating then! We arranged to meet at the Grosvenor Hotel on the Hagley Road in Birmingham the next day, where we would try out the game format with the man who presented the idea, Mr Peter Holmans.

I left Wrexham with a spring in my accelerator as I drove to Birmingham to meet Peter Harris. As I drove I took stock of what had happened to me over the past eighteen months. Up for the Cup, and Starburst took care of the light entertainment side of things, while my acting with Mel Smith in Muck and Brass had showed off another side of me. 'Not bad,' I thought, 'for a late starter in the game'. Things were getting really exciting now with the prospect of a game show in the offing. Remember that in the eighties game shows were at their most popular.

The Grosvenor Hotel is a pink-fronted building with lace curtains and delicate shrubs enhancing its overall ambience. It didn't give the impression that it was the home of weightlifters or rugby players, rather the home of the dressmaker or scatter cushion designer. As I was scheduled to be there on a purely temporary basis I didn't take too much notice of the finer details of the hotel's frontage; I was there just to meet the man who I hoped would make me a star.

I had never met Peter Harris before, but I knew who he was as soon as he walked down the drive. I was bedazzled by a tall, white-haired, well-groomed gentleman, wearing a short white fur coat, sporting a gold bracelet thick enough to tow a tractor, a Longines watch, and round his neck a heavy gold chain which was supporting a gold miniature of Kermit the frog (I later found out that he produced The Muppet Show for ATV). He swept up the drive of the Grosvenor (he obviously knew it well), and made me feel most welcome with his opening address. 'Hello darling, I'm sorry I didn't know what you did for a living, didn't mean it like that, I mean, well, you know how it is in this business, seen one, seen 'em all, c'mon let's get inside and see what we can make of this little lot!' He knocked on the door of the hotel to be greeted by the owner (I think he made cushion covers). 'Oh, Peter!' he cried excitedly, 'How lovely to see you again, and just look at you, all that gold, ooooh! I don't know whether to give you a kiss or weigh you in for scrap!' That was my first meeting with Peter Harris. It was to be the start of a most valued and enduring friendship.

We went into the function room at the Grosvenor to meet Peter Holmans who introduced the idea to ATV, and who was to become executive producer of the show, should it take off. The floor in the function room was marked out and a dartboard was put in place along with some chairs where the contestants would sit. We ran through what was in place as far as the rules of the game were concerned, and on reflection we didn't have much of a game plot. The two Peters talked long and hard trying to put some more flesh on the skeletal format they had, and the day drew to a fairly inconclusive close. I went home in a fairly dejected mood, as I could see my prospective career as a game show host slithering to a standstill. A few days passed and I heard nothing. Then out of the blue Peter Harris rang me at home and said they were doing a revised pilot at ATV studios on Broad Street in Birmingham. I was overjoyed at the prospect but still had reservations about the game's survival. In the studio I met Jon Scoffield again who was most encouraging. He really did seem determined that the game should succeed and, what was more important, he wanted me to be the presenter. I found out much later that Peter Holmans was totally against my selection. We stumbled through the pilot and it would appear that it was good enough to make a series. Peter Harris and Peter Holmans, along with floor manager Keith Lascelles, P.A. Barbara Bradbury and yours truly went out for a Chinese meal to sort out a few minor snags and to decide on a title for the show. At the end of the meal we all agreed that Bullseye would be the name of the game.

The next stage was to get the set built in the studio and to trawl for contestants. Programme associates were set in place, and audience researchers and question setters were appointed. Before we went into the studios to record the programmes we had been told the transmission details.

The series of thirteen half-hour programmes were to be recorded in time for the ITV winter schedules, and the transmission time was to be at seven o' clock every Monday night. This was called a protected slot. What happened was this: Crossroads went out at half past six till seven o' clock, and Coronation Street went out at half past seven till eight o' clock. These shows attracted massive audiences, so it was thought that the half hour between these two programmes would be a great place to put Bullseye. Remember in

1980 we didn't have the dreaded remote, so the powers that be reasoned that no-one would be bothered to get out of their chairs to change channels so they would sit through whatever came on for the half hour between. The challenge facing us therefore was a daunting one. We had to at least sustain the viewing figures that Crossroads was getting, and we had to hold those figures for Coronation Street to pick up. It was very much a win-or-lose situation; there was no grey area. If we didn't hold the audience we were dead, and if we did, then the network might go for another series. We were to be delighted, disappointed and downright dumbstruck, all within the first six weeks of the series hitting the screens.

A Monday night in early September saw us record the first two episodes of a programme that, despite the fiercest of criticisms from all angles, survived for almost a decade and a half. The first two episodes were so good that Jon Scoffield called us all in to his office to discuss our future. 'Thank you for coming', said Jon warmly. We all relaxed, though we really weren't all that convinced that the two shows we had recorded the previous night were all that good. We were to learn how good they were. 'What do we all think about last night's efforts?' asked Jon. The embarrassing silence that followed gave us all the answer. 'Burn them both and try to get it right tonight!' snapped Jon, and promptly walked out of the room. We stared at one another in disbelief. The Head of Light Entertainment had just written off £46,000. Back to the drawing board was a phrase that came to mind. Needless to say, we spent a long Tuesday attempting to save a critically ill programme. At the end of that long day we went into the studio to record two more episodes of this very embryonic game. To be absolutely honest we did little better than the day before, so when we were called into Scoffield J's office the next morning we quite expected the same reaction. And guess what, we were right. 'I can't keep burning these shows', said J. S., 'so I suggest that you do the best you can and we'll offer them to the network for them to do whatever they wish with them.' We went on to record the remaining 11 shows and began to pray. I honestly thought my career in the business was finished. Television exposure is all right if it's good exposure. Any other sort is professional suicide; remember Charlie Williams in The Golden Shot? Look what happened to him.

I was honestly dreading the first transmission; I would be ridiculed beyond belief, and the press would have a field day terminating my career. From being a fairly well-respected jobbing comedian I would be transformed into the nation's village idiot within weeks. I honestly believed that as a reasonably intelligent comic with a fair command of the English language, I could just walk into a studio and present a game show. I'd compèred corporate functions with ease, and conducted 'in-house' competitions at large company gatherings, so what was the difference?

You arrogant pup Bowen, just who did you think you were?

My problem was I'd missed the big picture. I thought that Bob Monkhouse was ordinary, and I thought that Brucie was just a variety act with a game show suit. The fact of the matter is you can't just walk in and 'do' a game show. It takes hours of practice and dedication. It takes time to learn how to work with cameras and lots of other people. It's not like working on your own on a stage where you are the only element in the equation. The big problem I had now was that 13 episodes of Bullseye were edited and ready for transmission, and the network had decided to run them on Monday nights at 7 p.m. from late September until Christmas! The die was cast. I would be a non-event by the New Year.

*I say, how very depressing!*

Throughout the time we were recording, Peter Harris had been a constant source of encouragement to me. He never at any time throughout that recording period shouted at me or suggested that I could have done better. I suppose he knew that I was fully aware of my inadequacies.

At the end of the recording, we had a party at the Strathallan Hotel for the crew and all who had worked on the show. Jon Scoffield was in attendance. We heard that evening that there were no more Bullseye programmes to be recorded at ATV Birmingham studios in the foreseeable future. Apparently the powers that be on the ITV network had seen the stuff we had done and had decided that enough was enough. We were all quite philosophical about it all, even Jon appeared only slightly disappointed; I, however, had pangs of conscience because with hindsight, I really thought I could have done better, but couldn't we all. The Peters, Harris and Holmans stoically accepted the sad decision and the Holman Peter would appear to have been correct in his assessment of my capabilities. He was gracious enough not to say 'I told you so' to the ever-loyal Jon Scoffield. The party came to a sombre close, and we all went our different ways, anticipating with some degree of apprehension the transmission of the first episode of Bullseye to the nation.

It was a Monday night in late September when the first episode appeared on the nation's television screens. I was sitting at home with Phyllis, not too eagerly awaiting the outcome of our efforts in Birmingham some weeks earlier. The show came and went after which I asked Phyllis what she thought. 'I'll go and make us a coffee', she tactfully suggested. This told me everything I needed to know!

I had enjoyed over a decade in the very transient world of show business, but so far had been privy to the more permanent side of things, with my diary having been almost full since I began. I'd had more than my fair share of television work, and certainly more than the 15 minutes of fame that some wordsmith or slick gimmick writer had said we were all allotted. Isn't that nonsense really? I mean, Phyllis would pay millions to remain unfamous! Anyway, here was I, involuntarily standing at a crossroads. There were several directions on offer, none of which I could choose. The great British Public would decide which direction the Bowen career would take; and it would not be too long before they made this decision. Alongside this uncertainty there was, however, another positive element rising to the surface, and it came, once again from the legitimate side of the business.

CHAPTER EIGHT

# *Beer and Bully*

M Y FORAGING into the world of the thespian once again (remember Muck and Brass) brought further opportunity to show off
in the world of the television commercial. These engagements can
prove very lucrative and can also raise one's profile if the commercial
becomes popular and is transmitted regularly. My career to date
had not encompassed the TV commercial so when I received a
phone call from a certain Stanley Joseph I was taken completely by
surprise. Stanley was a principal at the prestigious ATS casting agency
based in Leeds at the City Varieties Theatre. I had come to their
notice as a result of my appearance in Muck and Brass, where they
had one or two of their actors in the series. Barbara Peasland was
the face of ATS when I attended an interview for a commercial for
Tetley's Bitter. There were several of us there at the City Varieties,
all hoping to get some of the action proposed by Tetleys as they
launched their brand-new advertising campaign for their fine bitter
beer. The interviews were quite chatty and seemed to have no
connection with acting whatsoever, in fact I wondered after the
meeting why on earth we had bothered to turn up at all. 'We'll let
you know' came the predictable response from the client, so we all
trooped home feeling fairly despondent. I wasn't too depressed as
I had my cabaret work to pay the bills, but I saw for the first time
the signs of real despair in some of the jobbing actors who obviously
had been 'resting' for some time. Memories of some of the cast in
Muck and Brass came back to me as I remembered occasions when
a round of drinks was an embarrassment to them. They did have
to watch their pennies very carefully. They really must have loved
their art, because they weren't taking home breathtaking amounts
of money, that's for sure. I felt slightly uneasy doing this acting
'bit', having had no formal training at Drama College, although my

year studying Dance and Drama at the Laban studio when I was teaching might have helped a bit.

There has always been a faint divide between performers in the legitimate theatre and variety acts, and to some extent I can understand why. Here was I, auditioning for an acting job as a part-timer, alongside people who had spent years practising their craft, and at the end of the day I drove home in a Mercedes and they sometimes caught the train or bus. I can understand the sense of injustice and inequality in this; perhaps that is why they take solace from looking at us 'turns' with an element of disdain. Well, some do anyway! But I digress.

The Tetley commercial offered the winner a chance not only to earn serious money, but also a chance to become a very desirable commodity, either as an actor, or as a cabaret act if that was your bag; because if the advert took off, instant recognition in the fame stakes was guaranteed, and that's the name of the game, like it or not!

A week passed by after the audition and nothing remotely connected to beer or Tetleys came into my life either through the letterbox or over the telephone lines. 'Ah well', I thought, 'I can still drink Tetleys beer even if they don't want me to extol its qualities on television.' I was resigned to remaining illegitimate for the second time in my life, but this time circumstances were considerably more comfortable and of course I had Phyllis and two fine children to bolster my ego. (I only had a small one by the way.)

The phone rang some two weeks after the auditions at Leeds and it was Barbara Peasland who told me that Tetleys wanted me to make one commercial for them where I was to play a longsuffering barman who was plagued by his regular clientele. We made the commercial at a pub in Todmorden in Lancashire; it took ten hours to shoot, and at the end of the day I wasn't at all sure that it would do big things for my career as an actor. Spending three hours saying 'Oh really, very interesting!' over and over again didn't really extend anything but my patience. There are only a limited number of ways you can say, 'Oh really, very interesting!', or so I thought. The filming of a TV commercial was opening a whole new bag of tricks to me. The obsession with detail and the minute interpretation of the writer's concept of the plot turns the whole exercise into a marathon. Along with the writer's demands for accuracy, the client has to be satisfied that he is getting value for the vast amounts of money he is spending; the director has to be satisfied that all the filmic options have been captured, I have to do exactly as I am told; which is precisely what I did!

Tetleys looked at the finished product after it had been cut, edited and had all the wizardry added, and then they booked a transmission slot to show the commercial. The future of the concept of the longsuffering barman in his pub was in the hands of the marketing department at Tetleys, who assessed the impact of the commercial on the viewer, and then decided whether or not to continue with the idea. It went out on a Monday night in September 1982 at about 9.30 p.m. I didn't actually see it but neighbours told me they had. The whole commercial was only 30 seconds long so there was little point in asking what it was like. All I could do was just wait and hope. The idea was that the barman would feature in every commercial, being tormented in varying ways by the locals who would trick or con him in as many ways as the writers could find. This would only happen if the original premise caught the viewers' imagination. The months went by with no one speaking to me, so once again my acting career was on hold. Fortunately I was still making enough people laugh to allow the acting to hang loose. Thank God for the clubs!

Eventually the telephone did ring and once again it bore good tidings from Barbara Peasland who, after three months of waiting and hoping, was able to tell me that Tetleys liked the barman idea and were going ahead with a series. The barman was to be called Alf and the storylines had been written and accepted for ten commercials. My ship had come in again; this time I was on the commercial side of legitimacy. If it paid the bills who's bothered about a pedigree; it's a mongrel's life for me I'm afraid.

*I say, how awfully materialistic!*

The Tetley commercials ran for five years in the North of England and Alf became a familiar face behind the bar as he struggled to keep abreast of his conniving locals. However, 1986 saw the beginning of the sharp rise in popularity of Bullseye, and this gave Tetley's a problem with Alf. The ironic situation developed where Jim Bowen was replacing Alf in the eyes of the public and in consequence was overshadowing Tetley's beer. People were saying, 'Did you see Jim Bowen in that advert last night?', rather than 'Wasn't Alf funny in

**'Alf' the barman in his flooded pub. We spent eight hours up to our waists in cold water. Never again!**

that Tetley commercial last night?' I had become too famous for the product. Bullseye had made me bigger than the product I was advertising. The series of commercials we had made had become a kind of sitcom with Alf being the star and the beer being the supporting character. So, I had to go! The bosses at Tetley's were extremely charming about this unusual situation saying that it was time to say our farewells to Alf, at the same time wishing me every success with my other supporting partner, 'Bully'. They took both Phyllis and me out to a most exclusive restaurant for lunch where they presented me with a plaque, which pronounced firmly that I really was a true Tetley Bitterman. I still treasure the memories of those riotous days when we filmed those commercials; from being filmed stuck in a pub flooded up to the waist, asking what the weather was like outside, to trying to serve a pint of bitter through borrowed glasses lent to me by one of the mischievous locals, I wouldn't have missed it for worlds.

If I were to be offered the same contract now to make that type of commercial, I would probably be able to purchase the Lune Valley and still have enough change left for Lancaster! Who's counting anyway?

Throughout the traumas of being dropped as Alf, and wondering about the future of Bullseye, family life remained constant. Phyllis, as ever, was a rock, and our two children were shaping up really well. Sue was doing well at Lancaster Girls Grammar School, and Pete was doing minimal damage at Arkholme C. of E. Primary School. Domestically it was a very stable period for us all, as throughout the seventies the telephone had rung often enough to allow us to move into Station House at Arkholme; this was an old Victorian railway station, which was to become a major feature in our lives.

The property needed developing, but its structure and its seven acres of adjoining land (formerly the railway sidings) were to house us safely and happily for the next twenty or so years. Sue took advantage of the land by schooling her horse on an all-weather riding arena we built for her, and Pete used what was left to practise his motorbike scrambling skills. It might be worth noting that even at this relatively early stage of family life Pete was already in the 'what's left after Sue' situation. All will make sense, I promise.

The two children grew along parallel lines, giving us much pleasure on the way. Sue was to go to Durham University where she read Chinese and Business Studies, and Pete was to teach us both a hard lesson in parenthood; but that's later on in the story.

**Our much-loved station house, Arkholme, 1979–1995.**

The start of the eighties was a watershed in every aspect of our lives. The career was on hold, awaiting the public's verdict; the children were doing OK, awaiting the rigours of adolescence; the house was keeping us warm and occupied, and thankfully, Phyllis was still there to make sure that everything turned out for the best. You'll be pleased to know it did ... eventually!

The atmosphere in the lounge at Station House after the first Bullseye went out was delicate to say the least. Phyllis, as promised, brought in the coffee and we sat looking at each other, wondering. I knew that the programme was awful, or rather, I was awful, and Phyllis knew that I was awful.

The worst thing about being married to someone for a long time (especially someone who's bright) is that you know what they are thinking, and you know that they will tell you what they are thinking; I was prepared for the worst. 'The problem is that you're not your natural self. You don't give off that warmth and affection that I know you can do when you're dealing with people.' How could I be warm and tender when I was concentrating on cameras, lights, contestants, scores, scripts, directors, and floor managers to mention but a few distractions?

The bottom line was that I wasn't prepared enough to tackle a game show of such complexity. I know you won't believe me but there were eight cameras in that studio and not one of them was my friend. The cameramen were, but the cameras weren't. The red lights on their heads were my enemies, especially when they were lit, 'cos that meant they were loaded with ammunition and they were firing at me!

We drew a veil over the evening and got on with our lives, until the following Saturday when the *Daily Mirror* came out. I got a phone call from the Arkholme Post Office-cum-newsagent at around half past seven in the morning suggesting that I didn't buy or read the said tabloid. I was down at the shop immediately to be faced by a very troubled newsagent. You see, the villagers had become part of the Bullseye saga. We had practised elements of the game in the local pub before it ever reached the studio and had spent hours working out the most acceptable target for the contestants to tackle as they went for the star prize. The magic '101 or more' was decided upon in the Bay Horse at Arkholme so consequently the entire village became a part of the show they had helped to give birth to. They all felt they were Bullseye's midwife, so any imperfection would obviously cause great concern. Their loyalty was about to be stretched to the limit by a certain TV critic (she was called Hilary Kingsley!) who wrote in the *Daily Mirror*, 'What is this balding, innumerate, illiterate geriatric doing on our screens at primetime presenting such a shambles of a game show?' She carried on with similar vitriol and I must say that the effect it had on me was devastating. For the first time I was experiencing the downside of being in the public eye; and I wasn't prepared for it. I couldn't see the point of subjecting myself to this sort of abuse when all I was trying to do was present a simple game show. That evening I went out for a drink to the cocktail bar at the Midland Hotel in Morecambe which was sure to be quiet, as in the light of the morning's press I felt that people weren't on shopping list, at least for a while. I approached the bar to order my drink facing the barman, not looking into the room itself. 'I read the article in the *Mirror* this morning, Jim,' said a familiar voice from the far end of the room. Turning round I found myself looking at one of the most loved and revered characters in show business. Eric Morecambe was sitting in the bay window of the cocktail bar with his driver. 'Come on over and have a chat,' he said.

I had never actually met Eric before, though I knew of his connections with Morecambe, so to be invited to sit with him was really quite special for me. I muttered something about the article not bothering me, though why I should lie to someone like Eric I don't know; I was talking to a man who was told he had no future in the business when he first teamed up with Ernie. Who was I fooling? 'Let me tell you something Jim', said Eric, 'the most difficult thing to find in anyone's house is yesterday's newspaper'. Such a simple observation, but coming from such a respected source gave me a totally new outlook on the press in particular and public opinion in general. I was to remember vividly that conversation on several occasions, as I found myself riding the gauntlet of showbiz hype in the coming years. Thanks a lot Eric!

'We'll know how well we're doing after about three weeks,' said Peter Holmans. He went on to explain the viewing patterns when a new show appears on the box.

Peter's track record more than equipped him to predict the future in this context; he devised The Sky's The Limit with Hughie Green and was directly responsible for introducing us to the sexiest bum on telly, the one that belonged to Anneka Rice; you've got it, he produced Treasure Hunt for Channel 4. Apparently the viewing figures during the early episodes of any new programme follow the same pattern. The first programme attracts the inquisitive element of our public, along with the diehard television viewers. Dependent on the appeal of the first week's show, the second week's figures should be better. By the third week, word is out about the show, so people are either with it or have switched off. As the weeks progress through the series, a pattern emerges which tells the programme planners what to do about the commissioning of a new series. Our figures went like this:

| | |
|---|---|
| Week 1 | 7.5 million |
| Week 2 | 8.9 million |
| Week 3 | 10.6 million |
| Week 4 | 11.7 million |
| Week 5 | 12.6 million |
| Week 6 | 10.6 million |
| Week 7 | 9.4 million |

The pattern emerging after week 6 told us that the public had reached a verdict that the show wasn't great so they were tailing off in their droves. We had been given a prime spot on peak time television, and the show wasn't cutting the mustard at all. Every week we looked at the ratings and by week 9 we were suicidal as we sank to 7.8 million viewers. Then, some Aladdin somewhere must have rubbed his lamp because, quite inexplicably, the figures started to rise again. By the end of the series we were touching the 14 million mark. We tried to work out why there should be such a dramatic rise in the programme's popularity, and we could only come up with one conclusion; and this is how we came to it. We transmitted the best programmes first, knowing that new broadcasting depths were to be reached by the time we reached programmes 10 and 11. Remember Jon Scoffield burned the first two shows we made, and the ones being shown at the end of the run were the ones nearest to Jon's box of matches! We decided that the viewing public couldn't believe how bad the first few shows were, and as they switched off; the remaining viewers became even more bemused by the further drop in standards. They then told their friends, who switched back on to confirm their worst fears, and we confirmed them! The end result was that Jon Scoffield called us all to a meeting in Birmingham after the last show had been transmitted. We all sat round the table in his office, vividly remembering the burning ceremony, and waited in anticipation for the boss to arrive. A smiling Jon arrived and sat down slowly in his high backed leather chair. 'Well,' he remarked, 'I don't know how or why, but your programme has been in the top ten for the last six weeks. The planners obviously have taken note of this and they want us to make another 26 episodes for the network. They obviously don't think much of the programme because they've decided to bury you in the Sunday teatime slot, or, as it's affectionately known, 'the God slot'. Now, is there any chance at all we could make a decent game show out of this mess?'

We were absolutely delighted about the decision to give us another series, but we were somewhat daunted at the prospect of going out at Sunday teatime. I suppose, bearing in mind that less than 12 months earlier we had two shows burned, an offer of 26 new shows was good news. Jon didn't seem too optimistic about our chances, but spent some time with us as we tried to make the show more of a challenge to the contestants, and to upgrade the prizes on offer, especially the star prize (not a speedboat again!). That was in 1981. The rest, as they say, is history; and let me tell you, it makes very good reading.

We began to realise that what the public liked about Bullseye was its fallibility. They could all answer the questions at home, they could all play darts better than the guys on the show, and they could certainly present the thing better than that balding geriatric they saw on their screens each week. We were proud to think of Bullseye as the Coronation Street of the game shows. The contestants didn't have to pass beauty auditions, or have the dress sense of Beau Brummel. All they had to do was play darts well, and answer fairly easy questions. It was the working man's game show. We didn't get many contestants wearing cravats or suede shoes and M&S featured prominently in the wardrobe department!

The series gradually became a wonderful part of our nation's Sunday afternoon routine. The great British public took us to their hearts in their millions for a variety of reasons. There is no doubt that my groupies could walk away from me quite easily, they may have a little trouble running, but they certainly couldn't sprint away! What I'm saying really is that any appeal I have would lie with our more senior members of society; to attract younger fans on the other hand, we had in our armoury a secret weapon. He was the baby that was created by one Peter Harris. His name was 'Bully'.

At the beginning of the third series (1984) Peter decided that the character, which featured in the opening cartoon-type titles, should be given a third dimension. He was to be made of rubber and was to be dressed in a red striped shirt and blue jeans. Made by Bendy Toys, he arrived on the scene at the end of the third series and we

**Peter Harris's baby, Bendy Bully. The star of the show!**

included him in the prize agenda at the start of the fourth series. After a high pressure executive meeting in the social club, it was decided that everyone who took part in the show should be awarded a Bendy Bully, whether they wanted one or not! I wondered where Peter was coming from when he suggested the idea of a rubber toy as a mascot for a game show which featured a sport played by big, yes big, hairy drinkers whose primary interests didn't necessarily lie with rubber playthings! It turned out that he was exactly on the button; Bendy Bullies became as desirable as any of our star prizes, in fact at this moment in time they are bringing over £250 on the internet.

By now, as we entered our fifth series, Peter Holmans was warming towards me as the presenter of his show. I fully understood his reluctance to endorse my position in the early days of the programme. I think he realised that by now I had established a rapport with the viewers, and that I was perhaps becoming a valid part of the equation that formed Bullseye. It was almost by default that the public took to the show, with all its catchphrases, my northern interviewing style, the prizes that sometimes were inappropriate, and contestants who, at times made the whole quiz look like a romp in the park!

Series number six arrived, and by now we had all stopped asking questions; we just did the show to the best of our ability, at the same time being fully aware that to get it too smooth could lose us viewers. We knew what they liked; no place for ego in this arena, for the game itself was the star. All that the two Peters did was make sure that the wheels went round and didn't fall off. We never altered the format drastically; we were too frightened to do that. We just tweaked it a little each year. It was the premise, 'if it ain't broke, don't fix it' that became our simple philosophy. The real truth was that we didn't really know what gave us the appeal we obviously had; we were just riding on an animal that everyone loved. We couldn't understand it, but we didn't mind, we just kept quiet and let her go! Well done Bully!

It looked like the gods were watching over us, and we seemed set for a long and successful future in this unpredictable world that is show business.

From the outset it was looking like the eighties was to be a good decade for me, with firstly Muck and Brass and then Bullseye coming closely on the back of each other in 1981. After two or three years I was becoming a recognised face around the country and this television exposure had brought me to the notice of agencies that booked quite prestigious work both on land and sea. The corporate and cruise market is an area of show business where it's quite advantageous to know the right people if you are to be offered a chance to earn your living in this lucrative field. I didn't have an agent which in many ways is good (15–20% good, in fact!), but there are times when you could use a helping hand, if you know what I mean. I had lived up North throughout my showbiz life and as a result didn't come into contact with those career-enhancing brokers who almost invariably lived and operated in London. The only way I was going to get into this prestigious and lucrative market was to be seen working in the city by an agent of note, and incidentally working well. I obviously had no control over this so the whole premise was in the lap of the gods, or of Bernard Delfont; probably the latter because he'd met the Queen and everybody who lived at the Palace and all the posh houses in London. Seriously though it did seem that there was an element of the 'who you know' syndrome in our business and, on reflection what on earth is wrong with that? Better the devil you know than ... well you know the rest.

I needed the 'right time right place' rule to come into play; and would you believe it, it did! I was booked to speak at a lunch at the Savoy Hotel in London by Bob Willis (international cricketer of this parish), a fine man who ran a PR company of some repute. Bob had seen me speak at a boxing dinner some weeks earlier and, true to his word, he booked me again when a suitable opportunity arose. This particular lunch was in aid of the Variety Club of Great Britain; a most worthy organisation, and to say it was a high-pressure gig would be a huge understatement. There were people there who I had admired from afar for years, and here was I, sitting at the top table booked to entertain them. Anyway I did just that; the right people acknowledged my existence and saw me as a reasonable speaker (for a northerner). I was recognised by London. The prestige work was on its way ... or so I thought. Apparently it takes more than one swallow to make a summer, and it takes more than one good speech to make a difference in London, so the wait for the 'in' bookings continued. I was, however, still big in Rawtenstall!

It was around this time that Bob Monkhouse was celebrating his 40 years in show business and he invited me to speak at a tribute lunch at the Hilton Hotel at Marble Arch in London. I was not only flattered to be asked but terrified by the request, if only because I didn't want to let him down. I knew that the guest list would be formidable, but I also knew how much respect Bob commanded from his peers so I knew that I would be playing 'at home' so to speak and that the natives would be friendly. Phyllis was obviously invited and it was just as much an ordeal for her, as we found ourselves seated right in the centre of a top table of guests comprising an awesome gathering of talent from every conceivable department in our industry. Terry Wogan, Mike Yarwood, Dennis Norden, June Whitfield, the list went on. The whole occasion was recorded for BBC television, and was compèred by the fine late lamented early morning Radio 2 broadcaster, Ray Moore. This without doubt was the most demanding, frightening engagement of my career to date. The lunch was magnificent (I believe), and the atmosphere in that huge function room was unforgettable. Phyllis was very quiet.

I think I followed Dennis Norden who, needless to say, spoke beautifully, with style and an enviable ease of delivery. Ray Moore then introduced me to the audience, reminding them of my track record in the business and my success both as a comedian and a game show host; it was a very brief introduction! I got to my feet and spoke for twenty minutes about Bullseye, its teething troubles, shortcomings, frailties; in fact I could have gone on but discipline prevailed and I sat down on time as requested, to thunderous applause. I think they liked the honesty of it all, there's not a lot of 'owning up' goes on in our business and I think my northern honesty and simplicity won them over. (It could have been sympathy though.) The bottom line was that I had won again in London at a highly significant function. Surely now the offers of high-class society bookings would flood in.

After the lunch we stayed around at the Savoy, as our train home wasn't due to leave for a couple of hours. We decided to have afternoon tea there as neither of us had eaten any lunch! Bob came through the lounge to sit with us for a few minutes. He thanked me for turning up and quite revealingly said, 'You're a clever sod Bowen; people love you because you get it wrong and they hate me because I can only live with myself if I get it right!' Essentially he was absolutely correct. There is no greater performer than Monk-house, R. His preparation is the envy of the profession, his attention to detail is legendary and of course people don't hate him. Perhaps they can't take on board excellence and perfection; sometimes the general public like an error or two to creep in. Ask Dennis Norden, he's been showing them to us for years and don't we love 'em! Don't talk to Bob about it being 'Alright on the Night', in his case it always is! Thanks for the invitation to lunch Bob; I'm over the nerves now.

Whether Garry Brown was present at that lunch at the Hilton is something I shall never know, but soon after my small triumph at Bob's 40th celebration I received a phone call from Garry asking me if I would like to do cabaret on *QE2* in the near future. Here we go again, I must have been in the right place at the right time, though I don't know where or when; but does it matter? I was delighted to accept, and very soon I was offered a contract to appear on this beautiful ship as headline cabaret. I could take Phyllis and the family and we were all given excellent accommodation and a chance to see what life was like in the lap of luxury, being completely ruined by the best service in the world as we saw sights that I as a non-flyer would probably never see. It was to be the start of a long and endearing connection during which I was to make some of the best friends of my life. The ship has afforded me priceless and innumerable memories, which I shall treasure forever. Recognition had surely come my way now and I was determined to enjoy it with all its pursuant benefits and, I'm afraid to say, its shortcomings. I was later to speak at such gatherings as the 'football writers' dinner, and the Footballer of the Year awards ceremony. It did seem like the career was cooking on gas, as the saying goes.

CHAPTER NINE

# *The Red Book, China and Oxford*

HOME LIFE was continuing as ever, with Phyllis guiding us all through a fairly complicated domestic passage. It became more complicated as Bullseye began to enjoy more and more success. With this success came a disturbing but predictable loss of privacy. Fortunately none of the family was showbiz orientated, and they enjoyed an anonymity afforded them by living in a small village in the wilds of Lancashire. London and the glitz of city life were not part of their existence; their parameters were Pony Club meetings and local motocross gatherings respectively. Not for Sue and Pete the world of precocious show-offs that seemed to be ever-present on the edge of show business, with its pushy mums and ultra-proud dads. The only pushing Phyllis did was to make sure that the pair of them turned out to be decent youngsters who reflected our standards and ethics.

Phyllis and the children were soon to be unavoidably exposed to the glare of the spotlight during 1986 as I was to be featured on This is Your Life. I must admit, rather arrogantly I suppose, as Bullseye was becoming such a popular programme, that it crossed my mind that I could possibly become a suitable candidate. We talked briefly about the possibility and Phyllis said that if she were approached she would have to think carefully about what she would do. Having had that brief exchange I discounted the possibility because I knew that any kind of public appearance caused Phyllis immeasurable stress, and I wouldn't want that. So any thoughts or aspirations regarding This is Your Life were summarily dismissed.

We were on tour with the game, and we found ourselves in Dartford at the Orchard Theatre. The tour was not very long, and we were approaching the end, looking forward to going home. Mort Allan, a dear friend, was company manager for the tour and as I arrived at the theatre in the early evening before the show, he called me to one side and told me that Johnnie Hamp wanted to see me at home the next day to discuss a new series he was making. Mort was a little vague about the whole thing when I questioned him: 'Why does he want me to go home?' I asked, it seemed to me that he could have initiated the whole conversation on the phone in these early stages. We were in Dartford, and the following night we were in Folkestone. I mean it's a long way to travel from Dartford to the Lake District and then back to Folkestone in 24 hours, even for the possibility of a new series. Then I remembered the poor soul who got his diary out when he was offered Bullseye, so I asked no more questions and made arrangements to get home early next morning. It seemed quite convenient as I was due to take delivery of a new car, so I could exchange vehicles at home and enjoy the new car as I drove back to Folkestone. I rang home and told Phyllis I would drive up to meet Johnnie, and do the return trip in the new car. 'What a good idea,' agreed Phyllis, so the plan was set in stone. Later that evening I received a phone call at the theatre from the owner of the garage that was supplying the new car. 'There's been a problem with the car, Jim,' explained a very concerned garage owner. 'The delivery is delayed until weekend. I'm sorry, but it's out of my hands. Could we deliver the car to you on Sunday next?' I was disappointed but there was nothing I could do so the revised delivery date was agreed. This now gave me a problem, as I would have to travel by train to Lancaster, to be collected by Phyllis to get me home to talk to Johnnie. I researched train times and discovered that I could be in Lancaster by 12.29 p.m., so with Phyllis picking me up I could be home by 1 o'clock. My return train was 3.30 p.m. so Folkestone was just possible as I didn't appear until the second half of the show, which was around 9.15 p.m. It was very tight but possible; I was by now, however, wondering why I was embarking on this lunatic schedule. I felt sure that Johnnie would understand if I explained the timings, and would be more than happy to arrange a more convenient time and place for this meeting. I chatted with Mort who suggested that it would cause much less grief for everybody if I were to do as Johnnie asked. The next morning saw me leave Dartford early enough to allow me to catch the 9.35 a.m. train to Lancaster. I had to change trains at Preston and it was here that I should have cottoned on to the forthcoming happenings of the day. 'There's summat goin' on at Carnforth, Jim,' said the guard on the waiting train, 'They've fired up the Flying Scotsman for a special trip, so there must be a VIP about somewhere!' I thought nothing of this as most of the rail staff at Preston knew we lived on a railway station so this was normal conversation for me. The second train got me into Lancaster on time where I was met by Phyllis who whisked me off home. I commented on her hair that had obviously just been done and looked great. She demurely replied that she felt like a freshen up, which, on looking back, was totally out of character. As we drove past the Bay Horse in Arkholme I noticed a coach parked just off the main road alongside the pub. I remarked that it was unusual for the pub to take coach parties but received no reply from the speeding Phyllis, who seemed hell-bent on getting me home. I thought this was to give me more time to talk to Johnnie before my return to Folkestone. We arrived home and had the customary coffee, after which we went into the lounge. It felt a little strange sitting there because not a lot was said. We both just sat there waiting for our distinguished visitor to arrive to discuss this new series. Time passed and still no sign of Johnnie. 'It's not like him to be late,' I commented. 'Oh, I'm sure he'll be here soon' was the rather weak reply from Phyllis, who was now behaving slightly differently, though in what way I couldn't describe. I gradually became aware of activity on the railway line, looked out of the window onto the platform and was staggered to see a huge steam engine hissing to a standstill right alongside the platform. I ran outside to greet the train, wondering why it had stopped there, when a familiar face from my days at Thames Television distracted my attention. 'We're making a documentary about the Settle to Carlisle railway and we'd like you to do the commentary,' said the friend from the past. I was looking down the track towards the rear of the train. What I didn't notice was the figure alighting from the engine behind me and making his way along the platform. The friendly face kept my attention long enough for the legendary Eamonn Andrews to creep up behind me and tap me on the shoulder before uttering those famous lines, 'Jim Bowen, you thought that you came home today to meet Johnnie Hamp, but that's not why you're here, because tonight ... Jim Bowen ... This is Your Life!' I then saw the rest of the village get down off the train, and climb up on to the platform where they all surrounded me. Eamonn continued, 'Tonight in London, you will meet friends and family who will share memories with the nation as we celebrate your life'. I immediately looked at the time; it was 2.50 p.m. How were we to get to London in time for any celebration of any kind? It then began to dawn on me that there was only one way that this schedule could be adhered to. The title of the song 'The Only Way is Up' gradually came to mind.

### I say, how intimidating!

I have a fear of flying as you probably know so there was a logistical nightmare for the programme makers. After a few minutes, when the full realisation of what had happened hit me, I spoke nervously to the programme researcher and explained the position. Needless to say Phyllis had primed the crew that there might be a problem, so alternative arrangements had been made. For the sake of the pro-gramme they asked that I try to board the aeroplane they had organised, but there would be a car standing by the aircraft should

**That famous Red Book in Arkholme – with Eamonn and half the village.**

I 'bottle out'. The car would make it to London in time, but the shooting schedule would be put under extreme pressure.

Cars took us all to Manchester Airport where we walked out on to the tarmac to board the plane. The researcher, who kept me well apart from the other passengers on the flight including Phyllis, supervised me throughout. I remember sitting immediately behind Eamonn thinking, 'This damn thing will never go down with a good Catholic like Eamonn on board!' I was hoping God really would 'look after his own'. In fact, at that stage in the proceedings I was quite willing to discuss with God a pact that might ensure a safe passage; and then again, I'm not sure he'd have listened!

Phyllis and the village contingent walked right past me down the aisle of the plane, completely ignoring me, which didn't help at all. I just sat tight clutching the early evening edition of the *Manchester Evening News* that I was told to turn the right way up before reading! I managed the flight without too much nervous destruction and we arrived in London in good time. On arrival at the New London Theatre, where the programme was being recorded, I was ensconced in a private room, where from nowhere appeared a suit, shirt, tie, shoes, toothbrush etc. – in fact everything I needed to look cared for as I prepared for what was to be a very special evening.

At 7.30 p.m. Eamonn walked down the centre aisle of the theatre, up on to the stage and announced the subject of the evening's tribute. On cue I followed Eamonn through the auditorium on to the stage, where I walked to my allocated seat. Across from me on the stage were the village party, Mort Allan (who had suggested that I go home from Dartford the previous day), Pat Creswell (my secretary of some fifteen years), former teaching colleagues and a host of friends (sadly Cheatyballs wasn't present). As the surprise guests were announced one by one, the lovely thing was that none of them were surprises. By that I don't mean I knew who was in the programme; I mean that the programme had been so well researched that they enhanced the evening perfectly and no one was there who shouldn't have been. What a flattering guest list it was as well; Johnnie Hamp, Frank Carson, Jim Davidson, Mel Smith, Gary Wilmot, Faith Brown, Jimmy Cricket, and The Black Abbots not to mention my workmates from the dustbin era, National Service comrades and fellow students. Add to the list of guests Keith Deller, Bobby George and of course Tony Green, my Bullseye scorer. The

**All the guests together as the Red Book goes public at the New London Theatre.**

most charming element of the evening came at the end, when a group of children from St Paul's Primary School, where I was once deputy head, came running on stage to round off the celebration. After the show everybody went backstage to celebrate the evening by eating lots of nibbles and drinking plenty of wine and lemonade. I think the odd glass of beer was consumed as well. The memories of the night have faded now; in fact we said that the party should have been the day after the show because it was all too much to take in on the same evening. I remember we went back to the Regent Crest Hotel to top out the evening's jollifications. Frank Carson and Jim Davidson were really on form, so a floorshow was an added bonus for us all.

Looking back over the weeks preceding the big night I should have realised that something was going on. The vague answers to questions, the odd, unusual appointments that Phyllis and the children suddenly had, the surprising hair-do: how could I have missed all those clues? The fact is, I did, and if anyone asks if you know that you're being done on This is Your Life, I can tell you: you haven't got the faintest clue! In fact, for your further edification I can tell you that if the programme makers find out that the subject suspects anything at all, they cancel the show; ask Bernard Manning!

Furthermore, let me put an end to the notion that the programme is intrusive and an invasion of privacy. Quite the opposite in fact; it is a warm tribute to the subject and an evening of unforgettable memories. Anyone who could refuse Eamonn Andrews, or for that matter Michael Aspel, would join Mr Cheatyballs in my Hall of Obliterati, so there!

It appeared that our family was growing up alongside Bullseye in that they all had their teething troubles at around the same time and their growth was relatively smooth and positive. Sue was showing great potential at school and Pete qualified to go to Lancaster Royal Grammar School. Everything was going well and we were all enjoying life in the station. The time came when Sue had to decide what to do with her life as she approached the end of her time at school. She thought that a slightly different approach to a course of study could help her in her search for a place at university and so decided to study Chinese and Business Studies. Durham offered a suitable joint honours course, but the grades she needed were quite high. Her hard work at school rewarded her with the grades required by Durham and so she applied for admission to Van Mildert College in September 1987.

As you by now know our family name is Whittaker, so Sue, when filling in her application forms for Durham, quite correctly said she was called Susan Whittaker. This was good news for her because there was obviously no connection with the Bowen associated with Bullseye. She felt fairly certain that any connection with Jim Bowen from television would do little to enhance her chances of a place in a faculty studying Far Eastern culture. (After all, I came from Accrington!) Where the application form asked for her father's occupation she felt the need to ignore the question, so left the section blank. Ironically though, the interviewer asked her whether she had a father, to which she answered, 'Yes'. 'What does he do for a living?' asked the interviewer. 'Oh, he works nights!' came the reply.

She got into Durham University!

Her course ran for four years, the second of which was to be spent in Beijing to really get to the heart of the Chinese culture and language. Her first year went really well and she prepared herself for her second year abroad.

We all went to Manchester Airport to see our only daughter (aged

eighteen) fly out of our lives to the other side of the world for
the best part of a year. I remember watching her walk through the
departure gate to board the plane; she turned and waved as she
disappeared out of view. We stayed to watch the giant Cathay Pacific
747 lift off the runway, starting an exciting year for Sue, but for
me the departure of that 747 signalled the beginnings of a difficult
time at home. The significance of that flight departure was to become
apparent during the following few weeks.

For some unaccountable reason it marked the end of an era in
my life. I suppose it initiated the male mental pause kicking in. I
realised that Sue had virtually gone out of our lives and I didn't
like it. I had suddenly become of less use than I was when she was
at home. The self-esteem factor had been considerably reduced so
my desire to proceed wilted. To even write about my behaviour
during those months after Sue's departure fills me with shame. I
just curled up and 'couch potatoed' from June to November in
1988. I could see no reason to continue with the order of things
(though I never missed an engagement, which should have told me
something). The days, however, saw me lying on the settee, completely incommunicado wondering what the point of it all was.
Phyllis just carried on as normal, though she must have wondered
what normality was. To this day I cannot account for my behaviour;
I can say, however, that November eventually did come around and
the dark clouds of depression lifted. They do say that the most
difficult shot in golf is the distance between your ears. The same
rule applies when trying to fight your way round life's golf course.
I'm not a golfer, in fact I hate the game, but I can identify with
that philosophy. I struggled to master that small distance for weeks,
not understanding why there should be a problem, and in the process
I became an absolute liability. How Phyllis tolerated my selfish
behaviour I shall never know. Fortunately she did, and there was a
light at the end of a completely futile tunnel. I can identify to the
minute exactly when the end of this tunnel came into view.

Every year, on the last weekend in November, the Grand Order
of Water Rats holds its annual Ball at Grosvenor House in London.
It's always a spectacular affair with all the 'faces' in the business
turning out for charity. We had bought tickets to go to the event
back in June with two friends who were very excited at the prospect.
The morning of the Ball came and I was, as usual, drumming up

in my mind a reason to get out of bed. For the first time since the onset of this depressive state Phyllis became quite uncompromising in her attitude. 'Get up and get dressed!' she firmly announced. 'We are going to this affair whatever state you're in. Pete and Joan have been looking forward to it for months, so pull yourself together.' I reluctantly did as I was told and tried to appear interested. The arrangement was that we would all go to London in the Rolls and live it up for a couple of nights. Pete was to be chauffeur and we would all be showbiz posers for the journey. I felt about as able to pose as a shy gerbil and really struggled to get ready. We left Arkholme at around half past ten and travelled south on the M6 to London. By the time we had reached Birmingham I was starting to feel peckish so suggested we stop at Corley services for a snack. We went into Julie's Pantry where I ordered a double king-size cheeseburger with fries, and a coffee. The rest just ordered normal portions of everything. Phyllis took one look at the contents of my plate and said, 'if you're not ill after eating that lot you'll be very lucky!' Bear in mind I hadn't eaten properly for the best part of three months so my digestive system was in for a shock.

Julie's Pantry was my surgery that day. It was my psychiatrist's couch, my anti-depressant tablet, and my head repair shop. I cannot account for it to this day, but Julie's Pantry at Corley services marked the end of my mental aberration.

Even though the Corley experience had blown away the depths of depression, I still had temporary moments of doubt about my recovery, but as the weeks passed these moments became less and less frequent. The most confusing element of the condition was that there was absolutely no reason for me to be anxious at all. The series was doing well, the family were in good shape and there were no financial worries. I'm sure it was that damned aeroplane taking Sue to China that started it all. I never liked aeroplanes anyway, so I suppose this particular one had good reason to be hated. I bet if Mr Cheatyballs had been on the thing I'd have been all right! The good news for anyone finding himself down at rock bottom is that sooner or later things almost always come good.

The domestic scene rallied round and the feel-good factor became the norm again. Phyllis had, as expected, ridden the storm that had engulfed me and we were all enjoying the success of Bullseye as it entered its tenth season. By now I was acquiring 'cult' status with the universities, probably because they spent much of their misguided youth taking the mickey out of this essentially low-tech game. I didn't mind this at all because the feedback I was getting was that it was all good-natured fun; not only that but it seemed that I was in demand to present the touring version of the game at these places of high academic attainment. From the late eighties we toured the show round the holiday resorts and camps, and in the winter I found myself speaking at both the Oxford and Cambridge Unions, debating such significant subjects as 'North is better than South' and 'Big is not necessarily beautiful'.

My first invitation to Oxford Union was particularly memorable as you can imagine. Here was I, the host of an eminently working-class game show, being invited to speak on the ultimate debating stage. An academic arena that has seen celebrities speaking with razor-sharp wit, utilising all their satirical know-how; this famous chamber has witnessed the finest oratorical skills of guests and students alike; both scientists and world leaders have expounded their theories and ideals, so what on earth prompted them to invite me? I honestly don't know. However, my attendance there is recorded in the *Independent* newspaper and I unashamedly include extracts from my review which read thus:

The nearest I ever got to Oxford University – the Union!

*Bullseye! Jim scores again.*

On Tuesday night Jim Bowen stood up to deliver a speech in the chamber of the Oxford Union. Inside the building where prime ministers are nurtured, where Benazir Bhutto learnt to win an election, where Edwina Currie cut her political fangs, the biggest crowd for four years – 1,200 – was sardined into every available space. The moment the Union president announced Mr Bowen's name there was uproar. From the balcony a floor-stamping chant began. 'Jim, Jim, Jim,' it went on for what seemed like minutes. When the shouting subsided Mr Bowen began. 'Mr President, distinguished audience, thank you for that. But may I say I do feel you're taking the piss a bit.' This morning Ronald Reagan addresses the Union. But nobody expects the former US President to receive the kind of reception afforded the 54-year-old comic who presents a television darts show called Bullseye on a Sunday afternoon. Jim Bowen is a student hero. Such is Bowen's status at Oxford that at the last Union election many voting papers were spoilt by members adding his name to the list of candidates. On Tuesday students were in line across the Union quad three hours before he was due to appear, desperate to secure their place in the chamber

(Jim White, *Independent*).

## *I say, how terribly conceited!*

Since my entry into show business I had enjoyed more than my share of good fortune, bringing me the kind of success that everyone dreams of. It had afforded me an opportunity to do whatever was required to give the children everything that they needed to at least hit the road of life running; and I think this success compensated to some extent for my frailties as a husband and father. I use the word 'success' with humility because I genuinely believe that the first prerequisite in this business is luck; being in the right place at the right time helps but Lady Luck has to be on your side if you're going to make it (and that's not false modesty either). From my being in the right place in Liverpool in 1938, to being around when Peter Harris phoned me at that hotel in Wrexham, it seems that Lady Luck has taken a shine to me. Thank you Madam. We did have a little hiccup in June 1989; we thought she had deserted us, but she hadn't.

You remember when I went through the male mental pause

around the time Sue went to China for a year as part of her degree course? I recovered from that childish patch when I ate an allotment on a bun at Julie's Pantry on the M6. I thought I had problems then, losing Sue to the Chinese, but the end of that oriental-orientated year was to prove far more serious and frightening than any of us expected.

On Sunday 4th June 1989 I was compèring a Gala Charity evening with Jim Davidson at the London Palladium in aid of a leukaemia trust and we were approaching the interval at around 10 p.m. I went to the stage door for a breath of fresh air, and to have a chat with George, the stage door keeper, with over forty years' service in the job. He was always good for a tale or two and thoroughly enjoyed sharing them with us 'turns'. As I approached him he looked rather concerned and handed me the early morning edition of the *Sun* newspaper. The stark headline left me absolutely cold. '2,000 students killed in Tiananmen Square,' read the tabloid. I was totally numbed by the article as I tried to read down the page. I went backstage before the second half started and explained to Jim Davidson that things in China weren't too clever and that I really ought to leave the theatre at once. Of course Jim had no problem with that so I left the Palladium to return to my hotel. Mobile phones weren't as commonplace as they are today so the first thing I did was to ring Phyllis at home to decide what to do. Predictably, Phyllis was ahead of the game and had been watching Sky News since lunchtime when the story broke. Obviously neither of us could do anything but sit and wait, so I remained in London that night to return home next morning. Pictures of Tiananmen Square filled the news bulletins throughout the night. I vividly remember the images sent home of the lone student confronting the Chinese army tanks in the square. I'm sure you do, too. Eventually we received a message from a journalist working for the *Sun* newspaper telling us that Durham students had been located in the campus of Beijing University. They were all safe and sound and had been well away from the student activities in Tiananmen Square. The British Embassy was on the case rapidly, and all the UK students were gathered up and taken to the Embassy. From there they were driven to Beijing airport where they were flown home the next day. We went down to Gatwick to meet Sue and her fellow students where we were confronted with GMTV cameras and newshounds. The sight of that 747 (Cathay Pacific again) was as much a source of relief to me as the 747 flying out of Manchester the previous June was a source of concern.

Sue and her friends were interviewed by the reporters on their arrival at Gatwick, after which we loaded the car up and sped off to the safe haven of the station at Arkholme.

For the next two weeks Sue spent most of her time in her bedroom coming to terms with the tragedy she never really saw. Phyllis had kept all the broadsheet publications covering the riots and these brought Sue up to date on the whole chain of events. She never talks about it, even today; I suppose being a student she could identify with her Chinese counterparts and could sympathise with their difficulties. For all that went on during her time in Beijing, she still looks back with affection at her time spent there.

She resumed university in the September of 1990 and went on to complete the course, gaining a 2:(i) honours degree in Chinese and Business Studies. Now began the task of finding related employment, a challenge that faced most graduates as they enter the workplace. Her experiences in China, tanks and all, did nothing to subdue her desire to travel, so as there seemed little opportunity to take advantage of her degree in England she opted to go to Japan to teach for a year. There she would not only earn money but also enhance her CV considerably by having Japanese as an addition to her language portfolio. She returned from Kagoshima in Japan still facing no related job offers so returned to Durham where she studied for a time chasing a PhD. After several months' intensive study, the prospect of a further three years in the sheltered world of high academia began to daunt her, so she began to seriously search for a job. After attending a lecture in London given by John Manser, Sue returned to Durham and sent her CV to Robert Fleming's, (John Manser's stamping ground) in the hope that perhaps she might be considered for a position in the company. She was invited to London and after a series of intense interviews was offered a job on the Japanese desk, where she earned lots of money both for them and, I suppose, her. Sue stayed with Fleming's for five years, after which she sought financial advancement by going American, and starting work for Salomon Smith Barney as a dealer in Japanese equities, whatever they are. All I know is she can retire before me, the little sod!

CHAPTER TEN

# Dark Days, But Not Many

THERE is a famous saying that every man believes in heredity until his son makes a fool of himself. Pete progressed through the potentially risky periods of his upbringing relatively smoothly, and apart from the inevitable skirmishes that accompany domestic tensions arising from having an older sister, he reached 16 in good shape academically and socially. Both Phyllis and I were satisfied with his performance. His physical growth, however, became a medical problem. He was growing too quickly upwards and this was giving his knee joints too much to carry. The consequence was that both his legs had to be in plaster for three months, almost immediately one after the other. This meant that all his sporting activities, both physical and mechanical, had to be put on hold for the best part of a very important year for him.

This is where we missed the boat as parents.

We assumed that Pete was another Sue, and, surprise surprise, he wasn't. This enforced inactivity prompted him to search for fulfilment in other fields of activity, particularly at a time when he should have been concentrating on his A levels. Distractions were such that classroom interests were being easily sidelined by far more destructive forces. The rave scene was well in vogue and it was readily available to all who were seeking diversion. Sadly our Pete fell into that category. We were to find out later he fell quite dangerously into this fashionable way of life, which encouraged apathy in abundance, and a complete lack of interest in anything that wasn't hypnotically rhythmic. Basically we had failed to notice that our son had become a complete waste of space. He was totally unaware of his degeneration as a human being, and cared even less for any thing or person unless there happened to be a connection with the rave ethos with its ecstasy-addicted gatherings. This behaviour carried on throughout

his final year at Lancaster Royal Grammar School, and as a consequence he failed miserably in his A levels. (I remember someone
who got it wrong when it mattered as well.) However, he scrambled
into a subsidiary of Newcastle University at the Carlisle campus,
where his behaviour pattern was hidden behind the veil of college
activity. Then it all hit the fan. His bank manager rang me to
discuss Pete's financial position. It wasn't good; in fact it was
frightening. When we talked to Pete about it he was quite sure that
everything would turn out all right, and we believed him.

Unwittingly both Phyllis and I had become ostriches, burying
our heads deeper and deeper in the sand. We could not have done
anything worse.

I was travelling to London to make a commercial for a bur-
ger/chicken franchise when my mobile phone rang; it was Charles
Yates of the *Sun* newspaper. He coolly informed me that they had
pictorial evidence proving that Pete had been involved in the handling of drugs at a rave somewhere in the south of England. He gave
me details of Pete's car, his address in Carlisle along with details of
his recent travels to rave gatherings around the country. We had a
choice of two ways out of the dilemma. We could say 'No comment'
and leave the *Sun* to do the rest, or we could cooperate with the
newspaper and produce a positive article that might help thousands
of parents around the country who without doubt were in the same
predicament. Needless to say we chose the second option. (I was
frantically trying to take comfort in the words Eric Morecambe had
spoken to me in my hour of need, about how difficult it was to
find yesterday's papers.)

Pete appeared on the front page of the *Sun* alongside the story
describing his activities in detail. (So much for having a famous
father!) There were a few painful days to follow for us all, but Eric
was right, the papers were difficult to find after a day or two.
Fortunately the memory of the front-page exposé did stick around
for a while, especially with Pete. The worst, however, was yet to
come. The high-profile news article had alerted the authorities to
Pete's misdemeanours and as a result we were contacted by the police
who asked to come to the house to chat about things. The whole
drug scene was well out of our experience so we were glad to talk
to experts who dealt with these situations on a daily basis. They were
absolutely marvellous in the way they handled the whole affair.

It transpired that Pete had been 'shopped' by one of his so-called friends, who rang the *Sun* newspaper (for an agreed payment) to set up the photo opportunity, hence giving the *Sun* the exclusive story. The police explained that they would have to take him to Workington where he would be questioned about his activities, taking into account the evidence that had come to light as a result of the press article.

There we were, all sitting in the lounge trying to take in the fact that our son was being taken to prison. I must admit that at that moment, a sense of relief came over me, as I felt that someone was taking control of a situation we couldn't comprehend; and that is exactly what happened. Pete was whisked off to Workington police station where he was detained for questioning. The detectives who took him said that they were only allowed to keep him in custody for 36 hours, but such was my relief at the arrival of help that I suggested they keep him as long as it took to sort him out! After 24 hours we received a phone call from Workington police station. 'We're a little worried about Pete', said the voice. I immediately thought the worst until the voice continued, 'He enjoyed his break-fast this morning and this is not a situation we're used to. Anyway we've sacked the chef so it won't happen again!' Pete was returned to Penrith by the Cumbria constabulary where we collected him to bring him home.

The experience not only cured him of his rave tendencies, but has since been proved to be a massive learning process for him, as he got his life in order. The planned court appearance never took place, but the threat of a caution from the Chief Inspector at Workington added to the incentive for him to make good his future. Thankfully he sorted out his debts within the year and by the time he reached 19 years of age he had got the T-shirt of life; I can assure you also that Phyllis and I had grown considerably as parents as a result of that dark eighteen months.

The most disconcerting factor of the whole equation was that neither of us noticed any deterioration in the state of play at home. Bearing in mind that we had both been schoolteachers as well as caring guardians of our charges, it causes one to think how many other households are unknowingly the breeding grounds for deceit and malpractice.

The most damaging feature of an episode of this nature happening to a family is the trail of doubt and mistrust it leaves behind. Even when it is patently obvious that the problem has gone away, there remains a devil in the mind that stays there for an unreasonably long time; it erodes credibility with painful consequence, and it takes years to eradicate from the pattern of family life that was once so wonderful. I can say to any parents going through this 'mill of turmoil' that all does come out well; perhaps you could be a little more forgiving more quickly than I was. I look back on the whole business with a degree of regret tinged with a sense of inadequacy, but I can see that the big picture has a happy ending; after all, I went to the film. Pete is now enjoying a successful life in Tenerife and I can promise you that he is a son to be proud of, who has without doubt become a better person. Well done Pete!

The early nineties was a period when the family enjoyed the present, anticipated the future with excitement and looked backwards with relief and gratitude. With regard to our decision to go with the option Charles Yates of the *Sun* suggested, and be decisively up-front about the whole sorry episode of Pete and his errors, the positive feedback from readers and fans expressing support and approval told us that we had chosen the right option and the published article was a source of comfort to many families.

My dealings with the media have, to date, always been comfortable. It's part of the remit that goes with life in the public eye, and it always creates debate and confusion. Going into show business, by the very nature of things, is telling the world that you want to be noticed. Shy people don't do show business. They might say that they are shy, but I can assure you they are not. Show business is a licence to show off. Shy people don't show off; so shy people don't go into show business. They enjoy blending in to the background. I married a shy lady who hates the demands that are made on her private personage. That's not to say she doesn't support everything that I have to do as a result of making my living by having to be noticed. The underpinning she gives me is an invaluable asset; being the way she is she can almost invariably give rational information or a completely balanced judgement, because she can look at the big picture objectively. She's none the worse for that, in fact she's a damn sight more stable and responsible than most (Phyllis told me to write that!).

One of the problems with being in show business is that forces that aren't in the normal everyday scheme of things can influence decisions. We are mightily aware of image and ego, and the impressions we are making in this glitzy shallow world; all these elements can seriously damage the decision-making process. There is a definite place for the 'feet on the ground' influence on our lives as we work our way through the precocious environment, with its larger-than-life characters who constantly strive to impress, to succeed and to generally keep well ahead of the pack in the race for recognition. That's where Phyllis more than pays her rent. There is little chance of my getting too big for any form of footwear with Phyllis around. Now, having completely aroused and provoked your thoughts about shyness let me put this to you. Is an international soccer player shy? Let's take the talented Alan Shearer. Of course he could be shy, in fact he is, but he shows off his soccer skills, at the same time hiding the real person behind the numbered shirt. Don't ever tell me that the Harlem Globetrotters weren't show business with a ball and two baskets. Individual team members could be shy, and why not; we're talking athletes here, their exhibitionism is physical, it displays itself in the form of physical performance. Actors and variety artistes expose their minds and emotions, in many cases alone; nothing to hide behind there then.

I have a little more difficulty coming to terms with a shy actor. Anyone who can subject himself to standing on a stage in front of hundreds of people while he 'struts his stuff' is not, definitely not, shy. All this baloney about hiding behind the character they are playing, or letting the dialogue of the piece insulate them from recognition, is complete tosh! They go on stage because they want the approval of the audience. The whole business is about striving to be appreciated or, to put it less acceptably, they are seeking self-gratification. There's nothing wrong with that of course, as long as the end product is that the audience wins as well. The danger of this pseudo-shyness can be that the audience loses out, because the performer is too obsessed with the preservation of his own ego and image, and as a consequence the essence and integrity of the performance can suffer.

What a cynical observation about our more sophisticated members of the business! The bottom line is that stand-up comedians are acting their hearts out every time they go onstage, and without the help of a safety net in the shape of a written script or a preordained character.

That embittered diatribe is a prelude to a discussion about how we 'celebrities' react to the press. On our way up the ladder of fame in order to achieve recognition, we crave the attention of the media, whether it is newspaper, television, radio or just plain gossip. Publicity is the name of our game. Our function in life is to fill theatres, to appear in highly-rated television shows or to take part in as many public showcases as possible. The only way to learn the craft is to do it, and the reason we do it is because we want to become stars. Incidentally it would be quite nice if, en route, we were to become rich as well; so 'let not ambition mock our useful toil'.

So, where does that leave us with the press? I firmly believe that we can't have our cake and eat it. If we require the help of the press when we're upwardly mobile, we must expect to be fair game if any element of our lives, public or private, goes awry. A perfect example of how to handle the press is Sir Cliff Richard. One of the most enduring of our famous faces, Cliff has managed to handle every facet of his many years in show business with style and grace; more than can be said for many of us! I suppose I was fortunate in that I never had the appeal or resilience of Jim Davidson; I never actually courted publicity, or other women for that matter, so my minimal desire for wedding cake was more than satisfied; consequently, as a target for sleaze I must have been a bit boring.

I can also tell you, by the way, that one marriage in a lifetime tends to lead to more prosperity than the Middle Eastern attitude to matrimony.

Perhaps a realistic way of explaining management of the media is comparing it to good housekeeping and paying your rent. A lot depends on who's living in the house with you, and are they sharing the rent?

Another feature that enters your life when you become even a small piece of the nation's tapestry is the arrival of fans. These people enter your life completely uninvited and can take over your personal space with alarming speed, together with a surprising lack of consideration for your well-being. The same rules apply to fans as they do to the media. The two elements are born out of your success, and if you wish them to be there as you climb out of oblivion then you must be prepared to live with them, as your profile gets bigger. The people who at times can be the bane of your life are the same people as those who put you there in the first place. It has always been my philosophy that to ignore your fans, be they just autograph hunters or virtual stalkers, is the height of ingratitude. To give an autograph, or just a word of acknowledgement to a fan costs you nothing in terms of time or energy, yet is worth more than can be measured to the fan. I regard that element of the business as paying my rent. There are occasions when fans' behaviour can be boorish, verging on the rude and ignorant, but I genuinely believe that most of that is caused by nervousness to make the initial approach, so at least I give them the benefit of the doubt.

I console myself by thinking that the time to really get upset is when they stop asking for your autograph, and even worse, not even giving you a second glance. The time to be really concerned is when they come up to you and say, 'Didn't you used to be Jim Bowen?' Another regular ego-denting conversation goes like this: 'It is you isn't it? Yes, I was sure it was.' Then they walk away leaving you wondering who you are!

I remember Sir Alec Guinness, when asked how he avoided being recognised, replied, 'Avoid eye contact.' That was several years before it ever applied to me but he was absolutely correct; if you can keep looking down or away the chances are you'll get away with it. The only time that rule doesn't apply is where there is drink involved. Drink does take the inhibitions away from normally shy people and it gives them 'Dutch courage'. In these instances all the diplomatic skills you can muster are called upon. 'I think bloody Bullseye is crap', has been the cry of many a well-intentioned drunk late at night in the presence of his fellow carouser; the drill there is to walk away smiling at the person in question (secretly hoping it's the drink talking!).

It's the same with fan letters. When they do arrive it's always good if you can reply to them, but it isn't always possible as you can imagine. They come in all shapes and sizes; some of them are from doctors, or at least from someone who is used to writing prescriptions! Some are complimentary, some offensive and some are, quite accidentally, both. Letters arrive saying things like: 'Your show's awful and the sooner they get it off the telly the better. Will you send a signed photo to Mabel my wife, for some strange reason she thinks you're alright.' Of course you send them a large portrait of yourself, and you put a first class stamp on the envelope!

The bottom line is that we really should not forget that in this wonderful business of ours we have been privileged enough to enjoy the work we do, and get paid well for doing it, so the minor inconvenience of signing your name or acknowledging a fan is the least you can do.

CHAPTER ELEVEN

# *New Challenges*

I HAVE always enjoyed the camaraderie of the public house and over the years have been directly responsible for sending licensees on luxury holidays abroad on an annual basis. It goes with the lifestyle of a cabaret artist that a late drink is the only way to ensure a good night's sleep. Medically I'm sure that would not hold up in the surgery but it is embedded in cabaret folklore that a late drink is in cahoots with Morpheus and that's good enough for me!

Bearing in mind this flaw in my ability to sleep unaided, I was pleased to hear of a local hostelry going on the market. I immediately saw this as an instant solution to my predicament and proceeded to make enquiries into its disposal. The Red Well Inn was close to the station at Arkholme where we lived, so I made a concerted effort to hunt down the vendor and set about completing its purchase. The transaction was completed and we employed a charming couple, Eric and Pauline Freeman, to manage it on our behalf. It worked out very well domestically too, because it gave Pete a chance to get his overdraft down by working at the pub for 89p an hour! Three years passed during which time we watched Pete 'straighten up and fly right' and we had the excitement of creating a fun pub where we had live entertainment three nights a week, and I could sometimes stay for a few minutes after time to take my sleeping medicine!

In the halcyon days of the club scene, Sunday lunchtimes were legend in the weekly entertainment programme of Mr Working Class. The Red Well in Arkholme wasn't exactly the mining belt of the North East or the steel area of south Wales but I thought that a cultural influx might tickle the fancy of the residents of the Lune Valley's farming district. I rang Bernard Manning (you remember, the society entertainer specialising in children's parties?). 'Bernard', I said, 'I've just taken over a pub in the Lune Valley and

**Red Well. Taking my sleeping medicine in the surgery.**

I wondered if you'd come up and put us on the map, so to speak by doing a Sunday lunchtime for us?' I explained how many people I could accommodate and he kindly accommodated me. I put a poster up in the bar which stated categorically that the performance would not be suitable for the easily offended, but even bearing that in mind the tickets would be £10 each. I sold out within the hour.

Bernard arrived one cold Sunday lunch-time in November and explained that he needed to be away from there in time to get to Maine Road, Manchester, as he wanted to be in time to see Manchester City lose (he's a big City fan!). He also told me of their latest game plan, where the team wear their shirts back to front to make them think that they're attacking! He went on at 1 o'clock precisely, insulted and abused everyone in the pub, told politically incorrect gags by the dozen and walked off to a standing ovation. He was absolutely disgusting! On his way to his car he called me aside and said, 'Ring George [Roper] and give him a lunchtime here, there's not a lot of work about at the moment.' That's the measure of the man; make no mistake, Bernard Manning has a heart of gold. We had many memorable times at the Red Well with visits from Alan Shearer, Mick Miller, Duggie Brown and that fine politician Sir Cyril Smith. I had met Cyril on board *QE2* where he was booked as a visiting lecturer and we became good friends.

After we had been in the Red Well for a while I rang him and asked if he would do me the honour of coming up to do his after-dinner speech, a wonderful piece of oratory which he called 'The longest running farce in the West End', obviously referring to Westminster. He agreed, provided that the proceeds went to his favourite charity. Once again, this time by word of mouth, the tickets were all sold within two days. My driver Pete Rimmer went to collect him from Rochdale, his home town and constituency. Pete had always had a soft spot for Cyril because they both hailed from Rochdale and they both liked Gracie Fields! The function room was extra full on Cyril's arrival and I think he warmed to the evening immediately as he felt the genuine affection of the audience. Part of the deal was that we had to serve meat and potato pie, or hotpot, as an added feature to the evening, which of course we did. (We did red cabbage as well!)

We set a comfortable chair on stage and duly introduced Cyril to his adoring fans. He had spoken for just over an hour when he asked where the hotpot was. We then took what was scheduled to be a twenty-minute interval after which Cyril would answer questions from the floor. The second half never happened. Cyril went round every table in the room and spent some time with everybody. He was still there well after closing time and Pete had to really work hard to persuade him to leave. Now there is a man who's on my list of 'Glitterati'. I was to meet Cyril many more times both on and off *QE2* and was able to return the favour to him to help his beloved Liberal club in Rochdale. Cyril for King, how about that!

We stayed at the Red Well for three years and when Eric and Pauline left we felt we had all been part of a really special time. They went on to look after a large caravan site in Cumbria and are doing very nicely thank you. On the financial side I think I looked at the Red Well in the same way that other showbiz folk regarded their golf club. I preferred the nineteenth hole to be at the beginning of the evening rather than at the end. Besides, ladies could come in anytime they wished (I bet Mr Cheatyballs played golf). Thinking back now, as I write this very revealing exposé of myself, I am beginning to realise how very lucky I've been as I pass the fifty mark.

If I'd been batting for Lancashire I would have received a round of applause from the crowd for getting fifty, when in fact it should have been me applauding someone or other 'for the good times' I've had. They can't be measured in runs; in fact they can't be measured at all. The best thing to do with grateful memories is store them very securely, and make sure that they're easily accessible, because there are times when you'll need them. There are times as well when you ask yourself if there will be any more special memories to come your way; have you had your memories allowance or are there still some pleasant surprises to come?

Look at your list Jim: talk to me about being in the right place at the right time!

Adopted, Dustbins, GCEs (eventually), National Service, Teacher Training College, Phyllis, Teaching, Sue, Comedians, Pete, Wheel-tappers, Starburst, Muck and Brass, Up for the cup, Jon Scoffield, Tetleys, and Bullseye. Surely that's a good enough list for anyone to be more than grateful for. Let's read on because there's more good news.

One of the advantages of becoming famous is that you become an attractive asset to cruise ships. It took four years of Bullseye to qualify me to sail the high seas while getting paid, as against paying out. Garry Brown, a most respected agent who dealt almost exclusively with cruise ships, became aware of my existence and rang me asking would I like to do cabaret on board *QE2*. Once again I paused before I replied, not wanting to appear too keen. 'I'm not working at home whenever there's a ship sailing', I coolly replied, 'When can I go?'

The truth was that in the mid to late eighties the cabaret scene was shrinking as tastes changed; holidays abroad were becoming more and more in vogue and of course there were only so many acts that could fill these large venues. The complexion of our business was altering radically and 'diversifying' became the buzzword for us 'turns'. Cruising had only been seen as the playground of the wealthy, but opportunistic marketing and promotion by cruise lines like P&O, Fred Olsen and Cunard were making people realise that a cruise holiday could be just as cheap as a holiday of the more traditional type. The elitist label attached to these floating hotels was being discreetly lost in a tide of advertising, which would give Mr and Mrs Normal the confidence to pick up a brochure. The images of daunting formal evenings where it was essential to pick up the correct eating utensil with the correct hand at the correct time, were being replaced by images of discos impregnated with informality and of people actually enjoying active uninhibited parties. The age range in the seventies for cruisers was probably 45 to 100+, so the young executive who was still getting his financial house in order wouldn't risk his holiday money to be lulled into inactivity for too long. He would want to take no prisoners for the two weeks his employer had allocated him, and would try to drink hotels and resorts dry, and to misbehave and create mayhem as long as the money lasted. Life on a cruise ship isn't exactly conducive to that sort of behaviour, or at least it didn't appear so.

The arrival of the eighties was to see a whole new generation of younger cruisers. The good news for us was that the ships needed acts to enhance their already comprehensive entertainment itineraries; and they needed them quickly. And that's where Garry Brown came in.

I was booked to do cabaret on *QE2* towards the end of 1984, joining the ship at Southampton and sailing round the Mediterranean for 14 days. My contract required me to perform two shows in what was then the Double Down room, later to become the Grand Lounge. I was given two top grade cabins, which enabled me to take either Sue or Pete along with a friend; and I was paid money as well! What a contract that was; I mean, a fortnight's holiday for the family in return for two hours' work, and we lived in luxury as we sailed on the finest ship in the world.

There was, however, a more intangible price to pay for this incredible offer. Once the ship has left her homeport there is nowhere for you, as a performer, to hide, should you so wish; it is only when you leave port that this realisation dawns. Should your performance fall short of expectations there is nowhere for you to go, other than your cabin. You cannot get into your car and leave town, and perhaps leave an audience baying for your blood, and asking for their money back! The huge drawback to working on board ship is that you are living on a two-edged sword. Let me explain. The plus side gives you an enviable lifestyle for two weeks where you are pampered beyond belief. The other plus in the equation is that you are paid handsomely for the privilege. The bad news is that all the passengers on board know that you are being paid to be on board to perform perhaps two, or at most three times during the fortnight. They have paid serious money to cruise with someone who is being paid to do the same, with untold perks. Can you see how this confused, almost unjust economic equation can engender serious bitterness on the part of the paying customer? It's virtually a no-win situation for the passenger ... if you get your part of the bargain wrong, even though you don't get it wrong intentionally.

This was my first cruise, so please understand what was going through my mind as I was handed the ship's entertainment schedule. I was due to perform twice in the Double Down room (a daunting arena with shops forming a three-sided balcony), at 9 p.m. and 10.30 p.m. as we left Barcelona, some six nights into the cruise. In effect that was asking me to spend five nights worrying about the show, and if all went well I could enjoy the rest of the cruise. If all didn't go well I would be spending the remaining seven nights in our cabin. I wouldn't want to walk round the ship listening to whispers like, 'Wasn't he awful, and he's getting paid!' All these thoughts came to mind and as the cruise progressed they became more to the fore as we approached Barcelona. The resident cruise staff were very encouraging, explaining to me that the first show was never easy because the passengers had rushed from early dinner and were full of food and wine, but not to worry as very few acts did well on the first show. I was by now getting used to the idea of spending the rest of the cruise in isolation. The second show, they said, would be better because the late diners had eaten and drunk at a more leisurely pace and were more forgiving.

I remember the Ken Mackintosh Orchestra were the resident band, and excellent they were; any memories of my performances in that room that night are a complete blur. I couldn't have done too badly because I remember walking round the ship unaided and alone well after we left Barcelona!

The late Ted Rogers of 3-2-1 fame sailed on *QE2* some years later and sadly, for some unaccountable reason, got it completely wrong on the first night at sea. Rumour has it that he never left his cabin for 13 days and all he ate was toast. Apparently he wouldn't see anyone, even his cabin steward; the only thing they could get to him was buttered toast. I think they buttered it to help it under the cabin door! Only teasing Ted, you're sadly missed.

I discovered later that each act is given a mark out of ten by the cruise director and anything less than eight means no more *QE2*. I must have been OK because that cruise was the first of many, and it was to enable me to strike up a friendship with Colin Bryant, whose band, the Hot Rhythm Orchestra, was to feature large in my life aboard *QE2* in the coming years.

Memories of life on board are too numerous to mention, but I'm not going to let you get away without my recalling some of them for you.

Big names were a regular feature on the ship and one of the biggest we ever saw was Vic Damone, probably one of the greatest song stylists the world has ever known. He was due to appear in the Grand Lounge as it was now known, at the usual times, 9 p.m. and 10.30 p.m. By now I was working with the Hot Rhythm Orchestra in the Golden Lion pub every night and our performance times allowed us to watch the headline cabaret in the Grand Lounge. Long before Vic Damone came on stage Colin and the band and I were in position to watch the great man perform. He came on stage and completely mesmerised the audience (and these were the early eaters!) We all just sat back and marvelled at his style, his eloquence and his wonderfully gentle treatment of his audience. What we didn't expect to see was a little girl aged about nine years sitting on the front row fall fast asleep. How was the great man to deal with this situation? The little girl obviously would have no idea of the size of the reputation of the man she was inadvertently ignoring. As he came to the end of the song, which had encompassed the little girl's sojourn, he came down from the stage and crept up to her and knelt down in front of her as she slept. The whole room waited and wondered how Vic was going to handle this potentially embarrassing scenario. He did, and how!

He turned to his trio of musicians who were on stage and nodded, whereupon they played the intro to the definitive version of 'On the street where you live'. Ever so softly Vic began singing to this little girl who slowly woke up, gradually becoming aware that the whole room was looking at her, and that this man was on his knees singing to her. Such was the skill and warmth of the man that he managed to sing the whole song to the little girl, at the end of which he thanked her for listening. The smile on the face of the child said it all as the audience cheered Vic to the rafters. What a performer!

There was a sequel to that little girl's nightcap serenade, and I'm pleased to tell you I was in it. We left the Grand Lounge straight after Vic's show to start our evening's stint in the Golden Lion pub. My brief in the pub is to compère the goings-on and to introduce the band and the tunes as well as telling a few rather cheeky stories to the adoring fans who gravitate to the downmarket end of the ship! The Hot Rhythm Orchestra consists of six extremely fine musicians who play foot-tapping music to die for. The bar was full as we commenced our first set of the evening, and I went out front to welcome our audience to the proceedings. 'Well, what about that then,' I said, 'you're talking real class there', I continued, 'I hope you realise what you've just witnessed in there, that perform-ance in the Grand Lounge is as good as you'll ever see in your life!' I ranted. (I must stress that we did have a great rapport with the Golden Lion clientele!) As I was going on about the show a silence slowly fell upon the pub. It was one of those silences that gradually creep up and frighten you. I stared at the audience in confusion. Why had everything gone quiet? Suddenly I felt a gentle tap on my shoulder. There was Vic Damone standing right next to me. I was completely dumbstruck. 'Thank you Jim for those kind words, I really appreciate them.' All I could think of was how to get this brush with a superstar on record. 'Has anyone got a camera … please?' I pleaded. Of course one of our regulars did the necessary. It's only a Polaroid picture but David Bailey wasn't there so that'll do fine. Thanks a million Vic.

The captain of *QE2* is always fair game for the cabaret artistes on the ship and stories abound about the many gags we tell involving the skipper. One UK cruise had the privilege of the company of Max Bygraves as the main cabaret. We were as usual booked to do our stuff in the Golden Lion pub, and our work schedule still allowed us to peep in at the Grand Lounge show. I was sceptical about Max as I'd only ever seen him stumble through Family Fortunes on television and I wasn't that impressed. (Talk about the pot calling the kettle!) I was therefore very keen to see how this legend would handle the challenge of the first sitting audience in the big room. My scepticism was to be destroyed within 10 seconds of Max's appearance on stage. Before he spoke a word he had the audience in the palm of his hand. I think it's called charisma; or was it just that his many years in the business showed. His opening lines were: 'How nice to be here; I was just talking to the captain and he said he much preferred this ship to his last one, The Torrey Canyon!' The audience erupted with laughter, not so much at the gag but at the cheeky way Max delivered the lines, and the relaxed presence onstage that can only come with experience. He then went on to sing about a tiny house by a tiny stream, where a lovely lass had a lovely dream; he then asked the audience where the dream came true, and would you believe it, the audience knew, and what's more they sang the answer to him. Yes, you're right; it was *Gilly-gillyosenfeffercatsanellanbogan by the see-ee-ee-ee-ee*!

From that moment on Max had the most delightful love affair with over a thousand people, getting them to sing about pink and blue toothbrushes, and reminding them that 'Fings ain't wot they used to be'! Throughout the entire hour he never seemed to break into a sweat, he just cuddled the audience and en route showed me precisely what show business was all about. Sod 'im! Another great memory, thank you Max.

The crew on board *QE2* work incredibly hard living up to the demands of the high level of service expected of them from both passengers and the strict discipline of the ship's regime. Occasionally,

**The biggest star I ever met – and he didn't disappoint!**

**Max and Blossom. Sod 'im – he showed me all about showbiz!!**

as a reward to the crew they are allowed to grace the areas of the ship which normally are out of bounds to them. These restrictions are lifted when the captain sees fit and on one particular cruise I became involved with their celebrations.

The captain who made the decision to give the crew their party was Alan Bennell, the youngest of the *QE2*'s captains, and a man who enjoyed life to the full. One evening after we had finished our second show in what was then the Theatre Bar, Alan came over to our table where we were enjoying a nightcap. 'Jim, I'm thinking of letting the crew have a bash in the Grand Lounge next week, as they've had a particularly hard run, would you mind compering the evening for them?' I obviously agreed and plans were immediately set in motion. Roger de Courcey was the other headline cabaret (Nookie Bear came with him), and the Ken Mackintosh orchestra was resident on the ship, so they were approached and willingly accepted.

The next job was to inform the paying customers that they wouldn't be allowed into the Grand Lounge on the appointed night after their show was finished. This restriction was put in place by the captain to preserve the reputation of his crew, as well as being aware of the moral responsibility he shouldered for the passengers who were perhaps a little sensitive about liberated behaviour! One thing was certain, a huge head of pent-up steam would be released when the crew of *QE2* were given the freedom of the Grand Lounge. It was their rare opportunity to be extremely badly behaved, free from the demands of the passengers, and from their day-to-day routine, which in effect was a 24-hour commitment to serving the customer.

On the big night we were playing the Theatre Bar until 11.30 p.m. I stressed to all our patrons that under no circumstance should they attempt to gain entry to the Grand Lounge, as the crew party was to take place and things would be going on in there that they would not wish to see or hear. I explained that the language might not fall within their code of acceptance, and that patterns of behaviour could well not only offend them, but might tempt them into the ways of the flesh, ways that were not too familiar to them. I explained that the staff on cruise ships sometimes lost their way when let loose in the privacy of their own closets, and on the odd occasion could come out and do surprising things.

Our remit as responsible entertainers aboard *QE2* was to keep the passengers away from these potentially dangerous influences.

*I say, how terribly conscientious!*

As I was fiercely delivering this warning to the assembled crowd in the bar, the time was approaching 11.30 p.m. I became aware that there was movement amongst the audience, and the movement was leading to the Grand Lounge, the very place I had urged them to avoid. I knew that my pleas had gone unheeded; these people who were once my friends were deserting me, and ignoring my advice, in order that they might watch a scene of debauchery and sin (if they could sneak in!).

*I say, how terribly naughty!*

We were all backstage as the clock approached midnight, the scheduled start of the show. The crew were taking their places on the floor of the Grand Lounge with their six packs and bottles of wine, and other intimidating liquids scattered around, much like a picnic without solids. The wonderful thing about the gathering was that none of the audience sat on the plush seating. Even when the room became theirs for a night, they still respected the facilities, which were theirs to borrow and to look after, not to abuse; that's *QE2* for you.

Alan Bennell came backstage to thank us for doing the show and wished us all the best as we prepared to face a lively, slightly undisciplined gathering. They weren't so much an audience as a challenge; and it looked as if they were going to win! I finally cleared with Alan how naughty we should be and he categorically said that anything was acceptable as there were no passengers present to upset. I went to the curtain and peeped out, and on looking up to the surrounding balcony was amazed that it still remained intact, as at least half the ship's passengers were hanging over the sides in order to get a really good eyeful of the proceedings! I felt it my duty to tell Alan that in fact I thought he might be misinformed as to the passenger presence out there. 'Alan', I began, 'I think you should just pop your head out and just make sure that there aren't any passengers in the audience, and maybe a glance up to the balcony may colour your judgement as far as how naughty the show should be. We wouldn't want *QE2* passengers listening to the sort of thing that would get the ship a bad name' (Max Miller, Metropolitan, Edgware Road 1935!).

Alan went to the curtain and poked his head out to take careful stock of the situation out there. He returned to the dressing room and confidently announced, 'I've taken a good look out into the auditorium and I can confidently say that I see no passengers'. And I thought Francis Drake told lies!

The show lasted for three hours. I compèred the whole thing and was probably quite cheeky. We abused the passengers mercilessly cursing their fussy, infuriating habits; the ship's officers came in for even more annihilation and the captain's character was completely destroyed. Some-one even suggested that his parents were extremely disappointed when he was born as they expected a son! Roger de Courcey came on with Nookie Bear, and let me tell you that if you think Nookie is a children's entertainer then you'd better think again. He was absolutely disgusting, much to the delight of the audience. Roger was perfectly respectable; that's one of the perks of having a dummy as your spokesman!

The Ken Mackintosh orchestra played the night (or the morning) out and the crew went to bed tired and relaxed, more than prepared to continue to work tirelessly aboard *QE2*.

Alan Bennell was a much-revered captain and was extremely good with the passengers in that he socialised naturally, which really is an essential part of the job. Everyone wants to meet the captain of the ship and 1750 people can prove to be quite challenging in the socialising department. They expect to shake hands with the boss at least once on every voyage and most of them would be thrilled to bits if he were to spend the evening with him. Obviously this is not an option; in fact if you look at the numbers game in this context, the captain can barely spend five seconds of his time per head of the ship's population!

One of the ways the captain can spread his presence round the ship to maximum effect is to do a tour of the ship every evening, visiting each room where there is something going on. By doing that he can be seen by the majority of passengers, who can go home telling their friends that the captain spent most evenings with them, and that he'll probably be coming round when he's next on leave to spend a few days with them! A life on the ocean wave can seriously develop your sense of creative thinking!

*I say, how imaginative!*

**Roger de Courcey was quite respectable – Nookie was disgraceful.
Me and 'im after the crew show.**

**The Great Lady.**

During one of his tours of the ship I found myself caught in a most embarrassing situation. As I mentioned, our place of work on *QE2* was, and still is the Golden Lion Pub. There is a tremendous rapport between the band, yours truly and the audience which gathers there nightly in large numbers. My function is to link the musical items with badinage of a humorous nature, or just spoil the whole occasion by playing my trumpet or singing a jazz number or two.

One particular evening during our set in the pub I was jokingly speaking ill of the captain to the assembled throng by suggesting that his drink problem ought to be addressed fairly quickly, and perhaps his eyesight would better equip him to be a Premiership referee rather than the man in charge of the finest ship afloat. I also pointed out that his propensity for the ladies had not gone unnoticed. As we traversed the Bay of Biscay in a force 9 gale the previous night, someone noticed him on the bridge being distracted by a lady of some considerable stature offering him Jaffa cakes by the mouthful. As I was just about to incite mutiny, the entire pub went silent. I turned to my left to see Captain Alan Bennell looking sternly at me. He paused for a moment then strode aggressively towards me where I froze on the spot, awaiting his command to walk the plank. The revered Captain Bennell hove alongside me and whispered softly in my ear. What he said to me you will never know. We get engaged next Easter.

# CHAPTER TWELVE

# The End of an Era

A S WE CELEBRATED over a decade working on the majority of QE2's UK cruises with the Hot Rhythm Orchestra, life shore side was beginning to take on a new dimension. Bullseye was still capturing huge audience figures and seemed destined for an interminable run, having already completed thirteen years delighting the Midland Bank (as it was then called), not to mention Phyllis, who was ordering new pairs of trainers by the dozen!

However, like all good things, it came to an end. The Independent Television Network was undergoing senior administrative changes, which meant that the Heads of Light Entertainment within each of the regions were becoming a rare breed. One controlling body was replacing them, and this was to be responsible for the commissioning of all new and existing programmes. This body was called 'The Centre', and was headed by a certain Marcus Plantin. 'The Centre' in its wisdom saw fit to put an end to the lives of four very successful programmes, namely: Bullseye, Blockbusters, Boon and The Upper Hand. All four programmes were at one time or another in the top five positions in the viewers' ratings and Central Television made them all.

*I say, how coincidental!*

We found these decisions incomprehensible to say the least. Phyllis as usual reacted rationally by observing that thirteen years at the 'sharp end' of network television had afforded us a lifestyle to be envied by most of our peers, so to become bitter about these developments would be most ungracious. I did as I was told, came to terms with the revised scheme of things, and we got on with our very special lives.

During the nineties club and cabaret bookings, along with guest celebrity appearances, afforded me a steady, if sometimes bland, lifestyle, but the responsibility of paying the bills made me 'bite the bullet' and go out to work. The mid nineties saw the end of Bullseye on terrestrial network television, but Sky digital television was starting to make its presence felt throughout our nation and one of its channels, UK Gold, wisely thought that repeating some of the episodes of Bullseye in its familiar Sunday evening slot would prove a winner. A meeting between the interested parties took place and as a result over three hundred episodes of Bullseye were purchased for transmission at around teatime on a nightly basis. The negotiator of the deal, Peter Holmans offered me a 'buy-out' fee large enough to make Phyllis chuckle, so I willingly signed on the dotted line, thereby securing a peaceful time at home free from the worries of immediate penury.

The end of the century began to loom large and all seemed to be fine, if a little lacking in purpose and ambition, but I had the good grace to accept that I had had my share of success and thought that it was time to make way for these young upstarts who seemed to be taking over the nation's show business heritage. How dare these young blades appear so confident and assured in an arena where I had suffered traumas that would have killed a lesser man? They certainly were younger than the policemen I had seen recently patrolling the streets of Lancaster. I was in no way envious of them with their youth, good looks, talent and the whole world at their feet. Oh yes I bloody was!

In fact, I like to think I came to terms with being sidelined by show business quite gracefully. Retirement is not a word that exists in the vocabulary of us vaudevillians; what happens to us is that the phone stops ringing! Arriving elegantly at a stage in my life where longevity crosses the mind with increasing regularity, the ringing of the phone is a more than welcome intrusion into the ever more increasing gaps in the day. I am relieved to report that the phone did continue to ring regularly enough to make me feel secure in the knowledge that the end of the shelf was far enough away for me to still take an interest in things.

There is no doubt that the most influential element in my career was Bullseye. Without this most successful of game shows there would be little demand for the autobiography. Bullseye made an also ran into a star. It made history; it defied the odds on all fronts.

Even now, as I write these words, the internet is reminding everyone that it is still part of the fabric of television history. Statistics are there for all to read, quirky little known facts become salient points in arguments about how many times I said 'smashing' in the first episode. People are still convinced that the speedboats on offer as star prizes regularly were part of a marketing ploy to bolster a flagging cottage industry in the West Midlands. They are convinced that Peter Harris, who put the flesh on the bones of an essentially simple format, was in cahoots with the speedboat manufacturer (Fletcher's the name!) to supply him with a sample of his product should these boats be won. Of course that is complete poppycock. No one ever won the star prize on Bullseye. There is a red brick (or is it asbestos) university now offering a joint honours course in 'Darts the Bullseye way' and media studies. The sponsor is Horace Bachelor who lives in Keynsham, Bristol. He's fed up with showing you how to win the pools. How's your memory then?

Over the years as you can imagine the show has produced some characters, some of which are etched in the memory. One such couple hailed from Leominster, and somehow from the off they didn't seem to be the sort of couple who played darts. He was dressed in a tweed jacket complemented by cord trousers, checked shirt and a cravat. I mean to say, a bloody cravat! Not exactly the uniform of a pub darts team. His wife, a dear tolerant lady, was of the twin set and pearls brigade. He turned out to be a most arrogant man who behaved abominably towards his wife, telling her brashly to go and get him a cup of tea (and don't forget 2 sugars!), and generally treating her very much like a backward Labrador. Needless to say, within minutes of his arrival in the studio, none of us liked him. You will remember that there were three pairs of contestants on each show and eventually these were reduced to one couple who played for the star prize. Tony Green hated the man and whispered to me that he wished he was able to do something to hinder him should he and his wife reach the final, and try to score, between them, the required 101 or more to win the car. I stressed that he was not to attempt to do this, but agreed that it was sorely tempting! By some unbelievable turn of fate Mister Cravat and his subservient wife did get through to the final and both Tony and I were amazed and frustrated at his good fortune.

By the time the game had reached this stage, the audience had got the measure of this smarty-pants, and they didn't like him either! The problem was their reaction to his success was becoming obvious on screen, so they were giving our director a problem. Success should mean happy faces in the audience and he couldn't see many! They were supposed to be encouraging him in his battle to win the car, when in fact they really couldn't care less.

His wife had been answering the questions, so she had to throw the first three darts, hoping to score as many as possible towards the required total of 101, which they had to get to win.

Off camera Tony was nodding to me, whispering that she couldn't play darts so the chances of them winning were minimal and we thought that was a good thing. She took her stance at the oche and prepared to throw. I have to say she looked nothing like a dart player, in her smart pale green silk outfit with accessories to match. Tony suggested that she put her hand bag down as it might interfere with her throwing action (I thought he wasn't going to help her).

She threw the first dart ... treble 17 ... 51.

She threw the second dart ... single 19.

The third dart landed ... single 5.

Grand total scored ... 75.

This phenomenal feat meant that Mister Cravat smarty-pants only needed 26 to win the car. Tony was mortified. All his telepathic efforts to distract The Cravat from his task had failed. The audience weren't too keen either. He strode confidently up to the oche, not noticing our dejected expressions, and threw thus:

First dart ... single 20. He now needed 6 to win the car.

Second dart ... single 5. He aimed at twenty but slipped off to the 5. He now needed 1 to win the car. His attitude throughout the day didn't alter now. He actually turned his back to the dartboard as if to do a trick and neatly threw his final dart. Unfortunately the dart hit the wire and bounced out of the board. He had lost the star prize. You could hear the cheers in the studio restaurant some three floors away as the audience got to their feet and delightedly waved their arms about at his complete failure to win anything. Mister Cravat and his browbeaten spouse walked gloomily out of the studio with absolutely nothing to their names. When the show was transmitted some weeks later the cheering audience had mysteriously disappeared, to be replaced by a more subdued one from another show.

*I say, how very technical!*

As the years passed, Bullseye rested comfortably in the memory bank, only to appear on our screens courtesy of the 'wok on the wall'. I tried to rationalise its demise objectively and was encouraged by what I discovered. There is no doubt that the programme was taken off air at least two years too soon. To say I wasn't bothered would be to lie to you; however, it concerned me for reasons that may not seem to you to be the obvious ones.

Let me explain. The programme ran for 13 years on the network, and that's a long time for a game show to survive in today's throwaway culture. It afforded comfort and solace to all walks of life, and was doing no harm to anyone. Young children were being weaned off Play School on to a game show they thought they could understand; university students struggled to keep up with the advanced technology of the programme; and the recycled teenagers enjoyed the simplicity and naivety of the half hour of stress free television that was theirs for the asking every Sunday around teatime.

The fact that it was removed from our screens when it was enhanced our memories of the show, because it was taken out of our lives when it was most needed.

Nobody was given any warning ... Whoosh ... it was gone!

This probably accounts for the fact that people remember me, Tony Green, Bully, and all the catchphrases with heightened endearment because, metaphorically, we died prematurely. No one likes to see anything or anyone cut down in its prime.

'Quit while you're ahead' is the gambler's motto, and a wise one too. We were fortunate because we were told when to quit, we had no choice. The truth is, that had it been up to us, we would have gone on forever, and what a misguided decision that could have been.

Gone would be the genuinely affectionate embraces we now get, along with, 'Eeh, Jim, why did you stop doing 'Bully', it were't best show on't telly'. Gone would be the warm cries of, 'Look at what you could have won!' No more would I have the pleasure of being teased about the star prize always being a speedboat, and the winner always coming from Walsall, or somewhere equally distant from a jetty.

I think because we were taken off early, we weren't allowed to play ourselves out in the minds of our devoted viewer. We didn't outstay our welcome. I'm not sure that I would have liked to run the seemingly endless course of Family Fortunes, Catchphrase or Wheel of Fortune; all programmes that have obviously been successful, but, I believe have now reached their sell by date. They now have to suffer the indignity of being consigned to irregular scheduling, of being used as fillers; in other words being subjected to the network's whim. But it's the viewers' whim that concerns me. Whatever Bullseye was, it certainly wasn't wallpaper telly, and we came off the screen before we became polyfiller.

People remember Bullseye like we older chaps remember National Service. It always seemed better than it was because we only remembered the good bits. Buddy Holly, Ricky Valance, and Jim Reeves all died prematurely; did we perhaps enhance their talents in our own minds because they hadn't been around long enough for us to make an impartial judgement? Probably not in most cases but as more time elapsed we perhaps gave them the benefit of any doubt. I'd quite like to be given the benefit of the doubt please!

I think that perhaps in this day and age, when literally millions of pounds can be won in minutes (especially if you have a friend who can cough discreetly at the appropriate time!), our little quiz show on the telly with darts and questions might just disappoint you if you watched it today, and I wouldn't want that to happen. There are bits of my past I like, and 'Bully', even though he's only made of rubber, is one bit I would like to remember (and for him to be remembered) as he was.

*I say, how terribly poignant!*

CHAPTER THIRTEEN

# *New Home, New Opportunities*

ARKHOLME STATION had become our beloved home throughout the twenty exciting years that had seen us (or rather Phyllis) bring up our two children through all the vagaries that beset family life. It had somehow helped us cope; it had smoothed our path through uncertainty, with its thick Victorian walls protecting us from impending disaster. We loved the place and had no thoughts of leaving until one day we found we had time to reflect on our position. Sue was living in London earning vast sums of money (and still not sending any food parcels home!), Pete had gone to live in Tenerife where he had met a beautiful Spanish girl and was finding his domestic feet under her Hispanic supervision. It became increasingly likely to us that both the birds had flown the nest on a pretty permanent basis, so the station began to appear rather a large property for our requirements. The mocquette was looming large again and sure enough a meeting was called to discuss the future of our beloved railway station. It wasn't long before white smoke appeared from the building and the decision was made that Arkholme station would search for new inhabitants.

You can imagine the amount of 'stuff' that accumulates almost by accident as you indulge your magpie-like tendencies over the years. Antiques and memorabilia cluttered the nooks and crannies, shelves and cupboards and roof space and everywhere! It all just appeared without telling us. The cheek of it! Drastic action was called for and I was the man for the job. I began to take stock of our possessions round the house over the ensuing few weeks and in doing so began to realise that, short of moving to an aeroplane hangar, we could in no way accommodate all our chattels. I tried to rationalise the collection of soldiers' writing boxes from World War One, weighing scales of every conceivable style, illogical pieces of furniture that just happened to take our fancy. I failed to justify the presence of these dust-collecting items in our abode and eventually decided that the only contribution they made to our way of life at the station was an increased workload for Phyllis. They had to go!

One Saturday morning in the summer of 1995 I awoke around nine to find Phyllis as usual lying comfortably under the duvet showing no immediate intentions of facing the rigours of the day. For once at this time of day I was functioning fairly well between the ears and, having the freedom of the house, I daringly made a phone call to a Mr Alan Blackburn, an antique dealer of good repute (is there any such being?). I asked him to 'come up and see me sometime' to evaluate our wares. Over the next few weeks, one piece at a time, we salted away our disposable collectables and he reimbursed me accordingly. The gradual spiriting away of these items was not to go unnoticed for long. I was soon to be called to account for these disappearances by the keeper of the house and only after a detailed explanation of my reasons for the downsizing was I once again in the frame for being fed solids. We had been looking half heartedly in the property pages of our local chronicle for a replacement for our much loved abode with its five bedrooms, four bathrooms, seven acres of grounds, large garage, swimming pool and, most important of all, over twenty years of priceless memories. Sooner or later we would have to find somewhere, but as you the reader knows, to 'up sticks' and say goodbye to a large piece of your life only emphasises the passage of time and highlights the amount that is left of your allocation of this valuable commodity. So we faced the next phase together, Phyllis with her usual stoicism and reasoned approach to the whole exercise, and me, well I was just there, contributing little in terms of tangible offerings but in spirit I was doing my bit.

The river Lune has two banks, north and south (now there's a revelation), and its waters have always been a source of comfort to us; they give us that 'home' feeling, so any property we would be likely to purchase would have to be within a stone's throw of its course.

We were made aware of the conversion of an old cotton mill on the south bank of the river so decided to grasp the nettle and actually look round this building project with real intent to buy.

We were not disappointed. The huge mill, dating back to the seventeen hundreds, was being developed into luxury apartments. The builder was living in one of the units at the end of the mill, which he was prepared to alter to our specification. The deed was done; we had gone south of the river but could still feel its presence. The property afforded us magnificent views over the immediate gardens out to the river Lune and to the valley beyond. The move was painless as we had disposed of almost all of our trappings and were able to enjoy a whole new house and furniture experience. A local licensee, whose wife took full advantage of all the features of the property by converting the land and outbuildings into riding stables, which is now extremely successful, purchased the station almost as soon as it went on the market. We now found ourselves facing the second half of the decade having to come to terms with a new home, and a career in show business, which was, to say the least, temporarily lacking direction.

We slid into Low Mill quite effortlessly and instantly adapted to the changes imposed on us by our immediate environment. The responsibility of large areas of grass to be manicured faded from our vista (actually Phyllis was the immediate benefactor here). The property was deceptively large, with a lounge over forty feet in

**We didn't live in all the mill – just the bit under the water tower!**

length, taking up the entire width of the mill, at second floor level. Leading off the lounge was the office, which was quite unique in that it backed on to, and under, the adjacent fishing lodge. It was in fact, the water-collecting chamber to power the machinery of the now defunct mill. The large bedroom complex comprised a dual sink/shower/bath en suite facility taking up the first floor, along with an inner and outer hall. The ground floor afforded us a small self-contained flat. We had, as modern parlance would say, down-sized. The many apartments within the complex were beautifully converted and the feeling of security it gave us was most reassuring, especially in view of the amount of time we were spending on *QE2*. It looked as though we had found our final residence. It was as close to sheltered accommodation as we were likely to find without a caretaker, although the mill management were reminiscent of the escape committee in Colditz. I must say that Messrs Boardman, Riley, West and Winterbottom supervised the mill, its grounds and occupants with diplomacy and skill, making our stay there extremely enjoyable. The restrictions the management had to impose were minimal, but their implementation afforded us a comfortable relaxed lifestyle in beautiful, carefully tended surroundings. We were to stay at Low Mill for six happy years.

The move to the mill also highlighted the fact that we were now 'just the two of us'. It sort of underlined the new state of the union where the children had definitely gone and would, in the future, only ever feature in our lives on a loan basis. We were beginning to feel extremely lucky that both Sue and Pete had found stable relationships and were making their way on their own. Any doubts I'd had about the way I contributed to their development were starting to fade away and we were enjoying the family scene, albeit from a distance. Sue was coming home from London at weekends when she rode her horse at show jumping and cross-country events. Phyllis was seeing Pete once or twice a year when she flew out to Tenerife to stay with him. *QE2* dropped anchor there a couple of times a year so I was able to remember what he looked like (I don't do flying, remember). It was most rewarding to see the pair of them reflect in their behaviour the qualities we hold dear to us.

Speaking of visiting Pete, I have to explain the domestic scene at home when Phyllis goes Canary Island-ing. You will have gathered by now that when Phyllis leaves town for any period of time, not a lot of culinary activity goes on at home. On her departure Phyllis locks all the kitchen cupboards, immobilises the cooker and makes sure that the only commodity in the fridge is milk. She reminds me where the kettle is, shows me the sink and puts a label on the cold tap. You see I only do coffee. I don't do solids, not even toast. My routine each morning is: 1. Switch the kettle on. 2. Put the coffee in the cup. 3. When the kettle boils, pour the water on the coffee in the cup. 4. Open the fridge door to get the milk. 5. Pour the milk on to the coffee. 6. Stir the mixture. 7. Drink the contents of the cup. 8. Put the empty cup in the sink. 9. Lock the door on leaving. 10. Go to work.

Sad aren't I?

From a work standpoint during those years at the mill, looking back I can remember many highlights. The phone rang quite frequently so I was able to take engagements or not, as the case may be. I knew I was in a position to choose from the jobs on offer, though sometimes the cheque on offer persuaded me to take the job I didn't want. Examples of such undesirable jobs would be Christmas celebrations, works' parties, office shindigs – you know, the sort of boozy get together when everybody gets completely wrecked and just makes everything more difficult for the performer.

I was entering a stage of my life when just being there was more important than anything connected with the future. This new-found philosophy prompted me to think 'don't ask too many questions, just get on with it!'

All the years of hard grind round the club and cabaret circuit were being phased out by the slightly more civilised arena of the sportsman's or after dinner engagements. Tastes were changing and, as a direct consequence, the contents of my little entertainment package (which had paid the bills for many years, incidentally) had to be revamped and updated. Gone were the one-liners, the quick-witted (well-rehearsed) put-downs and the endless stream of jokes. The more sophisticated, upwardly mobile audience of this era had heard them all, and more besides. The demands of the dining Rotarian, Freemason or 'here-to-be impressed business contact' type guest had to be dealt a far more erudite hand than that offered by the stand-up comic whose style of delivery was becoming passé, old fashioned and not really 'cool' with this dress suited, nouveau audience. Stories became the more acceptable face of comedy; we had to become raconteurs, if you like. What most of us were doing in fact was dressing up gags, we were putting jokes into stories, we were conning the silly buggers into believing that we were almost as intelligent, almost as good as they were, but we really knew our place in the intellectual pecking order; especially when we picked up the cheque! 'Start the car!'

*I say, how very hard-faced!*

There are compensations for having been a bit famous. What happens is you become a target for innovation. Really big stars realise that you could be an interesting 'face' to appear on their show. A surprising offer came from the talented, innovative Ruby Wax, who had this outrageous idea of me appearing as a fairly smarmy game show host, where I quizzed the delightful Joanna Lumley. Joanna was asked to be very dumb, and to get the answers to my simple inquisitions horribly wrong. We all had a marvellous time recording this sketch; Joanna was hilarious and we all degenerated into disgraceful behaviour which, much to my surprise, Ruby, as producer, decided to transmit.

There had developed over the years a divide in the world of

**A rose between two thorns? I don't think so!**

comedy. It was quite an affectionate split caused simply by some of us getting older and some of us still growing up. The growing up element were sadly younger than us 'getting olders' and we didn't like it! These guys were clever and innovative, what with writing original material and being satirical, and it was all too much for us old-fashioned buggers. So the schism was created. Alternative comedy had arrived in the form of some very observant, intelligent chaps and lassies, and we were becoming 'old hat' and not too cool.

One of the new kids on the block was a certain Paul O'Grady, a scouser with a wickedly sharp wit, and a dress sense to die for. Paul had been spotted and became an overnight sensation (having worked the clubs for years!), and was to be the flagship heading the new wave of comedy talents. He was asked to present a television programme where two comedians of opposing styles were given the chance to perform in the other's type of venue. The deal was that I would do my show in Comedy Store (an alternative venue), and the other participant would perform in a workingmen's club north of Watford. I was approached to take part in this exercise along with a charming comedienne called Dolly Dupree.

**The three ages of comedy. Jim, Lily and Dolly – sounds like a group!**

The venues were agreed and I found myself at the Bearcat Comedy Store in Twickenham, which was in the basement of a pub and seated around seventy people. Dolly was to appear at Salford British Legion, a rather large forbidding club with a capacity of three hundred. The idea was that we discussed our tactics with Paul on camera before we did the gig, then Paul, as Lily Savage (you knew that anyway), would go onstage to warm up the audience then introduce us. I was first to go at the Bearcat and I suppose I found it fairly easy if only because of the size of the venue and the audience, having been used to the bigger clubs. I'd also been on the box quite a bit so that helped in my task of bridging the comedy gap (being recognised does give you an extra minute to prove yourself!).

Dolly was scheduled to appear in Salford a few days after me, with Paul again doing the compèring as Lily Savage. I had spent a couple of days with Dolly prior to the respective performances, and found her to be a charming character who was fighting her way through the world of observational comedy. A lady of considerable good looks and comparative youth, I really didn't think these factors were in her favour. I got the feeling that this comedic equation with its attendant challenges was extremely unbalanced.

The time came for Dolly to do her stuff in Salford and she followed a very strong northern comedian called Billy Bean. Billy was a Manchester-based act who was in his element in this type of venue. Bearing in mind that Dolly had only worked in comedy clubs in London, the prospect of entertaining the large crowd in this eminently northern arena must have been daunting to say the least. The programme went out and I don't think either of our careers suffered, nor was the comparison between alternative and old-fashioned comedy ever effectively made – incidentally I don't think it ever will.

I hope Dolly's doing well because we had a pleasant few days together putting the world of comedy to rights; I've since stopped doing that 'cos it hurts!

Another surprising approach came from Jonathan Ross, who had a late-night programme which ventured into the twilight areas of night life in the city. Around the time his show was running I had made a sort of Lancashire rap (yes, rap!) record telling the story of Bullseye the game show. It wasn't a record that was released, we tried to hide it, but some smart sod tried to wreck my career by

**Rapping in London's West End.**

giving it to J. Ross Esq. I think he came from Accrington. Anyway he heard the record and decided that I needed to be more informed about the rap culture. I was therefore sent out with a film crew to spend a night in London on the disco scene, where I ended up being the DJ playing the tracks and doing the posing bit. By the end of the night I was the only person slightly the worse for wear; everybody at the nightclub was drinking water, in fact they ran out of lager as I had drunk it all. It must be said, however, that they didn't stock very much as there wasn't much demand. How naïve can you get!

Production companies offer you opportunities to do pilot programmes in any medium. Heavy Entertainment Limited was a relatively new company with good ideas for broadcasting. The creative force behind this operation was a talented writer and producer called David Roper, who had a deep understanding and love of variety and music hall. He had seen me working somewhere and he offered me this delightful pilot programme where I was to be a team captain in a comedy radio quiz. Even better news was that Bernard Cribbins was to be the opposing team captain, and the lovely Pam Ayres was to be the chairperson. It sounded brilliant.

Each programme we would invite two guests to be on our respective teams and Pam would attempt to keep order as we struggled to win the day. The pilot became a series and we spent many happy evenings together recording the shows in venues as far apart as Chipping Norton in Oxfordshire to Richmond in Yorkshire, even gracing the cloisters of Eton (that's near London, you know).

*I say, how very posh!*

Working with Pam Ayres and Bernard Cribbins, along with the wide range of guest team members was most enlightening. Richard Stilgoe

**Pam Ayres.**

Bernard Cribbins.

(High Sheriff of Surrey, no less) was absolutely brilliant. His poetic skills were a joy and his incisive wit a revelation. Nicholas Parsons was a guest, well, not so much a guest as a takeover bid! Richard 'I don't believe it!' Wilson appeared on the programme when we recorded at Eton College – apparently Prince William was a fan of his, so we took the mountain to Mohammed! Security surrounding our visit was absolutely amazing, and the nearest available parking space was just outside Newbury; I ask you who'd be a Royal? The programme ran for two seasons and afforded me a refreshing change of scene as I tramped the showbiz trail.

Television was to feature again in my career, this time on a regional basis. Mentorn Television had this idea of taking stars born in the Midlands, back to their roots in a series called Now and Then. Their memories of seeing me record Bullseye in the Birmingham studios must have reminded them of me, and so Mentorn Television became my employer for a while.

It was a wonderful time for me as I was able to research and meet people like author Colin Dexter (remember Inspector Morse?), scientist and broadcaster Desmond Morris (does *The Naked Ape* ring a bell?), actress Sue Nicholls (Corrie), cartoonist Gerald Scarfe (married to lovely Jane Asher), actor William Roach (I promise you he's not boring!), musician Roy Wood (wishing it could be Christmas every day in Blackberry Way), and many more, such as Toyah Wilcox, Bill Oddie, Gwen Taylor, Christopher Timothy, Geoff Capes, Julia Watson and so on. The series ran for two seasons and it proved to be a massive learning curve for me. Most of these guys were heavyweights in the brain department. Interviewing people like Desmond Morris can be quite daunting. In fact the best way to interview Desmond is to just listen. We had a marvellous time together, me sitting there and Desmond talking. I didn't realise he was the one-time boyfriend of Diana Dors. He took me to a lake in Swindon where he honoured his contract with that extremely glamorous lady.

Then there was the lovely Colin Dexter. We met at the Randolph Hotel in Oxford where we talked about his roots. At first Colin was slightly apprehensive about the programme we were making about him, and he was a source of concern as we wondered how forthcoming he would be about his very private life. As we chatted at the Randolph I discovered that he was really keen on variety and those fine theatrical comedy legends. Max Wall was his favourite, and would you believe

**Ken – forty years married to Coronation Street. Me – forty years married to Phyllis.**

it, he was mine too. Bingo! I could do a fairly credible impression of Max, and I knew bits of his act. Needless to say I did my party piece and we were away. We became good friends as we traced his beginnings, from his old school, Stamford Grammar, where he taught Classics, right up to his phenomenal success as the creator of Inspector Morse. Did you know that, like Alfred Hitchcock, Colin appeared in every episode of Inspector Morse? You see, it's amazing what you can learn from a faded old comic's ramblings!

When I'd completed the first autobiography in 1993, just after I'd done the series with Colin, I sent him a copy and wrote on the fly leaf the following: 'Best wishes Colin, it was lovely to work with you. Please accept this book with my gratitude. In literary terms it's the equivalent of me giving the widow's mite to the man who has everything!' He graciously replied with a beautifully signed, limited edition of one of his works. What a man!

The middle of the decade was being awfully good to me, offering these lovely variations in my life and letting me meet all these wonderful people.

*I say, how very fortuitous!*

It was around this time that I was introduced to the RAF. I received a call from a Liverpool agency asking if I would like to tour with the Massed Bands of the RAF. This offer would enable me to completely indulge myself and do some really prestigious work with fine musicians in venues to die for. I willingly accepted the tour and was delighted to learn that the opening concert was at the Royal Albert Hall in London. It was the beginning of a fourteen-night nationwide tour that I shall never forget. We visited Symphony Hall Birmingham, Concert Hall Glasgow, Theatre Royal, Nottingham, Poole Concert Hall, and other venues of equal note. The camaraderie that exists between these guys is something to experience. I found myself becoming more and more part of the scene as the tour progressed. My driver, Pete, had been in the RAF in the fifties and still retained a sense of belonging. As a consequence, at every concert he could be found at the back of the hall standing to attention as the bands played the Royal Air Force March Past.

Squadron Leader Rob Wiffin was musical director of the Central Band of the RAF, and was appointed musical director for the tour. He proved to be a brilliant foil for me as we smiled and played our way through those memorable concerts. I was invited back the next year for a helping of the same, and once again the experience was unforgettable. This time the tour was directed by Wing Commander Robin Wilkinson, assisted by Rob Wiffin, who later that year was promoted to Wing Commander on Robin's retirement.

I often wondered how I was put into the frame to compère the Massed Bands tour. I was later to find out.

In the late eighties I was booked to compère a concert featuring the Band of the RAF Regiment at The Colston Hall, Bristol. I arrived at the venue full of a severe cold and feeling distinctly under the weather, where I met this good-looking flight lieutenant who also had a nasty dose of flu; he was Stuart Stirling. Between us we managed to get through the night coughing for Europe and in the process infecting the whole of Bristol. I remember his wife, Sue, spent the evening embroidering a garment of sorts. (Having worked with Stuart since, I think it was a cravat. He's that type, you know ...) Some years later I was to work closely with Stuart at Cranwell, when all was revealed. It appeared that Tom O'Connor and the late Roy Castle had done the tour for several years between them, and Stuart must have mentioned my name to the powers

**Reading the Riot Act at the Royal Albert Hall with the Massed Bands of the RAF.**

that be as an alternative. I remember working on *QE2* with Tom, who was most helpful when he knew I was taking over from him. Two years doing the tour had enabled me to establish strong links with the RAF, and Cranwell in particular. My place for the third consecutive massed bands tour was taken by that most accomplished of broadcasters John Dunn. My maimed ego nearly came to the fore then! Yes, I was disappointed at not getting the third year's tour; nothing to do with ego really, more to do with losing really enjoyable work. I think I know why I was sidelined for the job though. No, I'm not saying anything now in case the phone rings in the future. You never can tell who will get into a senior, decision-making position in this world. I mean, Marcus Plantin could become head of the RAF. Then heads would roll and I may be called upon to save the situation.

I don't think so!

Stuart Stirling was to ring me at the mill soon after I was sidelined from the massed bands tour, to ask if I would go to Cranwell to share a concert with his current band, the Band of the RAF College. It was to be a three-night gig in the Frank Whittle Hall at the college. I was delighted to accept and as expected we all had a really

From the RAF College Band, Cranwell.
Aren't computer generated graphics marvellous?

great three days. I have always had the utmost admiration for good musicians and I think the boys and girls in the college band felt this affinity and somehow this influenced the performance. I was asked back for a second run at the Frank Whittle Hall with Stuart and his brand new acquisition, the reformed RAF Regiment Band. This constant meeting together prompted me to discuss the possibility of doing a concert involving Stuart's swing section of the main band and the *QE2* combination of yours truly and Colin Bryant's HRO. The date was set, and what a night we all had. Imagine: both bands onstage at the same time, each band enjoying the performance of the other, applauding solos wildly and generally fully appreciating the combined skills and techniques on display. It was marvellous to be part of such a special evening. The audience were enthralled by it all.

Air Vice-Marshal Bill Rimmer was commandant at Cranwell during our visits there and he came to all the performances. I was to discover that Bill was a frustrated comic, and after each show we went back to the sergeants' mess to tell one another tales. I remember the first time we were due to go to the mess, Bill had to get an invitation from a senior mess member to enter the building as a guest. I found this quite strange. Here was Bill, the boss of the whole shebang, asking if he could enter a complex on a campus he commanded. He was an air vice marshal for goodness sake, that's close to God in the RAF! Apparently God would have had to ask permission to enter so I felt better about things then. We sat in the mess till late every night, Bill honing his comedic skills on us all. We laughed heartily at everything he said; you do tend to do that when it's an air vice marshall telling the gags. We later found out that Bill went on to become King of Cyprus, at least as far as the RAF was concerned. What a pleasure to know you Bill.

I was pleased to be able to continue working with Stuart and the Band of the RAF Regiment throughout the nineties and into the new millennium.

Over the years we have developed a sort of vaudevillian approach to the concerts in the Frank Whittle Hall at Cranwell. Stuart has a wonderful philosophy with regard to these shows in that he realises that our performance on stage should be primarily entertaining, which gives me a privileged licence to have fun with the audience. I am there as a sort of lubricant between the wonderful music being played by this fine band. His choice of programme is conditioned by a genuine desire to entertain rather than educate; to put a smile on the faces out there as well as to re-awaken their musical appreciation, and quite right too. I have seen more concert audiences driven to false appreciation and approval of an evening's performance, never to return, than I care to remember.

Play the tunes they know, and play them with the same enthusiasm you played them the first time and they'll come again. The majority of people attending concerts are not high flyers in the musical world, they don't know about modulations and sharps and flats, they just know what they like. The chances are they'll be upset if they don't recognise most of the stuff they hear. Imagine Tom Jones doing a concert and not singing 'Delilah'. The audience would feel cheated, and they would be absolutely right.

Squadron Leader Stuart Stirling has that down-to-earth approach to his craft that makes him rather special. A man who possesses a doctorate in music and still has the awareness to understand the common man's level of musical appreciation is a real showman. I look forward to working with him and the band of the RAF Regiment many more times at Cranwell in the future.

My association over the years with the military has given me great pleasure; whether it's my National Service memories I want to revive, or perhaps my appreciation of excellence, I find something stimulating about being with disciplined, dedicated youngsters who believe in what they are doing. I suppose I'm an old fart really, but I'm not bothered. When you reach an age that you feel qualified to comment ... you should! No, perhaps you shouldn't, you should think twice, because your comments could rebound on you when life bites back later on. It's not all about opinion; it's about getting on with life, for as long as the powers that be let you. Don't get stressed out with opinions. They're only thoughts anyway, and who ever paid the bills with thoughts?

*I say, how very practical!*

# CHAPTER FOURTEEN

# A Sad But Affectionate Interlude

THERE were to be sad times too in the mid nineties. Pete, my driver for over twenty years, began to have respiratory problems and, though initially they seemed fairly insignificant, a visit to his doctor revealed a more sinister scenario. It transpired that a valve in his heart was not functioning properly and treatment in hospital was necessary. This proved unsuccessful so Pete had to live with a less active approach to life. Ironically enough the first tangible evidence of his worsening condition reared its ugly head at RAF Cranwell. We were performing the concert with the college swing band and the Hot Rhythm Orchestra. Pete never missed the start (or the finish) of any shows I did, so it came as a surprise to me when he wasn't to be found backstage at the start of this particular performance. The evening drew to a close and Pete was nowhere to be found. We had a 6 a.m. start the next morning so I assumed that he had gone to bed. In fact he had gone to bed in the early afternoon, as the tiredness was becoming more and more of a problem. We returned home next morning and nothing was mentioned apart from Pete expressing his disappointment at missing the show.

*QE2* was soon to reappear in the scheme of things in the summer and we sailed off from Edinburgh in mid July 1999, to the Norwegian Fjords. Pete by now wasn't fit to drive long distances so John and Lynne Tinson drove us up to Edinburgh to join the ship. We all spent the afternoon on board, enjoying afternoon tea before John and Lynne left the ship to return to Lancaster. Four days into the trip a message came from Pete's wife, Joan, to say that things weren't looking good at home; in fact she really thought that perhaps he might not be around when we got home. He had been taken in to the Macmillan Unit at Royal Lancaster Infirmary the day we sailed out of Edinburgh. While in the Macmillan Unit he had been worrying about letting the side down by not being fit enough to drive us to Edinburgh, and talked of all the good times we had shared together over the years. It seemed almost as though he was anticipating events and Joan just thought we ought to know.

I had friends in high places on *QE2* and the time had come to ask a favour. I approached the chief radio officer and explained what I wanted to do. If I could get faxed messages of support and encouragement to Pete from as many sources as possible then I felt at least I had done something to cheer him up. We sent faxes from the captain, officers and crew of *QE2*, the Hot Rhythm Orchestra, and of course Phyllis and me. I then had to somehow contact RAF Cranwell to get the band to fax a message to Pete. Even in these days of high tech. communications, the Norwegian fjords were not the ideal place to be when having to send faxes immediately. The chief radio officer was brilliant. Somehow he sidestepped the mountains with his box of electronic wizardry and made sure that all the faxes were sent off from the radio room onboard almost immediately (they had to be faxes because I wanted Pete to be able to pin them up round his bed). We did encounter further problems when we found out that the RAF College Band was at Earls Court, London, taking part in the Royal Tournament. It was here that band sergeant Steve Humphreys came up trumps. I had worked closely with Steve when I toured with the Massed Bands. I knew he was based at Cranwell so I called him at home. Steve's wife answered the phone and dutifully contacted Steve at RAF Uxbridge, where the band was staying during the Royal Tournament. Steve then made sure that the required fax was sent. All the boys and girls in the band signed it and Steve did the rest. Eventually every party involved managed to get all the messages through.

When the ship arrived at Gerainger I was able to phone Joan. I knew instantly that the news was not good. Pete had passed away. She was obviously devastated but through the grief-ridden conversation she described to me how all the faxes had arrived (seven in all), and how Pete read them and had them pinned up round his bed as we had hoped. Joan did say that she thought she detected a smile as he read them out loud. That must have been little consolation, but well done everybody.

Pete's last words to Joan were: 'Ask Jim to do something for this place'. I did, and that's another heart-warming tale.

After the dust had settled a little on this forgettable time, we discussed what we should do about Pete's last request. He had always enjoyed the showbiz times, the fun occasions, so we decided that a fun night was to be the way to go. We had no trouble getting the venue or the acts to take part. In fact Pete would have been flattered if he had known how popular he was! The evening was presented at Morecambe's largest venue, The Dome. It seated over 600 people and it sold out within days of it being advertised. Mort Allan, a good pal, sorted out the opening of the show by recruiting a local dance group and the rest of the show fell into place as our friends in the business lined up to take part. We organised a huge tombola stall, enabling every one who bought a ticket to collect a prize. The whole evening was a tremendous success and we were able to send a large cheque to the Macmillan Unit at Royal Lancaster Infirmary.

As you can imagine, over the years Pete and I had met and worked with many celebrities. One of the best was the doyen of the game show, and king of the stand-up, a certain Robert Monkhouse. Pete and Bob had talked very briefly on a couple of occasions, probably about cars. I knew Bob was a very good cartoonist and I dared to ring him at his home to ask if he would kindly draw one for us to auction at the evening performance, explaining the reason for the request. The silence that greeted my request was extremely disquieting. It seemed ages before Bob replied; I really thought I had gone too far, as I know the demands made on these high-profile stars are enormous. His reply eventually came: 'I'm sorry Jim, I'm not prepared to do that'. I was mortified; I felt I had abused the friendship of a man for whom I had the highest regard. 'Put me down for a grand', he whispered. I was absolutely speechless. It took a moment for me to gather my thoughts. 'I don't know what to say, apart from thank you', I clumsily replied.

'Just don't say who sent it', said Bob.

I did as Bob requested, but a sentence in the souvenir programme for the evening read: 'A thousand thanks to a dear friend'. What a gentleman! You'd better believe it.

Pete's widow Joan was there with her two lovely daughters and I'm sure that the evening went some little way to helping them face the future. They must have known then that they need never be alone during the difficult times that lay ahead for them. Life had to go on, as they say, but I missed him very much for a long time. It was a mind-focussing time for me, and perhaps Pete's departure made me hold on even harder to the things that were precious to me, and there were many.

*QE2* had been a large part of our lives since the early eighties and as the new decade approached the dawn of the new millennium (what a con that was!), we found ourselves spending more and more time working aboard this fine vessel as the popularity of her UK (Southampton/Southampton) voyages increased. In the 1998 season we spent almost three months at sea. This was made up of nine cruises varying in length from 10 to 15 days. It seemed that the bulk of the spring and summer months were spent packing and unpacking. It felt like we were on leave when we came home. National Service all over again, without the sergeants! Things, however, were to change. Fashion, market forces and some fairly aggressive accounting was to see the demise of *QE2* as a regular cruise liner out of Southampton on UK sailings. The American owners of this eminently British ship discovered that the transatlantic route, taken up to now intermittently by *QE2*, was far more profitable than when she plied her trade carrying us Brits round the Med., or taking us up to see the Land of the Midnight Sun, or to see Casablanca, or for that matter taking us anywhere 'cos we didn't spend enough on board! We were constantly working the discount system, looking for upgrades in the cabin war and generally being, as they say in Yorkshire, careful wi't pennies. We became the victims of our own good housekeeping. The upshot of it all was that transatlantic cruises to and from America featured far more frequently in the *QE2* brochure than ever before. As a consequence of this rearrangement of the ship's itinerary, changes were afoot with regard to the entertainment on board and, yes you've guessed it, our lives were to be rearranged as well. 1999 saw us entertain on four UK cruises on *QE2*. The beginning of the year also saw a slow down in terms of live performances, as well as a reduction in cruise work, so the atmosphere at Low Mill was one of reflection and recuperation. Life went on without too much excitement, which, after the packing and unpacking of the previous year, was quite pleasant.

## CHAPTER FIFTEEN

---

# *From Sea Waves to Airwaves*

'Is THAT JIM BOWEN?' asked the voice on the telephone. I knew the answer to the question, which began a conversation with Steve Taylor, a BBC Radio executive, who was in a position to make decisions that could be career threatening or enhancing. From the timbre of his voice I was quick to grasp that he fully intended to fill my days with work. 'How would you like to present a radio programme?', Steve asked. I was well aware that the salaries of radio people weren't quite what I'd been used to but remember what I've just told you. The atmosphere at the mill at that time was one of reflection, a time for gathering thoughts, for taking stock, a time to wonder if anyone in the world wanted me. Bearing in mind the slowing down of my cruise work and the distinct lack of any great interest in me as a performer of any stature, I was, so to speak, vulnerable to scheming BBC executives offering me a chance to 'feel wanted'. I had done work on radio in the past in the form of 'one hour specials' where I interviewed guests of a local significance (if you can call the Duke of Westminster local!). I must have made some sort of impression for Steve to make the phone call I suppose.

I was starting to feel wanted again!

I must say at this point that throughout this feeling unwanted period Phyllis was thoroughly supportive and displayed absolutely no interest in my condition at all.

Steve offered me five mornings a week from nine till noon co-hosting a light-hearted, magazine-type programme with a bubbly young lady called Sally Naden. Sally was already on the staff at the BBC, so she would simply move from her job as a broadcast journalist to morning presenter. Sally had been a Tiller Girl in the Victorian Music Halls (!) so she knew something about timing and all that

148

show business stuff. We convened a working lunch type meeting at the Royal Oak in Hornby to discuss the whole idea and to decide whether or not it could work. From the outset Sally and I got on well so we decided that at least in principle the concept was worth further research. John Clayton, a senior producer at BBC Radio Lancashire, was to be the guiding force, introducing features and ideas to tickle the fancy of the listening public in the hope that ratings would eventually improve. Further business meetings brokered the financial arrangements so we were set to bombard Lancashire with a new morning broadcasting format, which we hoped would turn up trumps for Steve Taylor, manipulator of this parish. I could not, in all conscience, make a commitment to rising each morning at 7 a.m., driving some forty miles to Blackburn, doing a three hour live broadcast and then returning home at over sixty (that's years not miles per hour!). So a contract was drawn up. Well not so much drawn up as talked about loosely. It was to be on a day-to-day basis and the length of the agreement was never to be talked about and nothing was to be signed. I suppose that's a gentleman's agreement, I like to think so. On reflection, I suppose I should have been flattered that the BBC would see fit to take a chance on a man who they knew relatively little about in terms of regular radio presenting; then again they had in their armoury Steve Taylor!

March 1999 saw the first three hours of 'stuff' go out on the airwaves of Radio Lancashire. To describe the feelings and emotions going through my body on that first day in the studios as I faced the prospect of sustaining a three-hour stint on live radio is asking the impossible. I distinctly remember looking in bewilderment at a control panel with faders, mixers, switches, dials, microphones on flexible arms, not to mention the soundproof insulation with its perforated tiles (I think they were padded); all this framing the face of a producer who looked like he was in command, but the furrowed brow and the wide-eyed look gave him away. Yes, we all knew that there was no turning back and I really think we all wanted to! The features that John Clayton had created for the programme worked well, and Sally and I seemed to get on well enough to return the next day to do it again. The ensuing weeks were interesting and we got the feeling that John and Steve were going to be pleased with the developing programme. For the first few months John, as deputy editor of the station, produced the programme and even in these early days we enjoyed a positive response from our listener.

Every three months the BBC issue listening figures which obviously give some indication as to whether or not the programmes being transmitted are successful. To our dismay we were to learn that our figures weren't all that impressive. I must say I expected our pro-gramme to sweep the board and to persuade every pair of ears in Lancashire to listen to us, but this was not the case. It was a very dejected pair of presenters who went into the station manager's office that June morning. 'Don't worry,' said Steve, 'Our listeners take time to readjust to change. Sometimes it can take eighteen months for a new programme to establish itself'. We knew that the three-hour offering we were giving them was different from its predecessor, so a crumb of comfort lay there, but only a very small crumb. Our egos were dented, our confidence dashed and just for a moment we wondered whether or not to join the army! Steve Taylor and John Clayton massaged our egos enough to persuade us not to serve Queen and country but to come to work the next morning and to obliterate the ratings information from our minds. (I'll talk to you later about egos; suffice it to say for now that they are a devious element of show business people's make-up that none of us own up to having.)

As we entered the second half of the year presenting the pro-gramme, our confidence was growing and our creative juices were flowing wildly.

Phyllis and I often go out with friends for a little drink. We call it the Mafia meeting. Not exactly a gathering of a mob as we have all passed the stage where our behaviour threatens society even in drink. It is at these soirées that we put the world and one another to rights. During one of these alcoholic evenings at the Strathmore Hotel, Morecambe, one member of our group, a certain Lynne Tinson, was discussing the meaning of life and why we were part of it all, when she observed (bearing in mind we were in the Strathmore Hotel where life and movement are difficult to detect anyway) that as we approached the time of our lives when perhaps we might become confused, or 'daft', she would prefer it if she could be happy in that confused state, as against being miserable. 'Happy daft', now that is a state of mind which seemed to all of us an attractive option as we skulked in this inanimate hostelry. Please bear in mind that this observation on later life was made by a lady who would like the epitaph on her headstone to read, 'what the hell was all that about?'

'Happy daft', what a glorious description of the three hours of 'stuff' we were delivering each morning to our increasing band of listeners.

The 'Happy Daft Farm' was born. Thanks Lynne!

The preposterous licence this title gave the programme initiated a new freedom of expression, within the ranks, and it eliminated the fear of taking risks with our listener. We were to learn that our listener enjoyed taking a risk with us. We didn't know it at the time but we were creating a family; we were to find out, almost by accident, that there were people out there whose lives now needed the 'risk' experience; they needed a journey into the world of the irresponsible. These people were reaching the stage of their lives when the phrase 'time waits for no man' really was becoming significant, so 'Sod it and let's get on with it!' became their battle cry. We were climbing in the ratings war and the possibility that this influx of listeners was coming from homes and institutions where supervision was the order of the day in no way concerned us. We were winning!

Our listeners were getting into the psyche of it all and they were spreading the gospel of its 'take-a-chance' mentality. We were getting new converts by the million, well … a lot anyway!

It seemed that our listener wanted to cast off the cloak of respectability, responsibility and just downright inhibited behaviour; they wanted to take a look on the bright side of life. 'And why not', as Barry Norman would say.

The Happy Daft Farm gave these born-again rebels a licence to be naughty and outrageous; they could sing on the radio, howl in unison with the farm animals and generally, while doing nobody any harm, behave just as they pleased.

*I say, how adventurous!*

Thinking about it now, they were taking no risks at all; the people taking the risks were Steve Taylor and John Clayton. It was their jobs on the line! The BBC was giving our listeners the platform to rediscover themselves, and in the process entertain their fellow listener (fortunately!).

The programme was now beginning to spawn a wide variety of

talent as a result of one of the regular features within its format. 'Give it a go', a dated reflection of the Wilfred Pickles era, gave listeners a chance to come into the studios at Blackburn and 'strut their stuff' in any way they wished. Scarf juggling went down very well, as did ventriloquism. We did realise, however, that some performers warranted an opportunity to shine on a more clearly defined stage. Hence the 'Happy Daft Farm on Tour' came into being. As each act performed in the studio (10.35 a.m. every weekday morning) we secretly auditioned them with a view to asking them to take part in a variety show at a theatre near them. The response was overwhelming. We were able to cast enough performers to present several shows around the county. We travelled from Bacup to Preston, Lancaster, Chorley, Southport, even Colne, as the listeners proudly showed off their talents to their peers. The whole adventure was an astounding success.

Stories abound with regard to the daily helping of nonsense we discharged to the county each weekday. Seeking to inject an element of surprise into the programme John Clayton suggested a 'spin the bottle' idea. The deal was that we would read out a list of topics, for example, favourite holiday, best school story, hospital experience, wedding tale and so on and then invite the listener to tell of their experiences relating to one of the listed topics. The idea took off and the contributions were hilarious. John suggested one day that one of the topics could be 'funerals'. Bearing in mind that this was live radio with no tape delay to give us at least some sort of protection I did for once question his judgement. I was overruled and the subject was allowed into the game. I was praying that the bottle didn't settle pointing at funerals, but yes, you've got it; second time round that's exactly where the bottle stopped. We trawled the airwaves for stories and sure enough one came up. It went like this: 'Hello Jim and Sally, it's Edith here from Rawtenstall. I've got a story about funerals.'

'Carry on', says I, nervously.

'Well,' she began, 'I'm sixty-three and I lost my mother two years ago and we were very close, oh yes very close, I thought the world of my mother, she were a saint my mother were, oh yes she were a saint! Any road, before she died she explained exactly how she wanted to be looked after when she popped her clogs [a local expression meaning to snuff it]. She said "Edith, I want none o' this mournin' an' bein' sad at t'funeral service. I want to be cremated and when t'coffin's goin' through t'final curtains I want you to make sure that you play *Sally* sung by my favourite singer, Gracie Fields. Now you won't let me down, will you Edith?" Well, Jim, I did everything she asked. I bought a CD of Gracie what had all her hit songs on includin' *Sally*. I gave the CD to the groundsman at the crem. 'cos it seemed he dealt wi't musical side o' things. I told 'im to press track 2 on t'machine after t'vicar 'ad done 'is prayin' bit, an' then we'd hear Gracie singin' *Sally* as me mum disappeared through t'curtains. Sure enough as t'coffin went through t'curtains we could all hear Gracie singin' me mam's favourite song. Then somethin' strange 'appened. I think t'feller in charge o't'CD player must have leant on a button or summat 'cos all of a sudden Gracie suddenly started singin', "Wish me luck as you wave me goodbye!" Well, everybody got their 'ankies out and started wavin' me mam goodbye! Eeeh, I don't think there were a dry eye in t'church. Everybody were bloody well laughin!'

The atmosphere in the studio was unbelievable. We were all looking at one another with tears in our eyes, John had that triumphant look, as if to say 'I told you so', and both Sally and I thoroughly enjoyed the 'near to the edge' broadcasting experience that was becoming almost the norm for Happy Dafters.

A popular feature on the programme was the 'Action Line'. As its name suggests, it was a facility which enabled listeners to ring in asking for help or information about virtually anything. A listener could be looking for a manual for a specific model of sewing machine, or perhaps offering for collection a budgie cage or un-wanted piano. The requests and objects on offer could be interesting to say the least! One morning a listener asked if anyone could provide a unicycle for a child whose ambition was to join a circus. You will agree, not the most usual of requests. Sally challenged our listener on this score, suggesting that if anyone could come up with a unicycle, she would, as they say, 'show her bum in Debenhams' window!' Within ten minutes a unicycle appeared in reception at the studio in Blackburn! Sally was now in the unenviable position of having to honour her part of the bargain. The phone lines went berserk with listeners trying to find out when this promised revelation would take place. We decided to capitalise on the whole idea, and in the process benefit one of our less fortunate customers.

The programme was a versatile beast, if a little 'off the wall', and we did pride ourselves on our ability to embrace any topic whatsoever with sensitivity and good grace. In fact the secret of its success was that its whole premise was that our listener should feel comfortable with Sally and me, come hell or high water.

One of the guests who appeared on the programme just prior to the Debenhams incident was a Blackburn bus driver. Nothing special about that you might say, but in this instance you would be quite wrong. This relatively gentle, unassuming man spoke with such devotion about his adopted son, Sam. The word bravery can slip very easily off the tongue, but when we heard Sam's story the word took on a totally new significance. Life had been most unkind to Sam. He found himself on this earth with problems too large for either Sally or me to comprehend. Wheelchair bound, Sam had been deprived of sight, speech and the ability to hear well; all this compounded by virtual immobility resulting from cerebral palsy. We found ourselves totally humbled by this man who chose to adopt Sam. I mean ... why? Why, we asked, did this bus driver choose to inherit such a massive burden? What a crass question to even think of asking, and here am I saying we could handle any topic with sensitivity. 'Because he was there', said Sam's proud dad. His answer not only put us firmly in our place but also provoked a reaction from our listeners that melted the lines. He went on to explain how he was raising money to get Sam out to Florida to 'swim with the dolphins'.

Coincidence is a fortunate thing isn't it? There we were, arousing a huge response from our listeners on two counts: firstly, Sally's wild promise to disrobe in Debenham's window; and secondly a Blackburn bus driver's delightful chat about his son's swimming ambitions, both items taking place within days of each other.

*I say, how very opportune!*

Here's what we did. We discussed on air how we intended to get Sally to do the decent (or was it indecent?) thing and bare all to the shoppers of Blackburn. We then approached Debenhams and told them of our situation, or rather Sally's! It was agreed that on a pre-ordained Friday at eleven o'clock we would do an outside broadcast in Debenhams' window, and we would announce it on air. The great day arrived, and as we approached the shopping precinct in

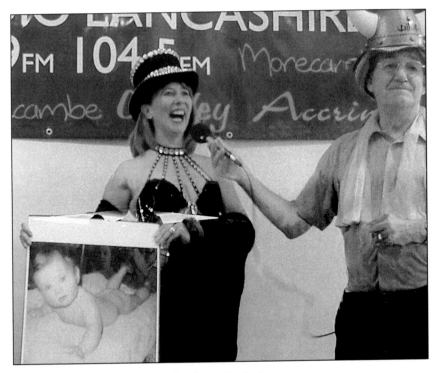

**Debenhams' window.**

Blackburn we were amazed to see hundreds of people crowding round the entrance of Debenhams. They had all come to see Sally pay her dues! Our producer, a very talented young man called Alec Makinson, had devised this scheme whereby Sally would hide behind a screen in the ladies' lingerie window and, as we played David Rose's arrangement of 'The Stripper', she would throw her garments over the top of the screen, one piece at a time. First came the shoes, then the skirt, then the blouse, followed by stockings, bra, old boot, miner's helmet, donkey jacket, empty paint tin, etc., and so it went on to screams of laughter from the crowd. Sally finally emerged in the Tiller Girl outfit she had borrowed from Blackpool Pleasure Beach looking a million dollars; more importantly though she honoured her agreement with our listeners to show her bum in Debenhams' window by carrying with her a photo of herself completely naked ... aged 9 months! Our listeners were delighted at such fun, and so was Sam's dad; we collected over £200 as we freely assaulted the assembled crowd with empty buckets. Well done everybody!

One of the Happy Daft Farm's best pals was a very talented folk singer who lives in Bolton and is appropriately called 'The Bolton Bullfrog'. Bernard Wrigley is a fine writer and an extremely accomplished musician who has written an endless supply of trails for the programme. He surprised us all when he turned up at the Debenhams' disrobing ceremony to sing this original composition:

*Sally's gone and done it now because of what she said,*
*If she hadn't spoken out of turn she wouldn't be so red*
*We hope it doesn't send her completely off her head*
***'Cos she said she'd show her bum in Debenhams' window.***

*It's all because of what she said about a unibike*
*On Jim and Sally's morning show, the one that people like*
*What you say can be recorded if you're speaking down a mike*
***And she said she'd show her bum in Debenhams' window.***

*The likelihood of getting a unicycle seemed so small*
*So she said that she would be prepared to go and show her all*

*She said she'd do it if a unicycle could be found*
*She was feeling smug – not many unicycles to the pound*
*But here come three or four of them doing wheelies round and round*
***So she'll have to show her bum in Debenhams' window!***

*But if she looked behind the shop she'd probably have a fit*
*For there is Jim with a metal saw making unicycle kits*

*So here we are at Debenhams, we've come from near and far*
*We hope that Sally's here as well and hasn't crashed the car*
*We listen to the morning show and think that she's a star*
***And she's going to show her bum in Debenhams' window!***

Many sincere thanks Bernard for all your help with the programme.

We kept in touch with Sam and his dad. I'm pleased to tell you that the trip to Florida took place, and as we looked at the photos of Sam playing with the dolphins we knew exactly why Sam's dad had chosen him. We also learned a bit more about interviewing people. Smarty-pants!

The programme was becoming a way of life for our patrons. A combination of face-to-face meetings with our listeners at the evening shows we did, together with the stacks of mail we were receiving daily, were making us ever more aware of the impact we were having on their lives. Towards the end of our second year on air both Sally and I were being made increasingly conscious of our responsibilities to our listeners. We were becoming a comfort zone for the stressed, a pair of ears for the lonely, a sympathetic mattress for the troubled to lie on; in fact, for many of our listeners, our being there was their only reason for them to get up in the morning! What a burden to carry if all that were true.

Another facet of the programme was the outside broadcast, or O.B. In the early stages of its life we felt it would be unwise to take the programme out of the cosseted environment of the studio, where crises could be handled quickly and unobtrusively; by now, however, we were growing in confidence. We had managed a small O.B. challenge when we ventured some 800 yards (sorry metres) from base to record Sally taking off her clothes at Debenhams in Blackburn. Dare we move farther away from the nest to transmit the whole three hours of stuff to our listener? The opportunity was to come to us with a bang.

Friday 23rd July 1999 saw the arrival of the Queen at Morecambe. We're talking human royalty here, travelling by car, not 68,000 tons of marine hardware sailing into Morecambe Bay. Yes, Her Majesty Queen Elizabeth and Prince Philip were due to arrive in Morecambe to unveil a bronze statue of the much-loved local hero Eric Bartholomew, alias Eric Morecambe, a man who brought sunshine into all our lives ... Now Morecambe is, as you well know, in Lancashire, and we broadcast under the BBC Radio Lancashire banner, so we felt it was our responsibility to 'go live' in Morecambe to describe to our listener the whole royal visit. Our first outside broadcast was a royal one!

*I say, how terribly ceremonial!*

Morecambe was closed to the motorist on 23rd July. I was due in position at 8.30 a.m. and bearing in mind the event was taking place a mere five miles from where I lived, I thought half an hour would give me ample time to get in place and liaise with Sal. However, I was stopped a mile from our O.B. van and told to walk the rest of the way. Crowd barriers were in place for about as far as the eye could see; cones had been breeding overnight and policemen formed an endless cordon around the Queen's planned route. 'Bollards!' I thought (and there were plenty of those about as well), as I began the long hike to my allotted station.

The royal party were due to arrive at the statue at 10.30 a.m. where, after the unveiling ceremony, they were to proceed some 200 yards (sorry, metres) to a huge marquee, where royal nibbles were the order of the day. Sally and I were situated some small distance from the entrance to the marquee, where it was anticipated that we would get interviews with the many 'celebs' making up the entourage. The Queen and Prince Philip arrived on time, and we could see all the action from our position. Then the royal party began to make its way towards the food hall (sorry, marquee). The total distance they had to travel could not have been the length of a cricket pitch. Crowds were gathered either side of the walkway all craning their necks to get a glimpse of the royal couple. Hands were outstretched in the hope of perhaps shaking hands with Ma'am or Phil; and some of them were successful. The establishment was well and truly represented by this fine couple. It took over 40 minutes for them both to travel those few yards to the tranquillity of the marquee. The Queen had time for everyone. Philip was his usual cheeky self, knowingly grinning at everybody with that 'I know what you're thinking' look in his twinkling eyes. As they approached our position by the entrance to the marquee I'm sure Philip winked at me. He probably recognised me as a famous star. On reflection I think he'd got something in his eye.

The VIPs followed on, all chatting to the public and obviously enjoying this special day for the people of Morecambe. As it turns out, the Eric Morecambe statue is one of the best tourist attractions ever to have been installed in this Lancashire holiday resort. We were still in broadcast mode as the procession passed by, so our mission to talk to 'celebs' was still top of our list of things to do. Robin Day approached, so Sal put on her interview hat and approached the imposing figure. We knew Robin had always had an eye for the ladies, so the chances were Sal would come out on top, if you'll pardon the expression! Pauline Clare, Chief Constable of Lancashire, was next to come close to us as we trawled for 'celebs' so I attempted to protect my criminal record by approaching her. She was absolutely charming.

The joy of communicating to the masses is that you don't actually know the precise impact you are having. You can choose the soft option and only believe what you want to, or you can take the factual route and believe the listening figures. Of course Sally and I chose the soft option. I think it's called shelving responsibility, or becoming a counsellor by proxy.

*I say, how very convenient!*

The Happy Daft Farm was featuring prominently in the overall scheme of things as I approached the winter of 1999, but the early morning starts five days a week were making their presence felt. The respite offered by occasional trips on *QE2* throughout the year eased the rigour of the routine a little, so life was quite comfortable for this sixty-two year old. The work pattern seemed to be absolutely ideal and everything in the garden appeared to be lovely. I was still in the 'wanted zone' and the ego I didn't have was being given lots of attention by the collection of recycled teenagers who were my fans; and Phyllis was still serving me solids!

Alas! Gilbert and Sullivan said it, 'Things are seldom what they seem.' Yes, you've guessed it ... read on please.

# CHAPTER SIXTEEN

## QE2, A Life on the Ocean Wave ... Again!

OVER THE YEARS Colin Bryant's Hot Rhythm Orchestra has proved to be one of the most popular features on board *QE2*. Not only is the band probably one of the best of its kind in Europe, but the way the boys give value for money everywhere on the ship in terms of passenger management as well as the excellent shows they perform nightly in the Golden Lion pub puts them in a class of their own. Over the many years they have worked on the ship you can imagine the fan base they have built up, the friends they have made and of course the countless memories they have collected.

The phone rang one afternoon in November 1999 as we were enjoying our Complan after the morning's toil on the radio, waiting for the matron to pop in to tell us who we were (I don't remember pulling the cord to summon her presence). I picked up the handset to hear the voice of Garry Brown, the highly respected agent who had always negotiated our *QE2* contracts. Nothing untoward I thought, as it was around this time that the following year's contracts were discussed. Isn't it funny when you can anticipate the content of a call before anyone speaks a word? Such was the case this November morning when, even before Garry spoke, I knew our days afloat were numbered. As it turned out they weren't even numbered, they didn't exist, they were gone, extinct, dead, and defunct. The conversation began by my asking what dates we would be required in the year 2000. The conversation ended by Garry saying that my financial demands were over budget in the revised scheme of things, and would I mind terribly if I stayed at home next year. The question was rhetorical! What in fact he meant was that I was surplus to requirements and my nautical experiences

160

aboard *QE2* would end forthwith. I was not required on any voyages she would make during 2000. My luggage would not be registered on the ship's manifest; I was doomed to be land-bound for the foreseeable future.

Here was I, sixty-three years of age, being told that I was no longer required; I had become, in effect, excess baggage. It would appear that all the sterling work I had done with the HRO in that fine British pub on board the most prestigious ship in the world counted for nothing. No longer could I casually mention that I was trolling off for a couple of weeks to the sun, to be cosseted by flunkeys who moved with the speed of light to satisfy my every whim. No longer would there be any need for Phyllis to cut the labels off her bargain purchases in order to wear them with pride at the Captain's cocktail parties in the Grand Lounge on Upper Deck Aft. Our world was in tatters, we were inconsolable, so much so in fact that when I put the phone down Phyllis cancelled afternoon tea! The prospect of a trip on the high seas aboard an ocean liner was fast becoming an evening on a longboat drifting towards Garstang on the Lancaster Canal!

One of the many advantages of being a more seasoned member of society is that you can see the 'big picture' more clearly. You don't react hastily to disaster like those impetuous young things who can't handle crises with style, panache and good grace. Our generation has more about us. We did National Service. Not for us the knee jerk behaviour of those young people whose immaturity shines out like a beacon in the face of adversity. Our lot can brave it out. We've got stiff upper lips we have!

*I say, how very stoical!*

However, we really were quite disappointed about not rejoining *QE2*, but did appreciate the competitive state of the cruise market and so we looked back with affection on our time on the great ship. Our only lasting regret at the time was that we didn't get the opportunity to say goodbye to our many friends on board, who really thought we would be back.

The diary was extremely empty from November 1999 to December 2010, but were we downhearted? I think I'd like to phone a friend! You see, the problem with being in this confounded business is that however you try to pretend you haven't got one, you have.

It has to be fed and nurtured by tangible recognition in the form of letters or phone calls, or even emails. It needs reassuring that something will turn up and that it still has a valid place in the world of entertainment. I speak of course of EGO, the curse of the showman, the blight of the weak and the downfall of the less sensitive. See, I told you I would explain about egos didn't I? Now, pay attention at the back!

I, myself, me, haven't got one, so there's no problem there then. Are you sure?

I have to admit, however, that at this stage in my career I was beginning to feel slightly neglected again, and that the world was passing me by. The work was trickling in and we had no problems paying the bills, but there's more to it than that. It's not the 'money' bit; it's the 'feeling wanted' syndrome rearing its ugly head again. I wasn't back to eating allotments at Corley services again (remember that sad episode!), but I did feel the need to be sort of moving forwards, though why on earth, at sixty three years of age, I should want to move forward beggars understanding; moving backwards is the direction I should be thinking about at my age for God's sake! The end of the shelf is near enough without having thoughts emphasising the fact. Ego doesn't understand time; it's just there, the bloody thing!

The morning radio programme was still occupying most of my days, as well as influencing my night time habits with those early morning starts, so I suppose really I ought to have been grateful that I was being gainfully employed. Realistically I was in a most fortunate situation. The fact that *QE2* no longer required my services was compensated by the fact that I had been given a new career on the wireless. I was becoming quite a large fish in a local pool. The airwaves of local radio had heightened my profile considerably. As a result, the ego I didn't have was fortunately being more than gently massaged.

Word must have got round the shipping lanes of the United Kingdom that I had been given the hard word by Carnival cruises (who now owned Cunard) because the phone at home began to take messages from both P&O and Fred Olsen cruise lines. I was being offered work of a far less demanding nature by these two companies and though the remuneration was not quite as attractive I was delighted to cruise on P&O's *Arcadia* and Fred Olsen's *Black*

**On duty in the pub. (Costumes by Harrods)**

*Watch* during the year 2000. Both ships afforded us delightful hospitality and in return I gave two performances per cruise.

On our return from sailing with the opposition we were becoming aware, through the grapevine, that seeds of discontent were germinating aboard *QE2*. The Hot Rhythm Orchestra had come in under budget and was working its way through the season. Colin kept in touch with Phyllis and me at home, as he and the band completed their cruises. As the year progressed it was becoming apparent that both Phyllis and I were being missed. Colin and I had thought this might happen, but obviously it was not for us to comment. Everyone who had cruised with us knew that the combined package of the band and yours truly, in the Golden Lion pub, was a very strong feature in the entertainment programme on board ship. We could never understand why, when the pub was packed to the gunnels every night, and doing enormous business, our combined talents had been dispensed with. Carnival management could not have been looking at bar takings and, it would seem, despite all the efforts of the cruise director and the hotel manager, they were blissfully unaware of our existence.

As the season was coming to a close in the autumn of 2000, I had a call from Phyllis at the studios during the programme telling me that Garry Brown had rung and would like me to give him a call on my return.

***I say, how exciting!***

I arrived home around 1.30 p.m. and drank my glass of Sanatogen (I'd gone beyond Complan by now). Phyllis and I had a little chat on the mocquette about tactics, after which I rang Garry in his London office. Isn't it funny when you know what's coming before anyone has spoken a word. (I think we've been here before in this book!) Garry started by explaining that Carnival management had perhaps underestimated our combined input to the ship's entertainment programme, at least as far as the Brits were concerned, and perhaps we could enter into negotiations for the 2001 season sailing on *QE2*'s UK cruises with the HRO.

I was wanted again. Somebody up there does like me! It didn't bother me though. Oh really! Ask your non-existent ego, Bowen!

However, that little smattering of remorse on their part did soften my approach to negotiating the terms of a new agreement, but I have to admit to a teeny-weeny bit of smugness as I contemplated the deal. As you would expect, Garry brokered the details of the new contract with style, and we approached the end of the century good pals with Carnival and in good heart. In fact we had good cause to be of cheerful spirit because Garry had negotiated a lucrative contract for the 2001 season, signing me up for five cruises taking in destinations as wide ranging as the Land of the Midnight Sun in the north, and Istanbul in the Eastern Mediterranean.

The *QE2* as usual lived up to our expectations. The band was back and on good form and we all carried on just as we had done for the previous decade and a half. Everyone seemed pleased to see the combination of the HRO and yours truly back in full swing, and the pleasure of meeting old friends, passengers, officers and cruise staff was heightened by the temporary loss of contact.

I was particularly flattered when the president of the officers' mess announced that I was to be made an honorary member of the wardroom, and as such was entitled to my own 'page' in the bar. This was run on an honesty basis, each member entering on his page the drinks he has had during the evening. At the end of the

**The Musical Mafia from the Golden Lion pub (plus kneeling turn!).**

month he gets a statement of his account, which he then pays to the wardroom treasurer. The cost of drinks in the wardroom is reasonable to say the least, but the real benefit for us was that we could take the boys in the band up there during breaks between sets. Also it meant that if any of us had a celebration of any kind, like a birthday or anniversary, the wardroom afforded us a great bolthole to escape from the hurly-burly of the Golden Lion for a little while. 2001 did see us celebrating several milestones as the year passed. Birthdays seemed to come conveniently while we were at sea, and the officers were most accommodating in their tolerance of our brief intrusion into their exclusive club.

Another very special occasion took place in the Golden Lion pub when a group of the ship's engineers came down and surprised both Phyllis and me when they presented us with a magnificently mounted piston ring from one of the ship's engines. It was very special to us because it made us feel valued, and made us aware that they knew how much we respected all she stood for. Thank you, officers of *QE2*.

**A proud moment for us both. A piston ring as a present! Thanks, boys.**

We saw changes on the ship, not only in personnel, but also in entertainment policy. The band was asked to perform midnight matinees on almost every cruise. This only reflected the high regard that the cruise director had for Colin and the boys. We always enjoyed the midnight gig as it gave the band a chance to really put on a theatre-type performance, as against the slightly less organised approach of the Golden Lion. This always surprised the passengers because the Grand Lounge somehow brings out the best of every performer, and the band and I just loved showing off. I had to be a little more sensitive about my material because if it offended anyone they would have a problem walking out unobtrusively in the Grand Lounge. In the pub it was easy, they just got up and walked away unnoticed; I'm pleased to say it hasn't happened too often over the years.

I presented the Bullseye game in the Grand Lounge when we were at sea, usually in the afternoon at 2.30. We always got a full house, which I found quite endearing, bearing in mind the show had been off the air for 7 years. Along with *QE2* goodies the winner always got a Bendy Bully, and the response the little rubber sod still evokes was really amazing.

**Christmas in September in Accrington – Happy Daft or what?**

On the last day at sea used to I do a talk in the Grand Lounge entitled 'Bullseye, the inside story'. It was really an excuse to talk about my autobiography. It later became a vehicle for me to tell stories (most of them true) about the development of the game, with slightly enhanced tales about contestants and their adventures in the studios. It also gave me a chance to go down memory lane and talk about the old days, Opportunity Knocks with Hughie Green, Take your pick with Michael Miles, and more recent shows like Wheeltappers and Shunters, about which I could talk first hand. Bearing in mind I worked every night in the pub with the band as well, I suppose I was good value! I must bear this in mind if they ask me back again, though truth to tell I'd probably do it for nothing ... That reminds me, I must go to the doctor's tomorrow, I think the pills are wearing off!

# CHAPTER SEVENTEEN

# Awards, Commercials and More Telly

T HE RADIO PROGRAMME was still going from strength to strength. People throughout the county were going Happy Daft in huge numbers, so much so that our station manager saw fit to enter our programme for an award.

*I say, how very showbiz!*

The only award I ever received in my life was a corporal's stripes for collecting waste paper during the war (World War Two that is!), so the whole experience of even being nominated was daunting. The Frank Gillard award is a prestigious one (especially if you're nominated), but we tried to analyse the content of our programme and decided that to categorise it would be difficult, so all thoughts of winning were put on the back burner, in fact they were taken out of the kitchen altogether!

I'm delighted to report that our assumptions that we were unable to be categorised were wrong. The Happy Daft Farm won the Gold award in the 'best sequence presenter' category, so well done Alec, Sally and Bernard.

The citation reads:

The judges felt that Jim Bowen played terrifically well on radio, with a bright, warm and funny personality. Jim's a seasoned professional – and that shines through – his approach with both listeners and guests and use of quirky material produced some great listening.

Although only my name was mentioned in the comments, we all appear on the certificate. I should think so!

The year 2000 saw diversions a-plenty with offers of voice overs

**Award-winning trio – Sally, Alec and me.**

for programmes, commercials, advertisements, and some pleasant little guest spots on television.

The most lucrative area of our business is without doubt the TV commercial. I'd had a brief taste of this kind of work, but purely on a regional rather than a national basis. Now there is big money! Actors pay their bills by doing them, sacrificing their art by talking about toilet cleaners on screen. We of the illegitimate world of variety pay our bills also by doing commercials. We have little art to sacrifice, but we will also talk about bathroom cleaners; our bathrooms will probably not be ensuite, however!

The place to live, without doubt, if you are to become a target for the PR agent looking for clients, is London. That's where the business is mostly done. So, if you want to be where the action is, 'go south young man, go south!' As you, the reader well know, I am essentially northern and always have been. Not for me the wine bar mentality, the lounge with sandpapered floorboards and Eastern rugs scattered about artistically. No, I'm the Tetley bitterman, the bag o' crisps man; meat and potato pies are my bag, not the pizzas or the paellas of this world. Basic, that's the word to describe yours truly. In fact I'm not of the showbiz ilk at all. I seem to have made my living in this business by default. I never moved to London when I got the call. I don't actually remember anyone calling, but one day in the seventies I did get a slight urge. Phyllis said it was wind.

Bear in mind these facts: I'm northern, by nature and location, I'm not exactly a high fashion item on the showbiz menu, I'm a veteran comic and my claim to fame is being connected to a low-tech, northern-type game show for some years. Do you therefore wonder at my surprise when I get a phone call from a very prestigious London entertainment agency?

Patsy Martin runs an extremely efficient office in the city called Personal Appearances, where she represents many famous celebrities; and she was ringing me? She wanted to know if I was free one day in February to film the opening credits to Who Wants to be a Millionaire?, that fine programme hosted so marvellously by Chris Tarrant. Was I free? In terms of film offers I was in the Bermuda triangle!

My non-existent ego slowed down my response. 'Of course I'm free!' I immediately screamed, and so the deal was done.

I was to be at Walthamstow greyhound stadium at 4 p.m. on Wednesday 31st January to meet the film crew and the director. Needless to say I was there by 2.30 p.m., just in case they changed their minds!

The premise of the opening credits was that five game show hosts would record sketches comparing the new with the old. I, for example, would wonder how Millionaire could succeed when there were no darts involved; Tom O'Connor would ask why there were no tunes involved (Tom presented Name that Tune in the seventies); Ted Rogers did his 3-2-1 finger routine as he tried to understand the triumph of Millionaire. The whole concept was a lovely idea.

It was a bitterly cold afternoon at Walthamstow. The film crew arrived around 5.30 p.m. as they had been filming the evergreen Nicholas Parsons at Hurlingham polo club earlier, and had experienced delays. This had nothing to do with Nicholas. The crew did look a bit knackered to me though!

By 6.30 p.m. we were ready to film my contribution. The idea was this. I was to sit in the stand overlooking the dog track, next to a greyhound. I was to ask the dog how Millionaire succeeded when there were no darts involved. I was then to ask where the speedboat was, whereupon the greyhound was supposed to look sideways at me. The whole idea rested on the dog looking to its left on cue. I can only say this to you: never buy a greyhound, they must be the thickest dogs in the world. We couldn't understand it; the track they chase round goes anticlockwise so if the dog is at all interested in the thrill of the chase, it ought to run round the track after the hare at least favouring the left. We had got a dipstick of a greyhound. I lamely suggested that we help it to turn left by putting a small piece of lead in its left ear, causing it to lean a little. I then further suggested that we place the lead in its ear using a pistol. No one was amused. The night wore on and eventually we managed to get all five cameo sketches filmed, despite our retarded canine friend. These little gems were shown at the top of Millionaire for several weeks. There we were, five ageing presenters bemoaning the passing of our meal tickets, and bitterly accepting the success of Millionaire. Shortly after we had made these small cameos, Ted Rogers sadly died. The rest of us were very disappointed in Ted because, as a result of his demise, the show's sponsors, The Alliance and Leicester Building Society, took the commercial off air. I suppose it would have seemed a little lacking in respect all things considered.

Ted's timing up to then had been good too!

Another such offer came from the Esther Rantzen programme. Esther often sailed on board *QE2* as a lecturer, and it was on one of these cruises that our paths crossed. She has a delightful sense of humour and her musical knowledge is quite considerable. She took an immediate shine to the goodies on offer in the Golden Lion pub and must have remembered the experience. Consequently, when her new series of That's Esther went into the studios for a further run she remembered us, and the phone rang! Sue Barr, a charming lady whose brief it was to research the programme, chatted at length with me and together we hatched up a satisfactory list of guests to make a one hour documentary about me. Obviously Esther wanted the HRO to appear on the show, which included officers from *QE2*, comedians I had worked with over the years, Johnnie Hamp, who discovered all of us in the seventies, and of course my relatively new colleagues at Radio Lancs. I felt tremendously honoured to be asked to feature in this prestigious daytime programme.

Around the same time Mr Grossman of Through the Keyhole fame entered the portals of Low Mill (for the second time) to try to confuse the panel as he stealthily moved around the property offering cryptic clues as to the identity of the famous occupier. I always worry when it's time for the panel to guess who the 'celeb' is. Sometimes the subject isn't as popular as he imagined he was, and the panel fail to guess his identity and that's awful ... well it's the ego thing again; it's been damaged hasn't it? Mind you, that doesn't apply to me, I haven't got one!

2001 came in with the force of a cuddly teddy bear rather than a lion, but all was right with the showbiz world, and domestically both Phyllis and I were still rubbing along together within the framework of a marriage worth forty-one years of anyone's life. I was affably drifting along, still totally reliant on Phyllis with regard to practically every aspect of my waking hours. The computer and all its extra bits were exclusively hers to control; emails were in her domain; www.com/something was beyond me; the feeding habits of the pets; the administration of the house; the garden; the milk run; the newspaper delivery; the list is frighteningly interminable. Thanks to her I had become a plank, a muppet, a man who had been spoilt beyond reason. I was a disgrace! Surely a man who admits to having all those frailties could not possibly have an ego!

*I say, how terribly humble!*

My weekly routine was still the radio commitment on a daily basis from nine till noon. We were enjoying exceedingly good ratings and the feedback we were getting was most rewarding. We filled the airwaves with insanity to such an extent that, on impulse one Thursday morning in September, Sally decided that we were too far away from Christmas. The advent of shorter nights, cooler weather and more rain was too depressing to face, so she decided, on air, to bring Christmas forward. The revised 'Happy Daft' Christmas day was to be 25th September. Within an hour we had sorted out a venue to celebrate the occasion and we duly gave our listeners the details of how they could celebrate with us. A bowling club in Accrington had rung in offering us their facilities, thus enabling us to proceed with arrangements to do an O.B. This was all done in three days, giving us just over two weeks to build a Christmas special programme.

We needn't have worried. The listeners warmed to the prospect of an early celebration and came up with a surprising range of ideas. It was decided that the ingredients of the programme should feature all things festive. Music, food, presents, Father Christmas, carols and an abounding spirit of goodwill must be the order of the day. The Salvation Army were 'booked early for Christmas', so that took care of the brass band and the carols. A Jacob's join was suggested, so the food supply was assured; we knew from the reaction of the listeners that we were on to a winner. To ensure that the event was not oversubscribed we had to allocate tickets, so we devised a quiz to select the lucky winners. Alec, our producer, set up all the items we intended to feature in the programme, assisted by Sally, and we arrived at the bowling club in good heart, if a little apprehensive. We were completely staggered by what greeted us. Decorations festooned the club; listeners were there by the dozen, laden with festive goodies to eat; fancy dress, hats, streamers, hooters, all kinds of seasonal adornment, were in evidence. All this on a pleasant Friday morning in September! The programme went like a dream with all the participants, musicians, singers, poets giving their all in the Happy Daft cause.

Looking back over the three years we presented the programme, we featured some considerable talents, both musical and literary. I thought it might be quite nice to allow our contributors the opportunity of 'going into print' under another banner. I was absolutely delighted when they all agreed, so it's with great pride that I enclose these excerpts of creative writing and I thank them all most sincerely on your behalf. I know you will enjoy their efforts as you read on and I promise my ego won't throw its Teddy out of the pram.

One of the most popular visitors to the Happy Daft Farm was a very talented poet from Chorley called Steve Morris. Only minutes after he had begun reading his poems on air, the phone lines began to melt. Here's why.

### A NORTHERN BYE-BYE BLUES

*Yer a borin' bugger Brenda*
*I've said it now so theer*
*I've been wantin't'gerrit off me chest*
*Fer nigh on fifteen year*
*Ever since our weddin' night*
*When yer went to bed at nine*

*Wi' a mug o' soddin' Horlicks*
*An' Gardeners' Question time*

*Yer a borin' bugger Brenda*
*I've never liked yer kit*
*Them big, thick, itchy tights yer wear*
*An' t' mufflers that yer knit*
*I'da' loved a spot o' passion*
*If only once a year*
*Wi' a chance to dive off t' wardrobe*
*An' swing from t' chandelier*

*But I'm glad I've found the gumption*
*To say what's on me mind*
*Yer a borin' bugger Brenda*
*An' I know it seems unkind*
*I've craved exotic travel*
*Per'aps Egypt or Assam*
*But all we got were campin'*
*In Prestatyn wi' yer mam*

*Yer a borin' bugger Brenda*
*I'm determined to break free*
*So I've drawn out 'alf o' t' savin's*
*That we 'ad in t' TSB*
*I saw this ad in t' paper sayin'*
*Don't live yer life in t' closet*
*In Thailand yer can be yerself*
*So I've sent of me deposit*

*Yer a borin' bugger Brenda*
*An I'm tryin' not to gloat*
*But I guess by now yer've realised*
*Just why I've left this note*
*I'm goin' to swim wi' dolphins*
*Make love beneath the stars*
*You get yerself that bike yer fancied*
*Wi't drop down handlebars*

*Yer a borin' bugger Brenda*
*But I'll miss thi in a way*

*Sat' day nights in front o' t' box*
*Wi' us supper on a tray*
*An' that brings to mind one final thing*
*Be a shame to overlook*

*Yer a borin' Bugger Brenda*
*So I've slung me bloody 'ook!*

Many thanks Steve for allowing me to steal this poem from your book entitled *A Sportin' Life* (first published May 2000; reprinted October 2000 by Howling Dog).

From time to time listeners sent in quirky pieces of writing that we read out at intervals during the broadcast. Some of them prompted telephone calls asking for copies of these items. Here's a popular one I hope you'll enjoy. If you were to learn it you would have a brilliant party piece to perform when you have friends over, or when you just feel like showing off!

### CHRISTMAS CAKE RECIPE

**Ingredients**

| | |
|---|---|
| 1 cup water | 2 cups dried fruit |
| 1 cup brown sugar | 1 cup butter |
| 1 tsp salt | 8 oz nuts |
| 4 large eggs | 1 tsp baking soda |
| Juice of 1 lemon | 1 bottle whisky |

**Method**

Sample whisky to check for quality.

Take a large mixing bowl, check whisky again, to make sure it's of the highest quality, pour one level cup and drink.

Repeat.

Turn on electric mixer, beat one cup of butter in a large fluffy bowl.

Add one tsp sugar and beat again.

Make sure whisky is still OK. Cry another tup.

Turn off the mixer. Break two eggs and add to the bowl and chuck in a dup of cried fruit.

Mix on the turnerer. If the fried druit gets stuck in the
beaterers pry loose with a drewscriver.

Sample the whisky to check for tonsistency.

Next sift two cups of salt, or somefink, who cares?

Check the whisky.

Now sift the lemon juice and strain your nuts.

Add one sable poon of sugar or something, whatever you can
find.

Grease the oven; turn the cake tin to 350 degrees.

Don't forget to beat off the turner.

Throw the bowl in the bin.

Check whisky again and again. Go to bed.

Who likes floody bruitcake anyway ...

Another item that was sent in to the Farm was a graphic description
of how to give a cat a pill. We read it out several times by special
request so I thought you might like to keep it for future reference;
also it might persuade you to keep this book handy to enable you
to read it to your friends. Maybe your friends might want to read
it unaided which would give you a chance to anticipate their laughter,
and that would mean you could enjoy the item over and over again.
See how I think of you! Here it is:

### GIVING THE CAT A PILL

1. Pick cat up and cradle it in the crook of your left arm as if holding a
baby. Position right forefinger and thumb on either side of cat's mouth
and gently apply pressure to cheeks while holding the pill in the right
hand. As cat opens mouth, pop pill into mouth; allow cat to close
mouth and swallow.

2. Retrieve pill from floor and cat from behind sofa. Cradle cat in left
arm and repeat process.

3. Retrieve cat from bedroom, and throw soggy pill away.

4. Take new pill from foil wrap, cradle cat in left arm holding rear paws
tightly with left hand. Force jaws open and push pill to back of mouth
with right forefinger. Hold mouth shut for count of ten.

5. Retrieve pill from goldfish bowl and cat from top of wardrobe. Call
spouse from garden.

6. Kneel on floor with cat wedged between knees, hold front and rear paws. Ignore low growls emitted by cat. Get spouse to hold head firmly with one hand while forcing wooden ruler into mouth. Drop pill down ruler and rub cat's throat vigorously.

7. Retrieve cat from curtain rail, get another pill from foil wrap, make note to buy new ruler and repair curtains. Carefully sweep shattered Doulton figures from hearth and set to one side for gluing later.

8. Wrap cat in large towel and get spouse to lie on cat with head just visible from below armpit. Put pill in end of drinking straw, force mouth open with pencil and blow down drinking straw.

9. Check label to make sure pill not harmful to humans, drink glass of water to take taste away. Apply band-aid to spouse's forearm and remove blood from carpet with cold water and soap.

10. Retrieve cat from neighbour's shed. Get another pill, place cat in cupboard and close door onto neck to leave head showing. Force mouth open with dessertspoon. Flick pill down throat with elastic band.

11. Fetch screwdriver from garage and put door back on hinges. Apply cold compress to cheek and check records for date of last tetanus shot. Throw T-shirt away and fetch new one from bedroom.

12. Ring fire brigade to retrieve cat from tree across the road. Apologise to neighbour who crashed into fence while swerving to avoid cat. Take last pill from foil wrap.

13. Tie cat's front paws to rear paws with garden twine and bind tightly to leg of dining table. Find heavy-duty pruning gloves from shed, force cat's mouth open with small spanner. Push pill into mouth followed by large piece of fillet steak. Hold head vertically and pour half pint of water down throat to wash pill down.

14. Get spouse to drive you to the emergency room. Sit quietly while doctor stitches finger and forearm and removes pill remnants from right eye. Call furniture shop and order new table.

15. Arrange for RSPCA to collect cat and ring local pet store to see if they have any hamsters.

I hope you enjoyed that and you have some fun with it. Radio Lancashire's listeners certainly did.

# CHAPTER EIGHTEEN

# Time Moves On, and So Do We

THE MILL was ready for a revamp. It wasn't really but we'd been there for nearly six years and all that was possible to be done to it in terms of extensions, decorative alterations or merely cosmetic touches had been done. After having first cleared everything with the escape committee of course! The final improvement was carpets. We would completely re-carpet the mill with royal blue Wilton with a Prince Charles *fleur de lys* pattern. Then we would have completely rejuvenated the property. The phone calls were made and ultimately a contractor was employed. The job was completed in three days at a cost of ... Oh my God! But we were delighted with the outcome.

During the last couple of years at the mill, it had crossed our minds that there were rather a lot of stairs to climb or descend as we went about our daily activities, but friends had told us that stairs were good for our cardio-vascular systems so we felt reassured about things. It had also occurred to me that reversing the car down the drive could eventually prove to be a problem if my joints were to become less accommodating. But friends said I could get a reversing aid on my car so I felt reassured again. What in fact was happening was that we were subliminally becoming unsettled. We, or rather I, was searching for an excuse to start looking round for another spot to live. Neither of us actually said it but we were up for a change if the right property came along. We had, I suppose, been looking for the previous two years but nothing had come close to our requirements. We had to remain in our beloved Lune valley and the property had to be at least as good as the mill, with its 40 ft lounge and comprehensive, well-equipped bedroom, kitchen and ... well everything, really.

Early summer arrived and the sap was rising in the house-hunting department. The stairs at the mill were becoming more of a problem for us both. We could still ascend and descend with ease, but it was becoming a larger excuse for us to look around. My reversing problem wasn't going away either, despite the reversing aid I'd had fitted.

On Sunday mornings we sometimes go out for a little tour of inspection of the valley. Now it's nothing too specific, just a ride out, sometimes in the Rolls (Phyllis hates that), just to remind ourselves of how lucky we are. It could also be that at this time we were looking round for a comparable abode to move in to. It all happened the day after the carpet fitters had left the mill, having laid two acres of best Wilton throughout our three-storeyed residence. I had just paid the bill and felt the need for some fresh air so we went for a tour of the valley. As we approached the beautiful village of Melling, some four miles upstream of the mill, we slowed down as good drivers do. This move allowed us to take in more of the scenery (and the estate agents' 'for sale' signs). Would you believe it, a property we'd had our eye on for years had a 'for sale' sign in the garden. It was a Sunday morning so to phone the estate agent would have been futile. I knew that because I know for a fact that all estate agents go to church on Sunday mornings (along with double glazing salesmen).

We cheekily drove into the forecourt of the property and tried to appear nonchalant as the owner came towards us. Fortunately she recognised me (I'm not a 'has been' yet then!). 'Hello Jim,' she called, 'can I help you?'

From then on it was plain sailing. Trevor and Jane Brown proved to be the perfect vendors and the house was sold to us that morning. The views that 'The Lawns' enjoyed were without doubt the finest in the valley, and the property itself would make a perfect home for us in our dotage. It had a self-contained flat as part of its fabric, so when we became 'incompetent' and happy daft we could import a resident overseer to monitor our condition through traumatic times. The rooms in the house would give us all the facilities we required and we could adapt and rearrange to suit. We completed the purchase in July and moved in some weeks later. This gave both the Browns and us plenty of time to prepare to move. The house we inherited was absolutely pristine. All the keys to the house

**The view from 'The Lawns'. The Lune Valley – marvellous!**

and cupboards (and there were a lot) were neatly labelled, brochures relating to appliances in the house were filed in a kitchen drawer, and the complete set of the building plans were left for us to peruse.

*I say, how very efficient!*

Anyway, that's not bad, I suppose; three moves in twenty-one years. All of them were quite painless. The house had two acres of land at the rear, all of it meadowland, so not only could we enjoy the view we could walk into it. The land would need caring for but I figured I knew a man who would do that. I daren't lumber Phyllis with that burden again. Against everything logical, we were upsizing, at 64 years of age!

*I say, how awfully rejuvenating!*

We enjoyed working on the house. Well, I was back in supervisory capacity as we employed Tony to do whatever was required, and I do mean whatever! It was really a question of getting everything exactly as we wanted it. As with every move, your tastes are never quite the same as the previous owners so there was quite a list for Tony to look at. He started work on the property in August and at the time of writing this he is still there and going strong. In fairness to him we have been extremely self-indulgent and are sparing nothing in the refit. The views at the rear almost demanded a conservatory, and the lounge was given French windows so the Lune Valley can be enjoyed from every room in the house. In all the homes we have lived in we have never had views of any significance so I suppose we're making up for lost time. The work on the new house began to reassure us that we had done the right thing. The facilities we wanted were becoming apparent as Tony worked his way through the long list of the alterations we had envisaged. The conservatory became a reality; the interior decorations were turning the house into the kind of property we had imagined. Mahogany staircase spindles and newel posts arrived and Tony offered his resignation as the prospect of putting this complicated kit together was causing him stress beyond belief. Three weeks and a lot of mitring and sandpapering, coupled with tons of 'no nails' adhesive, saw the finished article in place, and it looks the business. Tony is receiving counselling for 'staircaseitis' but is due back from the home for the bewildered soon.

We have imported local talents in abundance as we gently change the façade of 'The Lawns'. Wrought iron specialists have given the house an air of increased elegance as they design and erect Buckingham Palace style railings along the stone wall fronting the main road. Professional tree surgeons have been consulted about a little pruning we would like; and we are seriously considering putting two lamps either side of the entrance without asking anyone's permission! We must now, however, start thinking about becoming thoroughly responsible citizens, as we are approaching a time in our lives when that's the way to be. I mean, I could well be asked to become a member of the Urban District Council, or even Squire of Melling!

*I say, how terribly grand!*

Seriously though, we have settled really well into yet another part of our favourite valley; all we need now is a following wind to allow us to put a little back into this part of the world that has been so kind to us. I'm doing my little bit by telling tales out of school to the residents in the valley by appearing in the surrounding village halls, where an admission charge of £3 can get you a seat to hear the same pack of lies that I tell the passengers on *QE2*! In one evening we can all have a bit of fun, and we can raise a few bob to augment the monies raised by those village stalwarts who spend hours making cakes and coffee to be sold at numerous coffee mornings. It's a 'no lose' situation really because I still feel wanted, the ego that I haven't got is satisfied, and it gets me from under Phyllis's feet for an evening. I'm waiting for the phone to ring again now as I write!

As the night work begins to ease down, show business has seen fit to give me yet another bite of the sequinned cherry. After almost four years of delightful broadcasting with Sally at the BBC, Phoenix Nights came onto the horizon and Hoss Cartwright (a hotel owner in Blackpool) was created by Peter Kay for series two of this staggeringly successful programme. Guess what? Yours truly got the job! 'Sunshine indoors!' was Hoss's hotel slogan and sunshine is exactly what came again into my life.

So began a resurgence of demand for this fortunate geriatric, with appearances on Richard & Judy, the Paul O'Grady show, and an incomprehensible flurry of requests to appear at universities once again (remember the Oxford Union?). As if this wasn't enough, the profile was further raised with a guest cameo in Peter Kay's Comic Relief version of Tony Christie's 70s chart topper 'Is this the way to Amarillo?', and Challenge TV (that's a satellite channel, you know!) has seen fit to transmit all 350 episodes of Bullseye four times daily, reminding me even more of the passage of time (did I really wear those suits?). And at the time of writing the Edinburgh Fringe Festival is looming large – I think I'll do it, I might as well take advantage of every scrap of life that's on offer, and be grateful!

How lucky can a fella get?

The radio career has made people aware that I'm still around and apart from enjoying the job I do feel fulfilled as a performer, and I know that the business will tell me when it's time to hang up the suit and content myself with life in the rural lane.

As my refuse collector supervisor so wisely stated, 'we're only here for a bloody weekend', so I mean to take full advantage of every scrap of life that's on offer, and be grateful.

I do believe that the most difficult calculation anyone in this business has to make is to work out when to go. I did mention earlier in the book that the telephone tells you, but as you approach decision time and the phone coincidentally stops – or nearly stops – ringing you can embark on a vast exercise in self deception if you're not careful. You can imagine that the phone has rung when you've been out, and you've forgotten to put the answering machine on, you can imagine that people aren't ringing because they think you're busy. Don't you believe it! Grasp the nettle; come to terms with having had a good run, and walk away.

I think I'll just nip into the lounge to see if there are any messages on the answering machine. You never know!

Coincidentally, talking about knowing when to walk away, the phone rang last week and the caller was a certain Johnnie Hamp asking me if I would like to do a summer season at Blackpool Opera House in a show celebrating thirty years of The Comedians. Obviously I gave this offer much thought, and told Johnnie I'd ring him back as this was disrupting my ideals regarding 'knowing when to pack it all in'. I didn't ring him back at all; how's that for sticking to your guns? But I have to be honest with you now, I just said 'Yes', and then I put the phone down!

*I say, how weak-willed!*

# CHAPTER NINETEEN

## *Tales out of School*

PEOPLE suggest that when you reach your fifties you're middle-aged. I don't see many folks around who clear the hundred mark (unless you're the Queen Mum, and she *was* special wasn't she?), so I tend to look along the shelf a little more often now, assessing the odds!

I remember Bob Monkhouse once opening his address by saying, 'Many years ago when I was young I said I was going to be a comedian, and people laughed ... Well, they're not laughing now!' How I wish that had been my line.

As I said earlier, never follow Bob, but at least that steal gives me a chance to say thanks to him.

The greatest compliment you can pay to your allotted time is to take advantage of it. As long as the messages life is sending me are encouraging I shall continue to 'be there', whatever anybody says! Consequently I shall extend my showbiz career despite public opinion and shall continue to look at life through alcohol-tinted spectacles. I shall try to earn my keep in terms of life points because at my age they're worth collecting – but I don't want a kettle or a toaster, I'd like more time!

I'm still available to do charity shows and auditions, and now that the DWP at Newcastle has begun sending me my pension I can afford an extra visit to the local library each week. Sammy the Labrador can sleep easily in her basket as the local pet shop has allowed me extra credit for biscuits, and best of all I can pick and choose the gigs on offer. (I shall probably do them all!)

Both Phyllis and I have discussed the children's inheritance and we think it only fair to leave them both a £10.00 overdraft to make sure they keep us in their thoughts!

**Sammy's heard about the food allowance.**

*I say, how awfully mean!*

Looking at the now depleted gang of The Comedians on satellite TV the other night made me think about the value of getting wrinkles. The older you get the more you find, but all I can say to you, my friend, is keep searching for them because they are your benchmark, your life's CV. So just grab every minute you're given because they are the human equivalent of the rings in tree trunks. The big difference is that you can remember the times, good and not so good, when your wrinkles became even more clearly defined. Pity the poor tree: lucky the person whose wrinkles are laughter lines. Remember, it takes two thousand muscles to frown and two hundred to smile. More importantly grab with delight the next few pages because I think I can feel this publication being given extended life, and I'm going to work on your wrinkles, though only 200 of them!

*I say! How physiological!*

Just to emphasise further the passage of time and the speed of its passing I think you should be reminded that The Comedians was on your TV screens 35 years ago, Opportunity Knocks with Hughie Green was there 45 years ago, and over 50 years ago you could hear Al Read and Jimmy Clitheroe on the wireless.

When I remember those flared-trousered, wide-lapelled humorists of the 70s, I find myself thinking, 'What wonderful storytellers they were'. And now I find myself with a second literary wind; I wanna

**The Comedians.**

tell you a story, in fact quite a few! Recalling those heady days of years ago has inspired me; so let's have some nostalgic fun.

Now, in the main these stories are true, though fantasy from time to time may creep in (that's because it's my book and I can do what I want), so be prepared. I could take you from Granada Studios in Manchester in the 1970s then, at the turn of a page, to sailing on the *QE2* in the 1990s. Or you could find yourself in the Studios at Lenton Lane in Nottingham where for 15 years we made the Bullseye television series, and in the blink of an eye you could find yourself enjoying a tale I heard in our local pub only last week.

Right, are you sitting comfortably? Then I'll begin ...

## A laugh on the ocean wave

Cruising over the years has become a growth industry as we have become more affluent as a nation and as our social insecurities have weakened. The prospect of high living is a great attraction and the lessening of formalities on board cruise ships encourage more of us to take the plunge as it were. The competitive nature of the cruise business has further encouraged growth as people realise that the deals available now are extremely inviting.

Since she was launched in 1969 *QE2* has always been the ultimate in terms of prestige within the cruise ship world. She still exemplifies all that is excellent and stylish about life at sea, and I was privileged to work on her for almost two decades from the mid-eighties, and enjoyed every minute of it. The ship's maiden voyage was at a time when computers weighed a ton, the internet was a sophisticated way of catching fish, mobile phones did not exist and texting was a form of crocheting!

The entertainment staff on board were controlled by the cruise director who programmed the ship's schedules with regard to leisure activities, both at sea and in port. Daytime and evening schedules were his responsibility in total so we are looking at a post carrying massive responsibility and power. The careers of many cabaret acts and cruise staff have been both ruined and launched by cruise directors. The word God comes to mind when defining their authority on board ship.

Life on board this most prestigious of ships was definitely not for Joe Public in those early days and cash on board was definitely King. Drinks were all paid for in cash, tipping was an accepted way of fast tracking service and was also a passport to many of the 'scams' that were operating in every public area on the ship.

Cruising then was very much an elitist pastime only to be enjoyed by the rather better-heeled members of our community. Today the computer has eliminated all cash transactions by debiting your onboard account to your cabin number. This was an excellent progression for the ship's accounting systems as it virtually eliminated any money laundering on the part of the ship's waiters, stewards, porters etc and in doing so protected the sometimes naive passengers (allegedly!).

Then, as now, cruise days at sea were punctuated by daytime activities which varied from shuffleboard to deck quoits to bridge classes, even golf lessons (snooker never actually took off for some reason!). During bad weather at sea indoor pursuits like bingo and horse racing were offered in the main lounges of most ships. As previously explained cash was king prior to the high-tech age, so bingo tickets were purchased in cash which did give rise to a financial grey area in terms of accountability on the part of the cruise staff. I must stress at this point that these financial loop-holes have been comprehensively sealed in today's cruise world, so please feel free to book a cruise, happy in the knowledge that you are not in the hands of villains and vagabonds, and that your time on board ship will be enjoyable and your monetary affairs very well protected!

However, this cautionary first story goes back to the early days and stars a legendary cruise director; a man who invented the phrase 'creative financial advancement,' quite within the legal con-fines of shipboard life. For the purposes of propriety he shall be called John Brown. I must stress that even now, decades after the time this story was given credence, John Brown is still regarded as the well-loved doyen of all cruise directors who have ever sailed the seas.

We must go back many years when *QE2* spent half its life traversing the Atlantic from Southampton to New York. This, of course, meant five days at sea so the entertainment programme involved much daytime activity on offer to the discerning passengers. As mentioned already bingo featured along with the statutory bridge, canasta, whist and sundry board games. For the more energetic, table tennis, deck quoits and golf or putting lessons were on offer. The weather affecting transatlantic crossings can, to say the least, be erratic so the need for a wide range of indoor pursuits continually stretched the imagination of the cruise staff. This is where the creative talents of JB came into their own.

In the Grand Lounge on *QE2* high profile activities took place purely because of its size; it was the premier venue on the ship, catering for upwards of a thousand people. JB realised that with such a large captive audience there was an opportunity to not only entertain but also to involve his captors in a scam which beggars belief. It went as follows.

While in New York on his fortnightly visit he passed a pet shop which was offering for sale … wait for it … baby turtles. John's mind whirred into action and he did not disappoint. He bought a dozen and after briefly learning how to look after them from the pet shop owner he smuggled them on board ship to the safety of his cabin. He developed the plot further and ultimately came up with a most imaginative idea which not only occupied the passengers at sea, but also gave him the opportunity to massage the financial systems in place on board to his advantage. Turtle racing in the Grand Lounge at 2.30 p.m.! The plan was set. However this was not to be normal turtle racing. This reptilians' confrontation was to have a twist. Apparently turtles, when away from their normal habitat have no sense of direction, so the race track, which was to be set up on the dance floor of the Grand Lounge, had to have individual lanes with raised strips bordering each one to avoid the turtles crossing lanes.

For this idea to have any entertainment content the passengers needed to be engaged, and what better way to involve holidaymakers than to give them a chance to have a flutter on the turtles? John set about constructing the lanes in the grand lounge, together with a 'parade ring' where the turtles could be inspected by the passengers. After all, when placing a bet it seemed only fair to John that the prospective customer should be allowed as much information as possible to help him choose the likely winner.

A table was erected on the side of the track to accommodate the bookmakers who were ready to take bets on the outcome of the five races scheduled to take place. Each race had five turtles in individual lanes lined up to travel some 50 feet to the finish line. All traditional racing protocol was observed. Starters orders were called after a suitable length of time had elapsed to allow the punters to study form in the enclosure.

Each turtle had a number painted on its shell to allow it to be recognised, either as a potential winner or as an also ran. Bets were placed and after an appropriate length of time the turtles were placed in their lanes to await the starter's whistle. It was during that 'appropriate length of time' that the dirty deed was done. Now please concentrate!

As the turtles were taken from the gathering ring to the starting line John went along the line of bookmakers to find out which of the turtles had been most heavily backed. This coveted information allowed him the privilege of predicting which turtle he would least like to see win. But how was he to achieve this aim? Well, I'll tell you but you mustn't tell anyone else.

Before placing the turtles in their delegated lanes he surreptitiously gathered up the most heavily backed turtle and quickly, quietly, discreetly smeared Vaseline on each of its innocent feet prior to placing the poor little sod in its lane. When the starter shouted 'They're off!' the instruction applied to all the turtles except 'Vaseline feet,' who just paddled manfully on the shiny dance floor to no effect. JB wins every time!

*I say, how criminal!*

In the 60s and 70s one of the most senior masters of *QE2* was the much respected, statuesque Lawrence Portet. Here was a man who stood very tall at the helm and a man to be feared by all. The story goes that one day at sea Captain Portet walked through the Grand Lounge during this bizarre racing event and quickly spotted some devious goings on. He called John over and knowingly asked, 'John, may I ask, is there any form of leisure activity taking place aboard this vessel which is not corrupt in some way or other?'

'I've no idea what you mean,' replied John quizzically.

He's still cruise directing now, but his cash flow situation has become somewhat restricted!

*I say, How impecunious!*

As I have said, I was privileged enough to spend much of the 80s and 90s sailing and working on *QE2* and stories emanating from my time on board are numerous and involve many famous faces. One of these notaries was the legendary fast bowler Freddie Truman, Yorkshireman of his parish. A forthright man was Freddie, to say the least, and he suffered fools badly. As in all walks of life Freddie made many friends and some enemies. In the professional game of cricket, especially in the 60s, rivalry was intense, so enemies were highlighted simply because of the high profile of the sport. Another famous Yorkshireman making his name in the world of cricket was a certain Geoffrey Boycott. Renowned for his self-preservation when he was at the batting crease, Geoffrey made few friends and I suppose, like Freddie, collected several enemies.

Having spent some time with Freddie on board *QE2* it became obvious that Geoffrey and Freddie didn't exactly rub along together. Their attitudes to the game were diametrically opposed, so you can imagine that when they were in a room together the atmosphere acquired a certain tension. Consequently, if in conversation with Freddie, Geoffrey was mentioned, these tensions came out and Freddie was always eager to point out his adversary's shortcomings. Similarly, if Freddie came up in conversation with Geoffrey ... the same rules applied!

Freddie took a cruise on the *QE2*, having been invited to talk to the passengers about his career in cricket. It happened that our drummer, Roy White, was a keen cricket fan and enjoyed watching the sport around the time Freddie was at his height. One night in the Golden Lion pub, where we entertained the passengers, we saw Freddie sitting on a bar-stool thoroughly enjoying the sounds of the Hot Rhythm Orchestra. It was getting towards the end of the evening and Freddie was savouring his glass of red wine (probably not his first of the evening), when our drummer noticed his sporting idol. At the end of the performance Roy suggested to me that we ask Freddie to come and sit with us and regale us with his notoriously funny anecdotes. I tentatively approached this giant of a man and invited him to join me and the band for a drink. I suggested that we would pay for his wine, because I knew that to a Yorkshireman this would certainly be a massive inducement! (I'm not suggesting that Yorkshiremen are mean but the word on the street is that they only breath in!) To our delight Freddie accepted our invitation.

Now F. S. Truman OBE, as you perhaps know, is no shrinking violet and as we all huddled round the table, totally engulfed by the fumes emitting from Freddie's huge pipe, we listened avidly to his riotously funny tales. Roy White, this sad cricket fan, seizing a gap in Freddie's rhetoric asked Freddie, 'What do you think of Geoffrey Boycott, Freddie?' There could not have been a better catalyst to Freddie's performance than the mention of Geoffrey Boycott.

'Geoffrey Boycott,' exploded Freddie, 'I'll tell you about bloody Boycott!'

He proceeded to describe an incident when he was commentating on the Roses cricket match at Old Trafford, between Lancashire and Yorkshire. Geoffrey approached the commentary box, opened the door and said to Freddie, 'Freddie, why do people take an instant dislike to me?' Freddie replied, 'It saves f***g time!'

To tell you another would perhaps be unfair, as I'm sure they will all be featured in Freddie's publication, but I'm sure he'll allow me just one more story which brought out his dry Yorkshire wit beautifully as he described an incident in Wales.

He began thus:

'I remember I was playing at Glamorgan, bowling to a particularly disgruntled batsman who was constantly complaining about the number of times I was appealing to claim his wicket. Eventually one of my more dubious claims for lbw was accepted, a little to my surprise. As the thoroughly disgusted batsman walked past me on his way back to the pavilion, he grunted at me, "That it was never ever out Freddie". I waited until he was still just within earshot and whispered back to him mischievously, "Look in tomorrow's paper, Taffy!" '

The stories continued well into the night, and Roy certainly slept well!

Passengers boarding *QE2* for the first time are sometimes in awe of the tradition and the history that surrounds this great vessel. This can sometimes affect their normally reasonable behaviour. The ship's purser relates the story about a lady travelling alone and finding herself unable to get out of her cabin. She telephoned the Purser's desk asking for help, explaining her predicament.

'Could you help me?' she pleads. 'I'm afraid I can't get out of my cabin.'

'What's the number of your cabin?' asks the Purser.

'I'm in cabin No. 3165,' replies the confused passenger.

The purser now decides to help the lady find her bearings in the cabin in order to help her get out.

'Tell me what you're looking at now,' asks the Purser.

'I'm looking at my bed, and to the right of it is a door into the bathroom.'

'That's fine,' says the Purser, 'if you look to your right you will see another door which will allow you to get out of your cabin.'

'Oh! I couldn't possibly do that,' replies the passenger, 'there's a 'DO NOT DISTURB' sign on the door!'

On one recent trip, sailing from Southampton to the Canary Islands, the weather in Southampton was particularly rough. Captain Paul Wright decided to delay the ship's departure until the following morning, allowing the weather to abate, and affording the passengers a comfortable night's sleep as the ship lay tied up alongside the Southampton terminal. The next morning at breakfast many passengers commented on how smooth the passage had been so far, but one or two stated that they did experience some movement during the night and expressed concern about this movement getting worse as the voyage progressed!

Being the Captain of *QE2* is an enormous responsibility and to reach such dizzy heights requires dedication and perseverance almost beyond belief. The job itself, however, carries many, many perks and the quality of life aboard ship for the captain seems, on the face of it, extremely enviable. However, with the appointment comes a most demanding workload alongside a 24-hour commitment to the overall safety and well-being of passengers and crew. As well as the nautical elements of the job there is a most punishing social diary. He is expected to attend numerous cocktail parties and private celebrations on board ship, not to mention having to dine with the more well-heeled passengers on an almost nightly basis. The tours of duty can last months rather than weeks and this can put tremendous strain on any relationships he may have shore-side.

A successful captain of a cruise liner must not only be an extremely capable mariner, but also a person who is at ease with people. The ability to tell a good story and to communicate effectively with passengers is an enormous asset to him. His prestigious status on board allows him to indulge himself in this pastime because passengers tend to listen in awe to his conversations with them, whether they are on a one-to-one basis or as members of a group.

Captain Paul Wright is one of that group of mariners who can tell a good story, and consequently can add an enormous amount to a cruise by way of his chats and his informative comments regarding the position of the ship and the pervading weather conditions. Paul is a Cornishman who rose through the ranks of merchant shipping to become captain of this most famous of cruise ships. For some years he worked for Cunard shore-side supervising the itineraries of the many ships owned by Cunard and Carnival line. Having spent some years on land he decided that it was time he found his sea legs again and ultimately was awarded the stewardship of *QE2*.

One evening we found ourselves exchanging life histories at one of the cocktail parties when he told me about his recent house move:

'When I was given the job of looking after *QE2*, I decided to move back to Cornwall from Miami where I had been land-bound for several years. In my search for a property I came across this charming terraced cottage by the sea. It seemed to me to be exactly what I was looking for as a single man who spent much time out of the UK. I purchased the cottage and ultimately managed to find time to go down there when my next leave allocation came up. I had been there a few days, renovating the cottage and generally finding my feet in the village. No one knew what my job was, and I quietly familiarized myself with my surroundings, enjoying the peace and tranquillity of this lovely coastal village.

'Now, along with the cottage came a mooring for a boat, one of the reasons I purchased the property. One beautifully sunny morning I found myself at the door of my cottage gazing out to sea, when my next-door neighbour saw me for the first time and made himself known. We began chatting and in the course of our conversation I told him I intended to get a boat.

' "Let me give you a piece of sound advice," my neighbour said. "Start off with something small. You mustn't be getting a boat you can't handle 'cos the currents hereabouts are unpredictable and you'll only get embarrassed if we have to come out to get you out of trouble!" I didn't have the heart to tell him what I did for living!'

One of the highlights of life on board ship is meal times. It is in the restaurants where friends are made, as passengers are allocated places at tables of six, eight or even ten covers. Several nights having dinner with a group of complete strangers can be a very enlightening experience.

My co-host on Bullseye was Tony Green, and in the mid eighties Tony and I were invited to cruise on QE2 to present the television game. We were allocated to a table which seated eight passengers. Two of the ladies dining with us at the table came from Huddersfield. It was their first time on QE2 and the whole experience was proving very exciting for them both. As the assembled diners relaxed around the table the conversation flowed freely and the two ladies from Huddersfield became more confident by the minute. During the serving of the main course one of the ladies was brave enough to address the wine steward.

'Tell me, young man,' she asked, 'do the crew sleep on board?'

'Oh no,' replied the waiter. 'I live in Rochdale and my shift ends at 10 o'clock tonight. With any luck I should be home before midnight. I'm not on duty again until six o'clock tomorrow night so I'll have almost a full day at home.'

The ship was at that time halfway across in the Bay of Biscay! I think it must be the ozone that affects the brain. Tony went on to further torment these two ladies, suggesting to them that the slight list of the ship was caused by too many of the crew fishing on the one side of the vessel, and that the slightest sudden movement was caused by one of them catching a large fish!

I remember quite distinctly being party to a conversation between one of the ship's senior officers and an adoring passenger who was discussing the leisure activities on board ship. The officer suggested that perhaps a game of snooker could be appropriate to while away the days at sea. The passenger's eyes lit up at the prospect of a game of snooker and he enquired as to the whereabouts of the snooker table. By now the officer realized he had dug a hole for himself and so dismissed himself, explaining that he was due on the bridge to put the headlights on as it was nearly dusk!

The captain of QE2 is always cannon fodder for the entertainers on board, especially comedians. He is frequently referred to as a drunk and his character is assassinated on an almost nightly basis by one or other of the entertainers. He, of course, knows exactly what is being said about him, if only as a result of the passengers reporting these slanderous comments back to him. Of course this is all part of the chemistry of cruising: the passengers being party to this 'secret' gossip about the human frailty of the captain. Almost invariably the captain joins in with this subterfuge and revels in the naivety of the passengers.

On one particular cruise some of the scheduled port visits were sidelined by bad weather, and so the cruise became something of a mystery tour. This situation gave us lots of ammunition with which to attack the captain, and we suggested that the change in schedule was in fact organized by the captain as he had a girl in every port. The passengers predictably reported our comments to the captain and this in turn gave him a chance to get his own back on those who perpetrated the rumours – I can assure you he knew precisely the source of this misinformation. Unfortunately I was one of the guilty persons, having suggested that the ship's diversion to Malaga was not as a result of bad weather but because the captain wanted to visit one of his lady friends. I was warned by passengers that the captain had retribution in mind for me. Sure enough on the last day at sea he got his revenge. Read on.

Every day at noon the captain reports the ship's position, speed, direction and expected weather conditions. This is broadcast to the whole ship. At the end of this particular broadcast, the captain informed the passengers that all taxis at Southampton could be ordered at the expense of Jim Bowen, who could be found in the Golden Lion Pub at 8 o'clock that evening where he would take bookings! I was inundated with requests.

Score at the end of the cruise: *QE2* Captain 1, Jim Bowen 0!

Lesson to be learned from this experience: never compete with the captain!

Even the *QE2* can be affected severely by rough seas and I remember at one particular cocktail party the captain was sympathizing with the passengers and trying to reassure them that things would get better. He told them of his visit to the stern of the ship where he had seen one of the crew hanging on to the rail. The captain enquired as to the state of the crew member who quickly replied, 'Just let her sink!'

The pressures exerted on an entertainer on board a cruise liner are far greater than those experienced by our land-based colleagues. The very nature of the engagement means that you are confined with your audience for the duration of the cruise. Unlike on land, where after your performance you can go home, this cannot be the case on board ship. Consequently, the importance of giving a good show becomes paramount because you have to live with your audience afterwards, unless you jump ship! A few years ago the late Ted Rogers (you remember, he of 3–2–1 fame) was the headline cabaret on a Mediterranean cruise on *QE2*. I always used to go and watch the cabaret in the Grand Lounge, mainly to support my fellow professionals, and maybe along the way learn something. Ted went onstage the second night of the cruise in the Grand Lounge at 10 o'clock. The room in itself is not the easiest to work, with its shopping malls forming a three-sided balcony. This encourages passengers to look at the goods on offer in the shops and can be distracting; audiences at the 10 o'clock show can be challenging to say the least anyway as they have just come from dinner and are still relatively sober. I watched Ted perform in this arena for the best part of an hour. Response to his efforts was minimal. Bear in mind that Ted had to do the whole show again at half past eleven, so he was in for a long night. After the first show I went backstage to reassure Ted that things would get better. Sad to relate his second show had even less impact. He was distraught at his performance and went to his cabin, never to be seen again on board until we docked at Southampton 10 days later. Rumour has it that all he ate was toast for the rest of the cruise, as that was the only sustenance that would fit under his cabin door!

Having watched Ted suffer that night, I was determined never to subject myself to such pressure again. Now the only time I work in the Grand Lounge is when I am supported by my friends The Hot Rhythm Orchestra. At least I don't suffer alone!

Over many years of cruising, as you can imagine, stories and situations arise which can beggar belief. The Great British Public can be incredibly stupid, naïve, ignorant, insensitive and downright unpleasant, albeit in most cases not intentionally. I blame the ozone permeating their brain cells, doing temporary damage and causing them no pain at all.

On one particular cruise on *QE2*, I was working as usual with the Hot Rhythm Orchestra in our place of residence, the Golden Lion pub. (This was the downmarket end of the entertainment spectrum on board this prestigious vessel but we did tremendous business in there, probably because we were a downmarket act!) The combination of the immense musical talents of the band and with my sometimes faintly humorous attempts at comedy was an awesome package, however, and we developed a tremendous fan base over the years.

The trumpet player was an outstanding musician of considerable repute called Mike Cotton. His musical CV was a most enviable read, especially to me who owned a trumpet rather than played one! During one particular 'set' in the pub Mike had performed especially well in a feature called 'I can't get started'. For those not in the know musically it's a piece designed to allow the performer to show off his trumpet playing to maximum effect. At the end of this number Colin Bryant suggested that we finish the 'set' with a simple up tempo number where I played my trumpet as part of the ensemble and sang the fairly basic melody in a cheerful manner to send the passengers off to bed in happy mood. As usual Colin was right in his assessment of the room and we ended the evening in good shape. As we were packing up our instruments a passenger came up to me to give his informed views on the show. Please note now that I was standing next to trumpet-playing icon Mike Cotton who was also packing away his instrument. The fan began thus: 'Jim, I thought you were fantastic. I had no idea you played the trumpet. Your talents shone out like a beacon on that stage tonight!'

Mike was still alongside me during this flurry of admiration trying to look inconspicuous when my informed admirer turned to him and said, 'Oh, and incidentally, I thought you tried your best!' Mike, ever the gentleman thanked the passenger, discreetly sidled away and left me in a state of confused embarrassment!

A little knowledge is a dangerous thing. I blame the ozone again!


## Tales from the pint pot

Conversations in pubs can prove extremely amusing, especially when told by the more senior members of our society. Farmers in particular have quaint philosophies and these can result in many hilarious sessions at the bar. One evening at the Castle Hotel in my village I found myself listening to two elderly farmers discussing the merits of their respective wives. (Before I put to print the following conversation, may I respectfully request forgiveness from all the ladies reading this book?)

It went like this:

First farmer: 'How's the wife Harry?'

Harry, without blinking an eye or hesitating for a moment: 'Well Tom, she's too old to breed and too nasty to keep as a pet.' I'm sure he said it with affection.

A regular in the same pub was a self-employed motorcycle engineer. He told us about a visit he had had from a consultant surgeon who had come to have his motorbike repaired. It was a particularly cold morning and the well-heeled surgeon came into the workshop to discuss his mechanical problem. As they mulled over the solution, the motorcycle mechanic, cold and damp, was bemoaning his earning capacity as compared to the consultant surgeon.

He asked, 'How is it that I can only earn a fairly average wage by repairing motorcycles and you seem to earn much more, yet we seem to essentially carry out the same type of work? I mean to say we both repair and mend things.'

'Ah' replied the surgeon, 'but could you repair the motorcycle with the engine running?' The silence that followed said it all!

## Right place, right time

I've always believed that life is a lottery and our numbers are allocated by the great Architect in the Sky, whoever he or she might be. Perhaps the only influence we can have on the path our lives take is that maybe we can put the numbers in the winning sequence. How we do that is by constantly looking at the big picture unfolding before us and trying to make reasoned decisions as to the route we take.

The word we're looking for here is ambition.

Nothing wrong with that I suppose so long as it is tempered with integrity and supported by a genuine belief that the ambition you nurture is fuelled by an ability to come up with the goods!

Having regaled you with such a profound philosophy let me now tell you the story of how this writer came to be offered a television series which ran for 14 years and which afforded him a lifestyle which was more down to luck than either ambition or the actions of the great Architect. Let us begin.

> The month and year: June, 1980
> The place: ATV Studios, Broad Street, Birmingham
> The cast: Jon Scoffield, Head of Light Entertainment;
>     Peter Harris, Programme Director on the staff of ATV;
>     Peter Holmans, Joint Managing Director of Chatsworth
>     Television
> Jim Bowen: Relatively Unknown Stand-up Comedian!
> Andy Wood: Devisor of Bullseye in its earliest form
> Norman Vaughan: Well-known Comedian/Compère

Jon Scoffield is a brusque man with masses of television experience, both as a director and as an executive, with a keen eye for new ideas and aspiring talent. He was approached by Peter Holmans of Chatsworth Television on behalf of Andy Wood with regard to an idea Andy had for a new quiz/game show. (Chatsworth Television was the much-respected production company that gave us Treasure Hunt and Anneka Rice's exceptionally attractive bum!)

Peter and Andy wisely enlisted the services of the then famous Norman Vaughan, who had made his name at the London Palladium as compère, and advertising Cadbury's 'Roses' chocolates – remember, the ones that grew on you! He had also had a spell hosting The Golden Shot. He was in fact quite a seasoned performer, which was probably why Andy thought it a good idea to take him along to give his presentation more credibility. I think the premise was that if the idea were taken up by Jon Scoffield for ATV then Norman would be the presenter. Unfortunately things didn't work out quite as Andy and Norman had planned.

The presentation was simple, with its two elements of darts and general knowledge appealing to Jon Scoffield, who reasoned that darts was the most popular indoor sport and that this island of ours was full of anoraks who made a career out of winning pub quizzes! The idea also involved teams of two contestants each, depending on the other's ability either at darts or general knowledge. Jon did, however, feel that Norman had had his bite of the show business cherry and offered to take the game on board, but without Norman as presenter. Andy reluctantly agreed to the acceptance conditions of 'game but no Norman'. The good news was that Andy stood by a gentleman's agreement he had previously made with Norman and the situation was amicably resolved. I think Norman's accountant had a little smile that said 'Thank you' to Andy! It now meant, however, that Jon had an embryo of a game show on his hands with no-one to host it. He did have, however, the 'in house' talent to create a credible product in the form of the two Peters, Harris and Holmans.

Peter Harris's track record in as a director in television was peerless. His directorial CV reads like a list of all that was good in television when the medium was still developing from the late 60s. He mothered Crossroads through its years with Noelle Gordon, he liaised with Jean Morton to create Tinga and Tucker, the early puppet series, after which he moved into light entertainment with ease in the early seventies, handling stars like Peters and Lee, Mike and Bernie Winters, Cleo Lane, and the ATV Thursday night variety flagship that was Starburst. The blockbuster series The Muppet Show became his to develop and he saw it grab the Sunday tea-time viewers in their millions. Little did any of us know that history for him and the Independent Network was to repeat itself a decade later in the form of a very different animal! Peter is still directing programmes as I write. William G. Stewart's 15 to 1 and Sky's Littlejohn now occupy his time; but more of Peter Harris later.

Now about the other Peter. He was the elder statesman of the group. In the late 60s he helped to develop Anglia television where he became Head of Programmes. He later went on to work as a senior producer devising shows like The Sky's the Limit and Double Your Money. You may remember that they both starred Hughie Green, who was later to present Opportunity Knocks! and who became the biggest star on our screens in that decade. Peter's expertise as the man with the eye to make the programme accessible to the growing masses of viewers was to prove invaluable as the format of the game at this early stage was, to say the least, sketchy.

Jon Scoffield still had to find a 'front man' for this newly acquired format so he selected Harris for the job. He gave Peter three names and phone numbers of current comedians/entertainers on the club circuit and told him to ring them in a specific order of preference, offering them the chance to take part in a pilot programme with a view to perhaps getting the ultimate prize of permanent show host, should the pilot prove viable.

Jon's decision to go for a club-type presenter was influenced by the fact that the game itself (involving darts and general knowledge) was essentially 'working class' (dare I use that expression?). In fact when the game eventually made it to the screen we proudly called it the Coronation Street of game shows.

Peter Harris, having been given his brief, then began telephoning the people on Jon's list in the order he had been given them. The first call was answered by a lady (I'll use fictitious names as you'll almost certainly know the people being contacted).

Lady: 'Hello, who's that speaking?'

Harris: 'This is Peter Harris speaking from ATV.'

Lady: 'ATV, what's that then?' (The lady's husband had been in show business for twenty years!)

Harris: 'ATV is a television company and I'm ringing to speak to your husband about working on a television programme I'm directing.'

Lady: 'He's out at the moment.'

Harris: 'When will he be back?'

Lady: 'Oh, later tonight I should think.'

Harris: 'I'll ring back later tonight then if that's alright.'

Lady: 'Oh, there's no point doing that 'cos he's always pissed when he comes home!'

There went the first choice candidate. The man at the top of Jon's list had been blown away by his wife, and he would never know the opportunity he might have had.

*Moral:* It helps if your wife has some inkling of the type of work you do and her telephone manner is socially acceptable!

Peter now moved on to candidate number two who was based in London. On dialling the number he hears, 'I'm not able to take your call at the moment, so please leave your name and number and I'll get back to you on my return'.

Candidate number two lost out. Show business opportunities are brief and instant. Jon Scoffield wanted a solution NOW, and that is exactly what answer phones don't offer. In show business answers have to be 'live'.

*Moral:* Never go out of the house unless you can have the telephone manned in your absence – in show business absence makes the caller go elsewhere!

Contender number three was called by the now despairing Harris to find that not only was there no answer phone but there was no reply at all. Number three.

*Moral:* Same as for candidate two!

It is now mid evening in the Harris household and no progress has been made in the search for the potential presenter. Having nowhere else to go Harris tentatively rings the Head of Light Entertainment at his home in Derbyshire. The slightly intolerant tone of voice greeting Harris did little to assist him in explaining the unfortunate sequence of events that had beset him in his recruiting efforts that evening. Jon Scoffield was not a man to suffer failure with tolerance, but he did offer Harris P. an alternative.

'You know Mr X lives in the Solihull area,' said Jon Scoffield. He was referring to a well-known entertainer who had up to now not been on the selection list.

'I know Mr X very well,' replied Harris P.

'I would like you to go and visit him now and offer him the opportunity to present this programme.' Harris P. was by now getting to the end of his tether so he readily agreed to make the journey across the Midlands to offer Mr X the job.

It was getting dark as Harris P. made his way to the home of Mr X, and his luck thus far in his search led him to think that there would be no one at home. He was, however, agreeably surprised as Mr X greeted him warmly in reply to his knock on the door.

'I've come to see you at the request of Jon Scoffield', said Harris.

'He is proposing to do a pilot programme involving darts and general knowledge. He has been given an allocated time slot on the network at 7 o'clock on Monday nights for 13 weeks, so if the idea takes off it would be good news for everyone.' (Bear in mind, dear reader, that in 1980 there were only two television channels of any significance, so a 13-week series was virtually a guaranteed fast track to stardom.)

Harris P. continued, 'Jon has asked me to offer you a chance to present the pilot and ultimately, if successful, the 13-week series would be yours.'

Mr X paused for a moment and said to the bemused Peter Harris,

'I'll just check how my diary is fixed to see if I can help you.'

His reply completely baffled Harris. Here was a man in show business being offered the chance of a lifetime presenting a game show and he felt the need to check his diary. Anyone in this business of ours who is offered a chance of such magnitude does not check if his diary will allow him to take up the offer. The sensible answer to Harris's question was a definite, positive, instant YES.

Harris was rather disappointed at Mr X's reaction and as he went for his diary Harris restrained him and suggested that perhaps the matter would be best left on hold just for now. Harris returned home, again without having finalised a presenter for the programme. Only a few minutes after he had returned home, the phone rang and it was Scoffield:

'How did you get on Peter?'

A weary Harris relayed the events of the evening to Scoffield, highlighting Mr X's efforts to check his diary, suggesting that his actions didn't exactly give the impression of excitement on his part. Scoffield agreed wholeheartedly and said without hesitation:

'Sod him, offer it to Bowen!'

And that's how I happened to get the series! I must tell you that every Christmas I send Mr X a diary!

## There's many a slip twixt brain and lip

Some friends of mine own a caravan park on the edge of the Lake District. Roy and Mel Smith are a charming couple who run the site extremely well; in fact it's probably one of the most beautiful leisure parks in the area. Mel, however, does tend to lose the conversational plot from time to time. On one delightfully dizzy encounter with one of the site's residents Mel really excelled herself. The story went like this:

Resident: 'I've got my three daughters coming up for the weekend to stay.'

Mel: 'Oh! That'll be lovely for you. Are they all girls?'

Roy: 'I'll just go and put the kettle on!'

## Frankly speaking

Frank Carson, of all the comedians in this country, is probably the greatest and fastest raconteur of us all. The problem with Frank is that he never ever ceases to be a raconteur. We were together staying in a hotel in Aberdeen, as we were due to appear on the breakfast programme the next morning. This meant us getting up at 6.00 a.m. to be in the taxi at 6.30 a.m. which would get us to the studio in time for the transmission. The taxi driver was a gentle, quiet Scot and with the best will in the world, at this time in the morning, was not in any frame of mind to take Frank's animated banter. I sat there in the rear of the cab as I was fairly certain that Frank would, as usual, be on form with tales and anecdotes of varying credibility, all delivered in an excited, noisy, garrulous manner. Within a minute I was proved to be correct. Frank began his early morning performance with:
'Good morning driver, did you know that my father saved the lives of over 4,000 men during the last war . . . He shot the chef!' The driver immediately began to wilt under the barrage of Frank's chatter. Ignoring the driver's complete lack of interest Frank continued his badinage. He began to tell a story which lasted the whole of the journey to the television studios on the other side of Aberdeen, a distance of some six miles. Even though it was told at that time in the morning, the story, which incidentally I had never heard before, warrants a place in this publication. So, with affectionate memories of that taxi ride in Aberdeen, and with sympathies for its driver, I recall the story for you, dear reader.
Frank began by reminding us that in the 1940s he was a member of the Special Boat Service, the Navy's version of the SAS. This was a highly specialised branch of the armed forces comprising men who were particularly fit and were probably quite brave. (Frank, even now, is in particularly good shape. As far as being brave is concerned ... well ... I'm sure he could have talked his way out of trouble!)
'It was in 1945 when I was asked to climb aboard a Sunderland Flying Boat [a sea plane] to take part in some parachute manoeuvres. We took off from Dublin Bay climbing out over Southern Ireland where we were drilled in training procedures up to the actual jump.

After an hour we started home fully expecting to land again in Dublin Bay (the aeroplane was equipped with floats to facilitate these on-water manoeuvres). I could see Dublin in the distance as the aircraft descended and, to my horror, realized that it was heading towards Dublin airport. It occurred to me that the landing surface at Dublin airport was infinitely more solid than that of Dublin Bay so I thought that a word to the pilot on the flight deck would be quite in order. I tentatively approached the door on to the flight deck and opened it to see the lone pilot whistling away as the aircraft was lining up to touch down on the unforgiving surface at Dublin airport.

"Excuse me sir," I said, "but with respect I think you are going to subject the undercarriage of this aircraft to pressures for which it was never designed." I realised that its landing gear didn't mix kindly with concrete.

"Ah yes!" replied the pilot cheerily, "no problem at all, 30 years of flying in the RAF, don't panic, easily remedied, vast experience don't you know?"

'With that the pilot coolly altered course and ultimately landed safely in Dublin Bay, its intended destination. When the aircraft had stopped, I went back on to the flight deck, suggesting that perhaps it had been as well that I mentioned the pilot's potential error.

"Oh no problem at all, young chap! I've been flying for 30 years, bags of experience don't you know? You can't buy experience." With that he got up from his seat, turned towards the cockpit door, opened it and promptly stepped out into Dublin Bay!'

## A load of Bully

Bullseye, ah yes! You can imagine over the years when we were making the programme we encountered many amusing, even hilarious, situations. We made 26 programmes each year for 14 years. Remember, there were three pairs of contestants per show, so with that number of contestants there had to be many memorable characters. Let me tell you the story of one who will remain forever etched in my memory.

His name was Bill, he came from Wigan and his partner was his young son-in-law. Bill was to answer the questions and his son-in-law was there to throw the darts. From our initial meeting at lunch time I felt that Bill did not look in the best of health. He was a frail man, aged around 60 and the size of a jockey. His son-in-law, however, was a sturdy, fresh-faced young man who looked in extremely good health. Throughout rehearsals in the afternoon all three pairs of contestants seemed comfortable with the programme, though Bill did seem to be suffering from the heat generated by the lights in the studio. The routine on recording day was that after rehearsing in the afternoon the contestants were taken off for tea in the restaurant. They were then given a chance to go to their dressing rooms where they could relax and discuss the prospect of appearing on a television game show. Almost all the contestants were nervous, but we managed to handle them quite well, particularly in the later series.

At around a quarter to seven the audience of around 400 were brought into the studio and seated in preparation for us to start recording at about half past seven. When the director was satisfied that all was ready to record the show he gave the word and the show's titles began. By now all the contestants were in place in the studio, the darts players standing alongside their partners who were sitting ready to talk to me, as I interviewed them at the top of the show. On cue I entered the studio from the back, coming down through the audience to the studio floor where I turned to face the gathered contestants. On the evening in question as I arrived on the studio floor I turned to see three pairs of contestants, the third pair looking distinctly uncomfortable. The first two couples seemed at ease with the situation and interviewed well, but the third couple comprising Bill and his son-in-law gave us cause for concern. Bill, who was the seated member of the pair, was sweating profusely and looked even frailer than he had during rehearsal. I interviewed the pair of them, getting incomprehensible grunts from the son-in-law and asthmatic wheezes from Bill, who seemed to be fading fast. As we approached the halfway mark of the game Bill had become a real worry for us. He had sunk down in his chair so far that all we could see of him over the desk was his head and shoulders. His ability to answer questions succinctly was becoming more difficult by the minute. His breathing became difficult for him as well, so much so that Tony Green, my assistant, shouted at the top of his voice, 'Stop!', as he was very concerned about Bill's condition. I must tell you at this stage that the only person allowed to stop the production of a television programme is the director, in this case, a certain Peter Harris. On hearing Tony's urgent request to stop recording, Peter came on to the studio floor to investigate. It was then that he saw poor Bill struggling to get his breath, sweating profusely and seemingly closing in on the Pearly Gates quite rapidly. The first responsibility of a television director is to make the programme as quickly as possible and to bring it in under budget. Any insignificant interruptions, such as the potential death of a contestant, gives him a problem, so they have to be dealt with instantly. Peter approached Bill, who by now was actually unlocking the Pearly Gates, and suggested that perhaps he could just give the cameras a smile as we arrived at the commercial break. Bill was in no position at this stage to sit upright unaided so Peter approached a burly security guard and suggested he come in, position himself under the desk, and put his arm up the back of Bill's jacket so that he could support him a little like a ventri-loquist's dummy. On Peter's instruction Bill would smile weakly at the camera, thereby giving the viewer the impression that all was well.

Once we knew that we were off air, we carried Bill out of the studio and laid him carefully down on a blanket at the rear of the studio. Such was his condition by now that we had requested that paramedics come immediately. I went back into the studio asking if anyone in the audience was related to Bill. Fortunately his daughter was there and she immediately left the audience to be with Bill. As she came to the rear of the studio she saw Bill lying almost motionless looking a serious shade of white. She seemed to show little concern as she went for her handbag, taking out a small silver flask.

'He will be fine in a minute,' she said, and without further ado unscrewed the top of the flask and held it to Bill's lips.

As the contents of the flask entered Bill's mouth the transformation was quite incredible. Bill slowly regained his colour, began to breathe normally and miraculously stood up, nonchalantly saying, 'Ah! That's much better!' and strode away as if nothing had happened. Appar-ently Bill enjoyed a drink on a fairly regular basis but as the studios were 'dry' he had tried to obey the rules. Unfortunately this, though the correct action to take, was an unwise one in his case. Since lunchtime that day Bill had adhered to studio rules and had been on 'on the wagon,' but as the day progressed his system began to miss its regular injection of potion. Consequently his state deteriorated and only he knew the reason why. Looking back at the incident it was hilarious, but at the time we genuinely believed we were going to lose a contestant to the Almighty!

## Putting the boot in

Professional soccer enjoys a higher profile now than at any other time in its history. Expectations of both players and managers are at an all-time high and their behaviour in public is now more than ever a subject for discussion. I was privileged to be at a dinner where, amongst many other soccer dignitaries, I noticed the towering figure of Sam Allardyce, manager of Bolton Wanderers Football Club. He was obviously having an extremely enjoyable evening, and though behaving impeccably he did seem a little the worse for wear. Sam is noted for the disciplined way he handles his players and it crossed my mind, taking into account that it was a Friday night and Bolton were playing Arsenal the next afternoon, Sam was perhaps behaving a little exuberantly. I jokingly approached Sam and said, 'Don't forget you've got a game tomorrow Sam!'

'I haven't forgotten Jim,' replied Sam. 'Remember, I'm the manager. I don't have to actually f***g play!'

Bearing in mind that Sam's performance as a manager was excellent, he had every right to 'do his thing'. I considered myself gently rebuked and slowly walked away – as I glanced back I'm sure I could detect a twinkle in Sam's eye. That was me put in my place. Well done Sam and continued success in your career.

Soccer stories always fascinate me and as I travel the after-dinner circuit I hear many of them. Forgive me if I steal one for your enjoyment. It involves the celebrated forward Denis Law and a certain Southampton goalkeeper who shall remain nameless.

Denis was always a robust player and the laws of the game used to be more flexible than today. This incident took place at The Dell, Southampton's home ground, in the early Seventies. Manchester United were the visitors and as usual were enjoying a successful run. The match was a sell-out and from the start tensions on the pitch ran high. Two minutes into the game and Denis found himself running into the penalty area to head a cross ball goal-wards. As mentioned Denis was no shrinking violet; he jumped to head the ball fearlessly, and in so doing severely struck the Southampton goalkeeper (who was renowned for being, shall I say, a bit of a poser) and sent him sprawling into the back of the net. The goalkeeper ran up to Denis, having dusted himself off, and said:

'You are a dirty b***d, Denis.'

'Yes,' replied Denis, 'and you'll be pleased to know that I shall be here all f***g afternoon!'

Needless to say Manchester United won the game and the Southampton goalkeeper had a nightmare 90 minutes! That incident took place when the game of football was played in a slightly more physical manner and any tackle below the neck was regarded as acceptable! Not any more I'm afraid.

It was around that time that Tommy Docherty was manager of Chelsea Football Club. He tells the story of when he bought Tony Hateley from a First Division club in the Midlands for many thousands of pounds. Tony's debut was at Stamford Bridge and it happened to be televised for BBC's Match of the Day which was to be transmitted that night. He had a particularly unimpressive match, so much so that Tommy realized he had bought a turkey. He was determined to sell the player at the earliest convenience but the fact that the match had been on television did him no favours, as Hateley's performance had been seen by the whole of the UK football world. Tommy went to work in his office at Stamford Bridge on the Monday morning determined to rid himself of this unfortunate purchase. Mid-morning Tommy received a phone call from the legendary Bill Shankly, who was managing Liverpool with great success.

'I saw the boy Hateley on television on Saturday night Tommy,' enthused Bill.

Tommy immediately saw an opportunity to offload his erratic purchase and quickly replied:

'Aye Bill, but I'm afraid to say that 70,000 wouldn't buy him.'

'I know that,' retorted Shanks quickly, 'I'm one of the 70,000!'

## Star turns

I've been privileged over the years to meet and talk with many show business legends. One of my most memorable encounters was with the great Lionel Jeffries. We met when I had invited him to appear on a programme I was producing called After the Show. It was an idea that I had where people in our business met at the end of their days' performances and found themselves discussing their lives and the situations that befell them. People in show business are by their very nature storytellers, and usually good ones at that. Lionel eventually proved no exception to that rule, although initially he was extremely reluctant to take part. Fortunately for me I was able to persuade him to come up from his home in Bournemouth to London to join in.

Once we had started to run the tape on our invited celebrity storytellers, Lionel, though initially less than forthcoming with his anecdotes, soon got into the swing of things and after only a few minutes we were having trouble shutting him up! He was an absolute star.

He began by telling the story of a celebrity lunch to which he had been invited as a special guest. He was allocated a place at the top table where Dame Edith Evans was being feted as one of theatre's legends. Sir John Gielgud was on Dame Edith's left and Lionel was seated on her right. During the course of the meal Lionel became increasingly aware of a rather unpleasant smell which prompted him to lean over to Sir John asking him if he had broken wind. Sir John replied that he had not but he was also aware of this smell. They both agreed that one of them should ask Dame Edith if she was aware of anything unusual. Dame Edith looked bemused for a moment, prompting Sir John to ask bluntly:

'Dame Edith, have you farted?'

'Of course I have my dear, do you think I always smell like this?' Lionel laughingly remarked that the subject of the smell was never raised again throughout the meal!

During the 60s and 70s Lionel was to feature in many British films alongside Peter Sellers, Margaret Rutherford, Dennis Price, David Lodge, Robert Morley and Bernard Cribbins, to name but a few cinema icons of that age. For my money he was one of the funniest actors of his time. (He told me that the role of the strictly disciplined prison officer Mr. McKay in Ronnie Barker's hugely successful series Porridge played by the late Fulton McKay was based on his portrayal of the long-suffering, inept police inspector in the film The Wrong Arm Of The Law starring Peter Sellers. His performance in this film, coupled with appearances in a string of British comedy films of the time, got him noticed by Disney, who were in the process of casting for the wonderfully entertaining film Chitty Chitty Bang Bang. Much to his surprise he was approached to play the part of the eccentric Caractacus Potts, a character of such comedic potential that he not only accepted with delight but made it his own by giving a most memorable sense of the ridiculous and a riotous insanity to this crazy man. Now here's where this story held, for me, a real sense of all that's great about showbiz. Lionel told it thus:

'I was completely unknown in America so the prospect of working in Hollywood not only excited me but carried with it no small amount of apprehension. How would the big names in the film react to this English intruder taking a plum role in this extremely prestigious production? How would I cope with the egos and cultural differences in tinsel town? I, along with my wife, flew out to the studios and we were accommodated luxuriously in a chalet-like house on a very exclusive estate. I was taken to the studios on my first morning in a limousine, passing en route film legends like Charlton Heston, dressed in the costume he was to wear for that particular scene (I think he was a Roman that day), also getting into his limo. The whole scenario was making me feel incredibly insignificant and inadequate in this larger-than-life world that was Hollywood. As the car approached the set allocated to Chitty Chitty Bang Bang I could see a hoard of people crowding round the entrance. I was confused to say the least when, as I got out of the car they all began waving autograph books at me screaming, "Could we please have your autograph Mister Jeffries! We think you're wonderful! We've never seen a big British star before and we're so pleased you're here! Please Mister Jeffries sign our books!" This went on for some minutes and by the time the furore had subsided a little, my confidence and self esteem had grown considerably. "Well, perhaps I'm not as unknown as I thought," I mused, and proceeded on to the studio lot with an air of self assurance that grew even more as the whole crew on set greeted my arrival with shouts of, "Welcome Lionel! It's great to have you with us. We all think you're marvellous! We've seen all your films and we think you're the best!" Then they all applauded long and loud. By now my doubts had eased considerably about my suitability in terms of status for the role. I was obviously far more famous than I thought initially so I set about the task of creating Caractacus Potts with renewed confidence and vigour!

'It was only some weeks into the making of the film, when I had established myself as a performer, that the director told me that all the autograph hunters who greeted me at the entrance to the studios on my arrival were film extras who had been hired to pretend to be my fans, and all the welcoming cheers on my arrival on to the set had been rehearsed. Apparently nobody on the film had ever heard of me!'

*I say, how's that for man management?*

In the eighties when we were recording Bullseye at the television studios in Birmingham we stayed at the Strathallan Hotel for the duration of the recording period of around two weeks. During one season Patrick Cargill was staying at the same hotel while appearing at the Alexander Theatre. I had always admired Patrick and remembered him from the celebrated 'Blood Donor' sketch he performed with Tony Hancock, as well as his successful TV sitcom series Father Dear Father. I plucked up the courage one morning to introduce myself (I was still relatively unknown at this time) and we got into conversation. He was an absolutely charming man and we chatted throughout the morning. I revelled in his anecdotes and I'm sure Patrick wouldn't mind if I were to let you enjoy one of them.

Patrick was in the legitimate side of show business, being an actor, whereas yours truly as a stand-up comic was a member of the less respectable element of the theatre.

Work in the theatre in plays and dramas depends totally on a strict interpretation of a script. All the moves onstage are carefully choreographed, and all movement and dialogue is strictly adhered to. In the world of variety there is much ad-libbing and very rarely do we give performances which are identical to the previous one. In the world of the 'illegitimate' theatre we are far less restrained and disciplined as we almost invariably have only ourselves to consider, unlike in a play where all the actors depend upon one another for the story to be told accurately. To stray from the script only serves to confuse the actors, in fact many of the legitimate members of our profession have great difficulty performing without a script. This situation is not too dissimilar in the case of the classically trained musician who relies forever on a written score. He or she in many cases has difficulty improvising, and few of them become great jazz musicians where improvisation is paramount. This in no way minimises their talents, but strict adherence to a script or a musical score on a regular basis can inhibit creativity. Now let's get on with Patrick's story.

He was appearing in the West End in a performance of Boeing Boeing with a mischievous actor who shall remain nameless (the late David Tomlinson comes to mind actually!). In one of the scenes he finds himself on stage with the aforementioned nameless actor. For no reason at all the telephone resting on a table next to him began to ring. He ignored it for a while but the ringing continued. He gazed across the stage at his fellow actor and knew from the cheeky glint in his eye that he was playing a trick on him. He found himself in the unenviable position of having to deal with a totally unwanted and intrusive phone call. The script did not call for the telephone to ring but it had to be dealt with if the play were to continue. For what seemed an age Patrick was frantically working out how to deal with this situation. If he were to answer the telephone what would he say? He had no help from the script because it didn't contain a telephone. He knew he had been 'stitched up' by his opposite player and he was determined to deal with this infernal ringing. Suddenly a flash of inspiration struck him. He picked up the telephone, looked across at his actor colleague and said, 'It's for you!' The smile on Patrick's face as he ended the story told me exactly how pleased he was with this wonderful piece of dramatic improvisation. Apparently the miscreant never ever again played tricks on Patrick on stage!

Tony Christie is probably one of the best male vocalists this country has ever produced, along with the likes of Matt Monro and of course Dickie Valentine, who started life with the Ted Heath Orchestra. In the 70s and 80s Tony was a massive club and cabaret star, filling rooms wherever he was booked to appear. I was privileged to be support act to him on a tour of the more prestigious cabaret venues in the UK. These were custom built in terms of sound and lighting to serve both performer and customer at the highest level. At the time Tony was a massive star and I was just about being recognised so I was somewhat in awe of him. I remember he had a Rolls Royce, registration number TONIO (TON 10), which really impressed me. Having told you all this you will now appreciate how amusing this little tale is. Here am I working with a major star in a top cabaret venue, a star of such magnitude that he is (in my star-struck mind) above the mundane, day-to-day rules we 'normal' people are subjected to, like careful driving for instance. In a Rolls when you are Tony Christie I couldn't imagine anyone querying your driving. How wrong can one be!

Tony told me the tale of how, as he was going home after the show, he was travelling rather too quickly through Chorley when he was pulled over by a good old fashioned Lancashire 'bobby'. Tony wound the window down to be glared at by this red-faced officer of the law who spoke thus to my hero:

'Nah then lad,' he began, 'I know tha's getten a Rolls and I know who I'm talkin' to so I'm tellin' thee now, tek a bit of advice from a friend. When tha'r drivin' this car, an' I know it's a Rolls an' I know that tha'r a big star, if tha' wants to keep askin' t'way to Amarillo an' tha wants to get there safely ... more o'th'anchor ... an' less o't' clog!'

Tony smiled sheepishly, apologised profusely and carefully drove off, noticing in his rear view mirror a smiling policeman, who nodded happily and turned to his traffic car. Good policing or what!

## After dinner stints

The after dinner circuit is a source of many an anecdote and as a member of that band of speakers I feel almost compelled to relate one or two of them. These are not necessarily my stories but as a tribute to my fellow speaker/diners I offer the odd sample. The first one involved that great Liverpool football legend, and giant of that iconic soccer side of the seventies, the great defender Big Ron Yeats. He tells of how, towards the end of his playing career at Anfield, he was invited to speak at the Prison Wardens' Social Club at Walton Gaol, Liverpool. He accepted and dutifully fulfilled his commitment. After the evening was over Ron made his way to his car which was parked in the secure grounds of the establishment. On arriving at his vehicle he realised that he had locked his car keys in the car, in fact he could see them clearly still in the ignition. He returned to the main prison building to ask assistance from one of the staff on duty. A warden speedily came to his aid explaining that of all the places in the UK to lock away anything inadvertently this was the place to do it. The warden then explained that he would go into the prison and carefully select the most appropriate inmate who could easily extricate the car keys causing minimal damage to the vehicle. He had a wide and varied choice after all because this would be child's play to most of the seasoned residents in this establishment! After a few minutes the warder returned accompanying the selected candidate, one who had been presumably chosen for the specific criminal skill of car theft! The three of them approached Ron's car whereupon he explained his dilemma to the prisoner. The aforesaid then explained that this was no problem and that he would deal with the situation immediately. Both the prison warder and Ron stood well clear of the vehicle as the craftsman sized up the situation. A few seconds elapsed before the prisoner quietly bent down, picked up a huge stone lying nearby and promptly threw it straight through the car window to gain access to the keys. So much for insider information!!

## Clubs and ducks

In the early seventies, just after the birth of The Comedians on Granada Television, all of us who had appeared on the programme found ourselves in great demand on the notorious northern club circuit, an area of show business we had already covered but now we had a higher profile. This meant that our money went up but so did the expectation that we would 'come up with the goods'. On some nights we had to appear at three different clubs (we called it trebling!) so you can imagine the state of us as we reached the last venue. Confused would be putting it mildly, wondering which gags we had told at which venue, added to which even at my tender age fatigue was setting in so the risk of error increased.

One particular evening the three clubs on the agenda were all situated in the Manchester area so the travelling strain was reduced, but the 'three club' syndrome was still there so much concentration was required. The first two shows went quite well but the prospect of the final performance at the Del Sol club in central Manchester loomed large. I arrived at the club at 11.30 p.m. so time was not on my side as a comedian because as you can imagine the chances of any sobriety in the club would be minimal and at that time in the evening customers have other things on their minds, all of which were commodities I could not provide!

I entered the club to see six people scattered round the room in various states of emotional fatigue and was told by the proprietor that the customers didn't usually get in there until just after midnight so at around 12.30 a.m. I would be going onstage. I was scheduled to do 40 minutes, and this was the first night of a week's contract, a Monday night no less; not the best night to start making people laugh, especially after midnight with all the other distractions available in a nightclub in downtown Manchester. I was by now feeling quite peckish having been out on the road since early evening so I asked if I could avail myself of the 'all day breakfast' on offer prior to my performance – after all, I had half an hour to kill before my show. I was duly served the meal which I scoffed heartily and afterwards I went backstage to prepare myself for the final show of a very long night.

After a fairly average introduction I walked out onstage to face at least another 9 people, which admittedly got the audience up to double figures, and for 40 minutes I died the death of a thousand men. My mouth went dry, the all day breakfast was doing little to help and the total indifference of the audience to my act did little to shorten the ordeal. I walked offstage to the sound of my own footsteps to be confronted by the manager who told me to leave the club never to return. He even suggested I take up another form of employment (I believe a plumber was mentioned!). Rather naively I asked him about payment for my performance, to which he smartly replied, 'You f***g ate it before you went on!' I wonder why I never, ever went back to the Del Sol in Manchester?

Throughout the years vaudeville has thrown up many varied and unusual acts, from Leslie Welch the Memory Man, who just used to sit on stage and answer questions on any form of sport, to the next act I'd like to tell you about.

The story was related to me by Eddie Large, the larger of the superb Little and Large comedy duo. They were starting in the business when variety shows were becoming less and less popular with audiences dwindling, leading to their ultimate demise, so they were privileged to see and work with some of these 'quirky' acts. One such act was 'Arnold, The Amazing Dancing Duck'. Little and Large were the opening act on a variety bill featuring this bizarre item. Eddie was fascinated by the name of the act and was determined to watch it on the opening night of the week's run at the Alexandra Theatre in Birmingham. The running order on the show was such that Arnold followed Little and Large, thus enabling Eddie to watch this mysterious 'dancing' duck. How did it work? How could a duck dance? How on earth did the duck learn such skills? After all ducks aren't the sharpest of creatures; it was all a fascinating scenario for Eddie to take in. All was soon revealed.

As Eddie tucked in behind the side drapes of the stage, having performed his act with Sid (Little), he prepared to watch this phenomenon. He was not to be disappointed. As he peeped round the curtain he saw this elegant figure of a man stroll onto the stage. He wore a morning suit, tails and all, stiff white dress shirt with matching bow, red rose in his lapel, white gloves, black patent leather shoes and immaculately slicked-down hair, Brylcreem-style; in fact he was the epitome of sartorial elegance. Immediately behind this strolling player followed ... yes, a duck!

The gentleman sat gracefully behind a grand piano situated centre stage and introduced himself and his partner.

'Good evening ladies and gentlemen, may I introduce you to my good friend Arnold [the duck], who this evening will dance for you.' Without further ado he bent down and picked up the duck which was by now standing alongside him and placed him carefully on top of the grand piano.

'Say good evening to the ladies and gentlemen, Arnold.' The duck appeared to acknowledge the audience by waddling round the piano top, initiating a round of applause.

'Now, ladies and gentlemen, Arnold will dance for you the waltz.' He began to play a waltz on the piano and Arnold duly obliged by paddling round the top of the piano in waltz-time. The audience reacted with disbelief, clapping loudly at this amazing feat.

'Now Arnold will dance a foxtrot for you,' said the morning suit, and proceeded to play a slightly more up tempo tune for the duck to dance to. The duck did not disappoint. He strutted his stuff with increased energy, raising even more applause from the audience who were by now completely baffled. More was to follow.

'Now Arnold will dance for your delight a quickstep, ladies and gentlemen.' Unhesitatingly the morning suit broke effortlessly into a quickstep tune and ... you've got it, the duck began an even faster paddling motion on the piano top. There seemed no doubt that the duck could interpret rhythms as it was surely dancing to the sounds coming from the piano with great gusto! The audience was by now completely blown away by what they were watching. David Attenborough had never seen this duck or he surely would have had it on his anthropological programmes! They went wild in appreciation of this piano-playing duck trainer and his pupil and cheered even more loudly than before.

Morning suit knew, however, that the performance had not peaked yet. In true vaudeville fashion he had left the best till last.

'And finally, ladies and gentlemen, Arnold will perform some Rock and Roll for you.'

The audience went silent as morning suit broke into a feverish rendition of *Rock around the clock*, the famous Bill Haley and the Comets hit. On hearing this the duck went completely ballistic and began to leap around the piano top in a demented fashion, quacking and flapping, shedding feathers by the ton, much to the delight and amazement of the audience, who were by now completely mesmerised by the whole theatrical experience. After this last dance there was nothing left to do but to lift the duck down from the piano top onto the stage floor and take a well deserved bow for their combined efforts. They both left the stage to thunderous applause, Arnold dutifully following morning suit back to their dressing room to prepare for yet another show-stopping performance for the second house audience.

Eddie was completely bemused by the whole episode, so much so that he followed morning suit up to his dressing room to have his curiosities satisfied. He gave it a few minutes before daring to knock (in case the duck needed rubbing down or something), then he took his courage in both hands and tapped on the door. It duly opened and there was morning suit in all his glory, now wearing long johns, his socks held up by suspenders, and carpet slippers, all discreetly covered by an ageing dressing gown.

'I'm sorry to disturb you sir,' Eddie began. 'I'm Eddie Large, part of the double act that precedes you on the programme. I was completely fascinated by your performance this evening and I just wondered how long it took you to train the duck to dance so effectively?'

'Not long at all really,' came the reply. 'I don't know whether you noticed as I sat at the piano I bent down and pressed a switch by my feet as I was placing Arnold on top of the piano. That switch energised a hot plate which began to gradually heat up. All I then did was accompany the duck's movements as the hot-plate got warmer. Obviously the hotter the plate got the faster the duck moved its feet, so all I was doing was following the duck's ever-warming feet. Simple, eh!'

Eddie thanked the artiste and walked away completely disillusioned.

'Oh and incidentally,' called out the dressing gown, 'on a busy week I can get through a couple of ducks quite easily!'
I wonder how Animal Rights activists would have reacted to *that*?

In the 90s, having worked on *QE2* for over a decade with the Hot Rhythm Orchestra, you can imagine we had put together a very professional package of music and comedy. We decide to take the show on the road and tour the smaller provincial theatres. Most of the venues were reasonably well attended and the tour became an annual event taking in maybe a dozen venues throughout the year. One memorable night we were booked to appear at Melksham Civic Hall in Wiltshire. We all arrived during the afternoon, settling in at our hotel in preparation for the gig. The show was due to begin at 8 p.m. so by 7.30 p.m. we were all ensconced backstage ready to do it. At about 7.50 p.m. I casually walked on to the stage and became aware of a worrying silence front of house. It was only five minutes to 'curtain up' and to my ears there was little evidence of an audience in the room. I then committed the cardinal sin of peeping through the side curtain to check the house. To my astonishment (and disappointment) the auditorium was completely empty apart from one couple sitting on the front row. I rushed backstage to tell Colin, the bandleader.

'There are only two of them out there,' I lamented. 'There are more of us than them. If we fought them, we'd win! What are we going to do?'

Colin instantly replied, 'We do the whole show as if the room were packed. We shall be completely professional about this.'

It was then my job to 'break the ice' with this solitary pair so I bravely went out onstage and addressed the couple.

'Good evening both,' I muttered, 'please don't be embarrassed by the lack of people here, we're going to do the full show for you just as we would were the house packed to the rafters!'

The man slowly stood up and replied, 'Well don't piss about too long, we're waiting to lock the place up!'

*That's show business!*


## Comic asides

One of the funniest comedians ever to emerge from the series of the same name was Eddie Flanagan. Of the dozen or so who appeared regularly on the series Eddie never actually made a massive impact. He was, however, rated by his peers as the funniest of all of us. He had the nerve to deliver a line and then wait for what seemed an age before continuing the tale. His expressions during these pauses were priceless and we all fell about watching him. His handicap (for want of a better word) was his wife. She had this unerring ability to say the most hilarious things in a wonderfully naive manner.

I tell this story with much affection, as Eddie and his wife were loved enormously by everyone who met them. This incident happened as Eddie was returning from doing a lunch-time show in Manchester with two strippers who Eddie had kindly taken to the gig as they lived in Liverpool. Eddie almost invariably took his wife with him so he found himself driving the car home from Manchester with his wife in the front seat and the two ladies he'd been working with in the back. The conversation turned to pets, whereupon Eddie's wife said, 'We've got a lovely poodle at home, haven't we Eddie?' Resignedly Eddie confirmed that that was the case. One of the girls in the back immediately replied, 'Oh! I've got two poodles, aren't they lovely pets?'

Not to be outdone Eddie's wife added, 'We got our poodle from

Lita Roza' (Miss Roza sang for many years with the Ted Heath Orchestra). 'She's a well-respected breeder you know.'

'Yes, I know she breeds poodles,' replied one of the girls in the back. The other then chipped in, 'I think she's bent you know!'

Eddie's wife quickly responded, 'She probably got that from her dad, 'cos I remember he had a bit of a stoop!'

Eddie lowered his head and drove quietly on. The silence in the car was deafening.

Most people on this earth, whatever their trade or profession, have aspirations to be someone else, if only for a while, someone they admire, someone who 'does it better', whatever it is! It prompts dreams and there ain't anything wrong with that, 'cos without dreams life can be very dull, even painful.

Comedy in particular delivers many icons to its legions, and I suppose these icons are exaggerated because by its very nature our business is larger then life, so our heroes seem larger or greater than those of say plumbing, where skills are generally seen as more parochial and mundane. (Nothing wrong with that, I hasten to add. We could well have a burst pipe soon!) The whole world of comedy divides opinion more than most spheres in pub conversations, even politics, though the participants in both professions could be put in the same category! I'll give you an example. How can anyone not find the late, great Tommy Cooper funny? As soon as he walked on stage he was funny. Opening the solitary gate in the centre of the stage and walking through it for no apparent reason was to me hilarious. Phyllis, who has been married to a comedian for the best part of half a century, can see no sense or reason in the man. She finds lovely Tommy totally unfunny. How can that be? I think that's why so many people want to be in this game of ours; it's the risk factor, the fear of getting it wrong because the chances of fouling up are greater than those of a plumber who is dealing with constant elements, predictable forces. There's only one way to bleed a central heating system, or unblock a sink; everything can be measured or calculated. The laws to succeed are etched in stone. Now with a comedian he's dealing with imponderables, the mood of the audience, the mood of his wife when he left home, the weather even can determine the chemistry of the room he's working in. Is the sound system right? Is the lighting adequate? Have the audience had enough or too much to drink? Do they like me anyway?

Putting it even more graphically, if a plumber has a bad day the only one to know is one housewife. If a comedian has a bad day several hundred know about it, and even worse he's on hand to face the music – his critics are in the same room!

To blow that theory out of the water, ask the patient of the surgeon who has a bad day – if he can answer! So it's all a matter of opinion isn't it? Oh! The fear of it all.

So how do we, the 'insider dealers,' choose our idols? Again it's all a matter of very personal opinion. Having said all that, I plump for Rob Wilton, a droll comedian from Liverpool who put the 'T' in timing, and Max Wall who put the 'L' in lunacy.

I'd love to tell you a couple of stories about these guys because they helped me to understand and appreciate comedy, even from a distance. Let's talk about Rob Wilton first. He was of the variety era, when a comedian could tour the theatres of Britain with the same act for years. This usually took the form of a sketch or routines which, over the years, the public came to know and love, even expecting to see the same ones every time they came back to the same theatre. (Would that it were like that now; instead, television gives away your entire act to several million people in one fell swoop!)

Anyway, back to Mr Wilton. The story goes that Rob and his friend Charlie were paying their respects at the graveside to a dear friend Harry who had sadly passed away. As they stood alongside the grave the coffin containing Harry was being lowered into the ground.

'He was a good pal to us was Harry,' whispered Rob to the grieving Charlie. 'You'll go a long way to find a better mate than he was.'

'You're right,' replied Charlie, 'I'll miss him a lot.'

'How old are you now Charlie?' asked Rob.

'I'll be 87 next birthday,' Charlie proudly whispered.

'There' not much point you goin' home really is there Charlie!' mused Rob dryly.

Talk about humour in the right place. I'm not too sure! I still think both Charlie and Harry would have smiled a little don't you? Whether these stories are apocryphal or not matters little really. The comedian in me wants to tell them again and again, 'cos they might give you a little chuckle, and that's the job of this book.

Ready for another Rob Wilton story? I hope so.

In the 1950s Rob was a massive star and filled theatres everywhere as a result of his radio shows and his extremely funny sketches in the theatres. (The Fire Station sketch comes to mind where Rob as the Station Officer has to ask the distraught lady reporting the fire if she could perhaps keep it going for a while as Harry the fire engine driver was at the bookmakers, but would be back soon!)

He was, not surprisingly, invited to appear in a Royal Command Performance at the London Palladium in 1953 when he was still at the height of his popularity. In fact he was top of the bill. If you remember, that was the year that Princess Elizabeth acceded to the throne following the death of her father George VI. She was by now of course married to Prince Phillip and it was one of her earliest duties as Queen to host the Royal Command Performance. After the show tradition has it that the member of the royal family hosting the evening goes backstage to meet the artistes taking part. As top of the bill Rob was last in line to be introduced to the Queen, a privileged position indeed! Now, you may not know this but there are certain things you have to do when meeting the monarch. For instance you must never be the first to speak, you must hold out your hand to be shaken and you certainly must never interrupt the Queen when she speaks. Bearing all these factors in mind, please read on! Rob was at the very end of the line when the Queen approached, shook his hand and moved off. Prince Phillip then closed in, shook Rob's hand said graciously, 'Mr Wilton, what a wonderful show tonight! In fact I wish it could have gone on much longer!'

'Well, your Highness,' Rob quickly replied, 'we could take a couple of crates back to your place if you like!' He escaped the tower by minutes!

Now Max Wall was a completely different kettle of fish. He was poles apart from Rob Wilton in every way. He was anarchic, manic, surreal and no doubt well ahead of his time. I suppose in modern parlance he would have been 'alternative'. The public and the establishment saw elements of his act as crude and his behaviour in the 50s when he ran off with Miss Great Britain was viewed with disgust by society. I think it left a slightly bitter taste with him, especially when he came back into vogue in the 80s. A formidable actor (his performance in Waiting for Godot was critically acclaimed

– as if he cared!), he trod the boards in his latter years in all guises but he will always be remembered as a Vaudeville patter merchant or as the definitive 'stand-up comic'. Every comedian I know loved, respected and even revered the great Max Wall. I watched him several times and never ever saw him do well. We are a very insecure breed us comics and when we don't do very well it hurts not only our pride but our confidence. You can imagine the goings on in the mind of the comedian who doesn't do well consistently over a period of time. I can tell you that most of us would pack it all in, despite our egos telling us otherwise. Which brings me to this story, that I hope you'll love.

Here we have a comic who 'dies' on a regular basis and can comfortably live with the situation. I wondered about how he could face an audience in the knowledge that the chances of him doing well were slim. I suppose economics drove him on, for even as a long-time performer at the highest level his financial state was not one to be envied (I think ladies and Guinness did a little damage to his economic well-being). Was it bravery or just stubborn persistence that motivated him, or was it the thrill of the chase? Whatever it was he fought on with a dogged determination, which I suppose at the end of the day tired him out and he gave up the ghost still in harness to the addiction that is show business, which was both sad and unjust.

He was booked to appear at the Sunderland Empire in the late sixties when variety was still alive but in intensive care. The audiences were thinning out and were becoming more difficult to please thanks to the advent of television, so the game was hard. Max topped the bill every night twice nightly for six nights, Monday through to Saturday in this notoriously difficult venue. Each night he went on last to perform his scheduled 20-minute spot and was received with complete silence and indifference throughout. He walked offstage each night to the echo of his own footsteps. Imagine that ... working every night knowing that your reception would be one of total disinterest! Max did just that, however, appearing totally unconcerned about his lack of success.

When the Saturday night came Max went on as usual for the first house and came off as usual to complete silence. The second house came and Max went on again, but – surprise, surprise – as he left the stage one solitary member of the audience clapped quite loudly. Max acknowledged the response and as he reached the wings he whispered to the stage manager, 'I'm staying on, I think they like me!' And then promptly returned to the stage to do an extra five minutes! Is that bravery or is it born out of a desire to ruin everyone's night at one go?! A comic ahead of his time if ever there was one.

Well, I'm sad to say that my fund of wrinklemakers has run dry. Actually my publisher has told me to stop. She says we're all having too much fun!

So, let's liken the end of this book to the end of a stage performance, because that's what it's been like for me.

At the end of a stage performance, if it goes well, the audience applaud loudly and you come back on stage and do what's called 'false tabs' or an encore. Having spent thirty years in the business and never having been called back to do an encore the whole sensation is completely foreign to me. So here I am having sweated blood to tell you my story; having agonised about how to make it all enjoyable for you; having had sleepless nights caring about this publication, I find myself in the same position again. I've finished now and still no sound of applause. Ah! But this is a book, it's not a live performance, there's no one out there in the auditorium, just you, sitting there, book in hand thinking, 'Thank goodness that's finished'. Well, you've been such a good reader I'm going to do an encore before I finally draw the curtains on what I hope you think has been a worthwhile exercise; it won't be a long one so you might as well read it.

CHAPTER TWENTY

# *Encore*

I T'S ALWAYS seemed to me that to justify an autobiography the
writer has to feel that there's a genuine interest in his story; or
that a publisher might see a degree of commercial viability in the
book. This, the second attempt to entertain you (maybe even to
inform and educate you), has been written for therapeutic reasons
as much as for any other. Certainly it hasn't been written for financial
gain, although I would quite like to come out of the exercise avoiding
a visit from the receiver! Even at this stage of my allotted time on
earth, I still can't resist the chance to make you smile, and without
sounding self-indulgent I think you might just have had a chuckle
or two during your read. I do hope so.

The adrenalin rush that accompanies the sound of laughter has
always meant a lot to me but I don't want it to become so important
that I can't live without it. It's nice to have the show business bug
on your terms, to have control over your own destiny and not be
manipulated by its glamorous, heady excitement. The smell of the
greasepaint, the roar of the crowd is all very well if you wear make-up
and your hearing's not what it used to be; but me, well I suppose
I'm not thoroughly impregnated with razzle-dazzle. I like a bit at
a time, that way I don't get addicted. As you well know by now,
I have little or no ego, so I'm not hurting too much as I draw this
literary exercise to a close. (If you believe that after wading through
this lot then I can only assume you've not been concentrating on
the detail in the work. Now please pay more attention!)

*I say, how terribly authoritative!*

Some years ago I treated myself to a hand-crafted trumpet made by
Sterling Instruments of Luton. I had it built with a brass body and
a copper bell or horn. It is a completely unique instrument and its

227

serial number was stamped number 0001. Along the length of the horn I had the maker engrave the words: 'it's not a rehearsal'. Not very profound I suppose but nevertheless a thought-provoking phrase. Life is for living and, unlike most show business productions, there's only one chance to get it right. No rehearsals for life, just the one shot. I know I'm not telling you anything you don't already know, but I could just be reminding you! Think Nike ... 'Just do it!'

That's the false tabs then; I hope the applause is there even if it's in the form of silent appreciation – but with a smile I hope. Thanks for reading the book, especially if you bought it. If you've borrowed it, no matter, I'll feel flattered to know that you have a discerning friend!

One day I'm going to fall into the 'Where are they now?' category, nothing is more certain, so I'd like to unashamedly steal a piece of poetry that was read to us on the Happy Daft radio programme by a wonderfully talented lady called Christine Taylor. A former primary school head teacher, and later a member of Her Majesty's Schools Inspectorate, she came into the studios and beguiled both Sally and me, not to mention over 200,000 listeners, as she read out loud on air this brilliant creation. It's an observational, retrospective look at our place in the overall scheme of things, and she gave me permission not only to borrow it for you to enjoy, but to put my name where hers is in the last line. A million thanks Christine for allowing me to put this wonderful piece of rhyming genius in the book; I know that it will put a smile on the reader's face. In fact that's what the whole book's been about.

It's been a pleasure putting it all together, if only to remind me of the good times, and of how lucky I've been. I hope I've also highlighted the notion that being in the right place at the right time is the most important factor in life after good health; and even that can be assisted if you live in the right place.

Ladies and gentlemen, I give you the work of Christine Taylor:

*WHERE ARE THEY NOW?*

*What happened to Roy Rogers? Where did Trigger go?*
*What happened to Gene Autry, the Cisco Kid and Co?*
*Where is Googie Withers? Where is Donald Peers?*
*Still beside a babbling brook, after all these years*

Who remembers Spangles and Uncle Joe's mint balls?
Burgon's and Sivori's before ice cream was Walls?
Dandelion and Burdock – now they all drink Coke,
Tizer, Vimto, Raspberryade, lost without a hope.

Once we all played hopscotch, kick can and rallyo,
Now it's the remote controlled computer video.
Who remembers Robin Starch, Rinso and Dolly blue?
Red Raddling and Ewbanks? Do you recall – I do!
Once we all ate tater 'ash, black puddings and cowheel,
Now we're into pasta, pizza, curried frozen meals.
We all liked Alma Cogan, Kathy Kirby, Vera Lynn,
Dennis Lotis, Ronnie Carroll . . . what's become of him?

What's happened to the Foxtrot? Let's have the big bands back,
Let's look into each other's eyes and go 'Ballin' the Jack'
Who remembers Woodbines and Senior Service too?
Ten Park Drive and Craven A, oh! I recall, do you?
Where is Cheyenne Bodie? Where is Wagon Train?
Down the Ponderosa, let them ride again!
Where are Sugar Butties? Where is condensed milk?
Where is Tapioca, semolina and that ilk?

Where is 'Six-Five-Special'? Where is 'What's my Line'?
Where are Bill and Ben and Weed? Lost in the mists of time!
But wait a minute, stop a bit; fast-forward twenty years,
I'll bet a penny to a pound these words will reach our ears:
What happened to the Spice Girls? Where did Oasis go?
Where is Peter Kay now? Who was Peter Snow?
What happened to East Enders? What's a filofax?
Who were Blackburn Rovers? What was Council Tax?

And the thought that's very sobering, and also very true,
Is that folk might say the very same of him, and me, and you,
So I'm going to be outrageous now, I'm going to have a ball
I'm going to make my mark and be recalled by one and all,
I'm going to think of something that will grab attention now,
I'm going to think of something that will make the world go 'Wow!'
So future generations will never say of me,

*I DON'T RECALL JIM BOWEN, WHO THE HECK WAS HE??*

## Latest News from Reuters

As this publication was reaching its finale, an event occurred at Kingston Hospital, London, which could have endangered the completion of this piece of literature. The author and his lovely wife became grandparents for the first time!

Robert James Graham (7 pounds 2 ounces) arrived recently courtesy of Sue and Glen, and I'm delighted to tell you that they are all doing very well.

I've had a word with him and the publication can go ahead with his blessing.

Herewith the smile of approval:

*I say! How very ... well, it's just very nice!*